Improve Your Chess Results

D1100183

Improve Your Chess Results

VLADIMIR ZAK

Translated by John Sugden

B.T.Batsford Ltd, *London*

First published 1985
Reprinted 1987
© Vladimir Zak 1985

ISBN 0 7134 2486 9(limp)

Photoset by Andek Printing, London
and printed in Great Britain by
Billing & Son Ltd, Worcester
for the publishers
B.T.Batsford Ltd, 4 Fitzhardinge Street,
London W1H OAH

A BATSFORD CHESS BOOK

Adviser: R.D.Keene GM, OBE
Technical Editor: P.A.Lamford

Contents

1 How Skill Develops – the Most Important Phases

The beginner only 'rejoices' when he can call checkmate to his opponent, or perhaps still more if he can win his queen (for in the eyes of the beginner this is, if possible, the greater triumph of the two). The master, on the other hand, is quite pleased, in fact royally content, if he succeed in espying the shadow of an enemy pawn weakness, in some corner or other of the left half of the board.

Nimzowitsch

The same chessplayer, pondering his next move, will come to completely different conclusions at different stages of his chess development. From observing my pupils, I have become convinced that over their formative years there are various methods of play which all of them, with astonishing regularity, will successfully employ, irrespective of their level of talent. Let us examine the most significant of these methods.

'Attack something – and if it doesn't move, take it.'

Every chessplayer in his first stage of development is guided by principles created by his own imagination. Forgetting that the ultimate aim of a game of chess is to mate the opponent's king, he strives for material gains above all else; to this end, he brings his most powerful piece – the queen – into play right from the first few moves, so as to do the opponent the maximum damage with its help. The novice cannot resist the temptation to give check, even when this involves loss of time and results in a worsening of his own position. Not worrying about the security of his king, he neglects to castle.

These and many other mistakes characteristic of the initial learning process are made by all adherents of chess. Only when moves cease to arise from momentary impulses (with some players this takes months) can the first stage be considered to be over.

A game between two novices aged about seven
Training Tournament
Leningrad 1978

1	e4	e5
2	♛h5	

Reflecting the accumulated experience of centuries. White plans a Scholar's Mate.

2 ... ♝c5

3 ♕xe5+

This speaks in the player's favour. Given the changed circumstances (Black has played 2 ... ♝c5 instead of the usual 2 ... ♞c6), White renounces his original plan.

3 ... ♚f8?!

Not bad! Black throws away a bishop, but does notice the threat against g7.

4 ♕xc5+ ♕e7

5 ♕xc7 ♕xe4+

6 ♝e2 ♕xg2

7 ♕xc8+?

Typical! The attraction of taking a piece is so great that the mate on d8 goes unnoticed.

7 ... ♚e7

8 ♕xb7? *(1)*

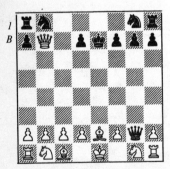

8 ... ♕xh1?

The diagonal is too long, the queens are far away from each other ... the rook is so much

nearer, and anyway with his last move Black was already planning to capture it.

9 ♕xa8? ♕xa8

Not before time, Black is the first to notice his opponent's undefended queen. After a lengthy struggle and numerous errors, White ... won.

One must first learn to combine, before attempting to play positionally.

Réti

These wise words by a distinguished grandmaster should be heeded. This is all the more indispensable since many trainers, from the very outset of their work with any young players, make their pupils play quiet variations of the Queen's Pawn Game and Caro-Kann Defence, instead of imparting to them a taste for gambit play. There is no need to demonstrate the perversity of such a 'method of instruction', which curbs the young players' flights of imagination and offends against the pedagogic rule that you proceed to the complex from the simple.

On taking up chess, children quickly develop a penchant for combination. They experience intense pleasure whenever some unusual configuration of pieces arises on the chessboard, even if only for a moment – whenever (let's say) a knight becomes stronger than a queen, or, as the result of a sacrifice (which may last for only one move), two pieces get forked, thus re-establishing material equality. Quite often, to a child, such a combination is an end in itself. He demands nothing more from it. It may improve his position, it may weaken it – the attraction of the combination is so strong that the young player goes in for it regardless.

One ten-year-old boy, with uncommon persistence, would begin all his games as follows:

1	e4	e5
2	♘f3	♘c6
3	♗c4	♗c5
4	♕e2 (2)	

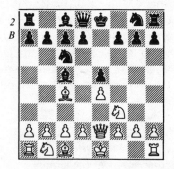

You would hardly guess that this move, which at first looks senseless, prepares a 'combination'. In actual fact, in reply to the natural 4 ... ♘f6, White continued with 5 ♗xf7+ (so 4 ♕e2 wasn't as

senseless as all that) 5 ... ♔xf7 6 ♕c4+ winning the bishop back. A few times, his opponents found the correct rejoinder: **6 ... d5! 7 ♕xc5 ♘xe4 8 ♕e3 ♖e8**, after which it emerged that White's position was very bad. In spite of this, the next game would begin in exactly the same manner.

Combinative vision manifests itself at an early age, and children are quick to notice and execute combinations which chance to turn up. Preparing combinations, however, is difficult for them.

The ability to do *that* comes at the age of twelve or thirteen, together with an understanding of the basic rules of positional play. Nor must it be forgotten that the imagination develops gradually, as the player grows familiar with archetypal combinations – all of which requires time.

Both opponents base their play on elementary traps.

A game between two girls of about nine
Training Tournament
Leningrad 1978
Vienna Game

1	e4	e5
2	♘c3	♘f6
3	f4	ef?
4	d4?	

The last moves by the girl players eloquently testify to their class of play. Black has committed an error which could have had unpleasant consequences after 4 e5 ♞g8 5 ♞f3 d6 6 d4 de 7 ♕e2! with a substantial lead in development. White, however, under the influence of dogmas learned by rote, and as yet unable to think independently and concretely, played the text move without hesitation (taking the opportunity to seize the centre).

4	...	d5
5	e5	♞e4
6	♝xf4?	

6 ♞xe4! was correct. Things could have been difficult for her if Black had replied 6 ... ♝b4!

But instead of this logical continuation, an incomprehensible exchange followed:

6	...	♞xc3?
7	bc	♝f5
8	♝d3	♕d7
9	♞f3	♝e7
10	0-0	0-0
11	♞g5?	

Her development barely concluded, White hastens to start active operations. The fact that this move is bad, and that after 11 ... h6 the knight has to go back where it came from, falls outside the field of vision of the young chessplayer beguiled by the many attractive ideas which arise from the nearness of the knight (and of the queen too, perhaps, shortly) to

the opponent's king.

| 11 | ... | ♞c6 |

Black falls in with her opponent's wishes.

| 12 | ♕h5 | h6 |
| 13 | e6? | |

It would be such a shame to move back! White had worked out the variation 13 ... fe 14 ♞xe6? ♝xe6 15 ♕g6, not noticing that 15 ... ♝f5 repels all her attacking tries. In any case, that same end could be attained a move sooner by 14 ... ♕xe6! But once again Black complies with White's wishes:

13	...	♝xe6?
14	♞h7	♖fd8
15	♝xh6!	gh
16	♕xh6	f5
17	g4?	

There was an immediate win with 17 ♕g6+ ♚h8 18 ♞f6, but to her misfortune White has noticed one more sacrificial possibility, and opens up the file for her rook.

| 17 | ... | fg (3) |

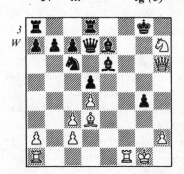

18 ♖f8+? ♖xf8!

An unforeseen reply. White had been counting on the capture with the bishop.

19 ♕g6+ ♔h8
20 ♘xf8 ♗xf8

In the end ... Black resigned on the 46th move.

In this example we observed how White attempted to win with the aid of a combination.

The strategic prerequisites for this were, of course, wholly absent. There were merely attempts, unsupported by accurate analysis, to extract non-existent combinative motifs from the position (18 ♖f8+).

This game confirms once again the familiar proposition that tactical complications occur a good deal more often in games by young players than in those by adults.

This is explained not only by the peculiarities of a specific age in life, but also by the players' level of mastery as it forms itself in the course of years.

It may sound strange, but combinations occur more rarely in a chessplayer's games the stronger he becomes.

In his *Manual of Chess*, Lasker wrote:

A combination takes shape in a player's head. Many thoughts – correct and erroneous, strong and weak, practical and impractible – strive for realisation. They keep being generated and contending amongst themselves, until one of them prevails over its rivals and is embodied on the chessboard in the shape of a move.

As the result of an immense amount of work on a multitude of ideas, a master will single out one of them, which will demand a precise analysis of variations and judicious positional assessment. In the process of selection, many combinative ideas are discarded.

The weak player is not in a position to carry out this task. In his case, the choice of move is determined not by the demands of the position but by fortuitous circumstances.

Tactical operations without regard for the position.

A little familiarity with the functions and 'specific gravity' of this or that piece or pawn in some simple elementary combinations – and already we are finding a certain connecting thread, we shall grasp certain methods of play, certain tactical laws.

Carlos Torre

In 1966 in Moscow, a new name appeared among the strongest young players of the Soviet

Union. Fourteen-year-old Mikhail Shteinberg from Kharkov shared first and second places in the USSR Schoolboys' Championship with Anatoly Karpov, later to become World Champion. A few months afterwards, in the USSR Championship semi-final at Oryol, Shteinberg attained the master's norm (no one else had ever succeeded in doing so at that age), and at the end of the year, in the international tournament at Groningen (Holland), he won the European Junior Cup (equivalent to the present title of European Junior Champion). Already one was struck by his maturity as a player – his ability to conduct a protracted positional struggle, his accurate and deep calculation culminating in a correct assessment of the end position, and his fine technique in endgame play.

To our deep regret, it was not possible for Misha to develop his gifts to the full. After gaining a mathematics degree at Kharkov University, he fell seriously ill, and died at the age of twenty-four.

I made his acquaintance at a junior tournament in 1965, after which he sent me several letters. In one of them, he writes: "Thank you. If it hadn't been for you, I'm sure it would have been ages before I looked at my old games again. Now I think they're very amusing."

Shkaleto-Shteinberg
3rd Grade Tournament
Kharkov 1962
Sicilian Defence

1	e4	c5
2	♘f3	♘c6
3	d4	cd
4	♘xd4	♘f6
5	♘c3	d6
6	f4	♗g4
7	♕d3	a6?

The ten-year-old Shteinberg hadn't been playing chess long, and was unacquainted with the standard manoeuvre which leaves Black a piece down. But at that age, the odd piece here or there often makes little difference. Rather, ingenuity and the will to win may prove decisive. The correct continuation was 7 ... g6, after which White can't play either 8 f5? gf 9 h3 fe, or 8 ♘xc6 bc 9 f5 gf 10 ef ♕d7. In either case, Black would emerge with an extra pawn.

8 ♘xc6!

An indispensable exchange. The immediate 8 f5 could be met by 8 ... ♘xd4 9 ♕xd4 e5 10 ♕f2 d5, when 11 h3? fails against 11 ... d4.

8	...	bc
9	f5	e6
10	h3	♗h5
11	g4	♘d7
12	♗e3	

White wants to pick up the

piece in the most convenient circumstances, but he could do so at once without unnecessary fuss – 12 gh ♕h4+ 13 ♔d1 ♘e5 14 ♕e2, with a perfectly sound position.

12	...	♘e5
13	♕e2	♖b8
14	0-0-0	d5

Black does everything in his power, but his trapped bishop and retarded development deprive him of saving chances. White has many ways of winning. One of them is 15 ed cd 16 fe fe 17 ♗f4 when all Black can do is hope for a miracle.

15	♗f4?!	♘c4!
16	♗xb8	♕xb8
17	b3	♗a3+
18	♔b1	♕b4

Finally Black has produced some threats. The simplest way to fend them off is 19 ♕e1! ♗b2 20 ♘xd5, or 19 ...0-0 20 ♗xc4 dc 21 ♖d4 ♖b8 22 ♘e2 ♕c5 23 ♕c3 etc.

19	♘a4	0-0
20	gh? (4)	

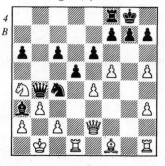

The black bishop has been *en prise* for ten moves and now White takes it at the most unsuitable moment. It was still not too late to win the game with 20 c3 ♕b7 21 ♔a1.

20	...	♕xa4!

A queen sacrifice always gives pleasure to a chessplayer – especially to a small one.

21	ba??	

The miracle comes to pass! There was no need at all for White to lose. To be sure, energetic measures are out of place here: 21 ♕xc4? dc 22 ba ♖b8+ 23 ♔a1 ♗b2+ 24 ♔b1 ♘e5+ 25 ♔c1 ♗f4+ 26 ♖d2 c3 etc. Yet by 21 ♕e1, with 22 ♗xc4 to follow, White would have preserved a winning position.

21	...	♖b8+
22	♔a1	♗b2+
23	♔b1	♘a3 mate

The majority of young players who possess excellent combinative vision will miss no opportunity to stir up a sharp tactical fight. Unfortunately, some of them don't for a long time succeed in eliminating one serious defect in their play – having achieved a won position, they relax, on the assumption that their task is over, instead of concentrating to the full and attempting to find the strongest continuation to finish the game.

Becoming absorbed in the analysis of one seemingly strong possibility such players will often forget about other lines. Sometimes this is done deliberately, with the aim of saving effort and time, but we should observe that mostly in such cases the effect is the opposite. We've all seen it happen – when once a player misses the strongest continuation, the struggle flares up with new vehemence; the dissatisfaction which inevitably ensues hampers the freedom of the creative imagination – often leading to oversights which culminate in ignominious defeat.

Vadasz-Shteinberg
Groningen 1966
Slav Defence

1	d4	d5
2	c4	c6
3	♘f3	♘f6
4	♘c3	dc
5	e4	b5
6	e5	♘d5
7	a4	e6
8	♘e4!?	

Theoretical manuals pass over this move in silence. To me, it looks no worse than the usual continuations 8 ♗e2 and 8 ab.

8	...	♘d7
9	g3	♘5b6?!

Black's desire to remove the pressure from his queenside pawn chain is understandable. But this is achieved at too high a price – the loss of two tempi.

It would be more natural to continue developing with 9 ... ♗b7 10 ♗g2 (10 ♗h3 is very strongly met by 10 ... c5! 11 ab cd 12 ♕xd4 ♘b4 or 11 dc ♘xc5) 10 ... h6 11 0-0 ♗e7 12 b3! with sharp play. Now White manages to create powerful threats on the kingside.

10	a5	♘d5
11	♗h3	h6
12	♘h4	

Of this move, Shteinberg writes: "White has no time to lose. If Black once gets in ... ♗e7, ... a6, ... ♗b7 and ... c5, White will simply be left a pawn down with a bad position. Up to this point Vadasz had played very quickly, whereas I had used up a lot of time on the manoeuvre 8 ... ♘d7 and 9 ... ♘5b6. But in the end, both of us got into time trouble."

| 12 | ... | g5?! |

Very risky, but what else is there? 12 ... ♗e7 is answered by 13 ♕h5.

13	♕h5!	gh
14	♗xe6	♖h7?

The game was played at the end of the tournament. Shteinberg was a point ahead of his opponent, and from the competitive standpoint a draw would have suited him. Perhaps this very consideration was what motivated Black's last move. A considerably stronger line was 14 ... ♗b4+ 15 ♗d2

♗xd2+ 16 ♔xd2 ♕e7 17 ♘d6+
♔f8 18 ♘xf7 ♖h7, and Black has
defended successfully.

15 ♗f5   ♖h8 (5)

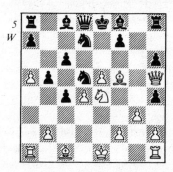

16 ♗g6?

To explain this bad move by
time trouble would be too simple.
Only 15 moves have been made.
But White has just sacrificed a
piece, and before doing so he
would necessarily have to devote a
great effort of analysis to probing
all the subtleties of the resulting
position. It's clear that Black's
most vulnerable point is f7. White
ought to concentrate his forces
against it. Most likely, he worked
out the tempting variation 16 e6?!
♕e7 17 ed+ ♗xd7 18 0-0 0-0-0; he
convinced himself that this doesn't
give him anything to speak of,
and, to economise on time, played
the text move – which quickly
leads to loss – without analysing
it at all.

This is just the sort of sorry end
that has occurred in many games
by young players lacking sufficient
practical experience.

And yet after 16 0-0! Black
would have been confronted with
difficult, scarcely soluble, problems.
For example: 16 ... ♘b8 17 e6 ♕e7
18 ef+ ♔d8 19 ♖e1 ♗xf5 20 ♕xf5
♕d7 (or 20 ... ♗g7 21 ♗g5!) 21
♕g6! The pawn on f7 is the basic
pivot of White's position, and he
has to guard it with all his strength
without being enticed by petty
material gains. A bad position
would result from 21 ♕e5? ♖h7 22
♕e8+ ♕xe8 23 fe♕+ ♔xe8 24
♘f6+ ♔f7 25 ♘xh7 ♗g7, and
Black wins without trouble. But
after 21 ♕g6! Black has no
defence against the threatened 22
♕g8, since 21 ... ♘e7 can be met
by 22 ♕f6 ♖h7 23 ♘c5 ♕f5 24
♘b7+ ♔c7 25 ♖xe7+, or 23 ...
♕d5 24 ♖e6! ♔c8 (24 ... ♕f5 25
♕xf5 ♘xf5 26 ♖e8+) 25 ♖xe7
♗xe7 26 f8♕+! ♗xf8 27 ♕xf8+
♕d8 28 ♕f5+.

16 ...   ♗b4+
17 ♔d1   ♕e7
18 ♘g5

Obviously White had pinned
his hopes on this move, but after
the simple ...

18 ...   hg!
19 ♕xh8+   ♘f8

Black obtained an overwhelming
material and positional advantage
which quickly decided the game.

20 ♗e4   hg

21	hg	♗e6
22	♕g7	f5
23	ef	♗g4+
24	f3	♕xe4
	0-1	

An undeveloped position is in many ways like the still unformed organism of a child: the one thing demanded of both of them is calm, healthy development, with no inclination to be sidetracked.

Nimzowitsch

Hjartarson-Short
World Under-17 Ch Belfort 1979
French Defence

1	e4	e6
2	d4	d5
3	♘d2	♘f6
4	e5	♘fd7
5	f4	c5
6	c3	♘c6
7	♘df3	♕a5
8	dc	♕xc5
9	♗d3	b5!?

A new move. Previously, 9 ... ♗e7 or 9 ... ♕b6 had been played. Faced with something unexpected, White reacts in a way that is far from best.

10 ♕e2?!

The gain of a tempo when White brings out his black-squared bishop (as planned) fails to compensate for the difficulties caused by the queen occupying a

square where a white knight wants to go. The calm 10 a3 a5 11 ♘e2 ♗a6 12 b4! was more in the spirit of the position, and would have halted Black's queenside initiative.

10	...	b4
11	♗e3	♕a5
12	c4	♗c5
13	♗xc5?!	

Why help the opponent to develop his pieces? White fails to grasp what is essential in the position – namely, development of the kingside in the most rapid way possible. This could have been achieved by 13 ♘d2! followed by 14 ♘gf3.

13	...	♘xc5
14	cd	ed
15	e6?!	

White's position is worse, and he tries to make up for it with complications. It's already too late for ♘d2? because of 15 ... ♘d4 16 ♕e3 ♗f5! 17 ♗xf5 ♘xf5, with a big advantage to Black.

15	...	b3+
16	♔d1	

16 ♔f2? is obviously worse; it could even be answered by 16 ... ♗xe6!? 17 f5 0-0 18 fe fe, with a very powerful attack.

16	...	f6!

Fourteen-year-old Short coolly repels his opponent's attacking tries.

17 ♘d2

He can't waste time. 17 f5 can

be met by 17 ... ♘b4 18 ♗b5+ ♔e7
19 ♘h3 ♖b8 20 ♘d4 ♘c2, or 20
♗d7 ♗a6. In either case Black has
a winning position.

| 17 | ... | ♖b8 |
| 18 | ♕h5+ | g6!? |

Playable, but Black could also
win without such refinements. For
example: 18 ... ♔e7 19 ♕xd5 (or
19 ♕f7+ ♔d6 20 ♕xg7 ♗xe6 21 f5
♘xd3 22 ♕xf6 ♖be8 23 fe ♖hf8 24
♕h6 ♖f1+) 19 ... ♖d8 20 ♕xc6
♖xd3 21 ♘f3 ♗b7.

| 19 | ♗xg6+ | ♔e7 |
| 20 | ♗d3?! | (6) |

Trying to confuse the issue after
20 ... ♘xd3 21 ♕f7+ ♔d6 22 ♕xf6
♗xe6 23 f5 which would not,
however, save White, if only
because of 23 ... ♖he8. But Short
concludes the game even more
simply.

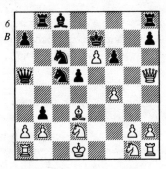

20	...	ba!
21	♕f7+	♔d6
22	♘gf3	

At last the knight is developed.
But then, that could have been
done twenty moves earlier!

22	...	♖xb2
23	e7	♕c3
24	♗c4	♖xd2+

0-1

*One may make mistakes, but
one ought not to practice deception
on oneself. He who bravely puts
his views into practice can, of
course, suffer defeat. Yet in so
far as he endeavours to understand
the causes of his loss, it will be
to his benefit ...*

*But he who no longer has the
courage to realise his conceptions
is losing the qualities of a fighter
and approaching his decline.*

Emanuel Lasker

Chekhov-Panchenko
USSR Young Masters Ch
Leningrad 1976
Sicilian

1	e4	c5
2	♘f3	♘c6
3	d4	cd
4	♘xd4	♘f6
5	♘c3	e5
6	♘db5	d6
7	a4	

Of course, Chekhov's knowledge
of the main variations after 7 ♗g5
is not open to doubt. However,
the move played also has its
positive points, chief among which
is the avoidance of a struggle full
of sharp tactical possibilities,

which Panchenko was clearly aiming for.

	7	...	**h6!?**

An ingenious move! Preventing the pin on his knight, Black concentrates his attention on the d5 point.

	8	♗e3	♗e6!

More accurate than 8 ... ♗e7 9 ♘d5 ♘xd5 (9 ... 0-0? 10 ♘xf6+! breaks up Black's kingside) 10 ed ♘b8 11 a5! with the unanswerable threat of 12 ♗xa7.

	9	♘d5

Forestalling 9 ... a6 and 10 ... d5.

	9	...	♗xd5
	10	ed	♘e7
	11	a5!	

With other continuations White couldn't bid for the advantage. For example, 11 c4?! a6 12 ♘c3 ♘f5, and with the elimination of White's black-squared bishop the weakness of the b6 point in Black's camp ceases to be a tangible factor.

	11	...	♘exd5?!

Led on by illusions, Panchenko strives to complicate the game; at the cost of serious positional concessions, he hopes to exploit the power of his central pawns. A more cautious line was 11 ... ♕b8!? 12 c4 ♘f5 13 ♕a4 ♘xe3 14 fe ♘d7 15 ♗d3 a6 16 ♘c3 ♗e7 17 ♗f5 ♕c7 18 0-0 ♖d8, and after castling Black succeeds in completing

the mobilisation of his forces.

	12	♗xa7	♕d7
	13	c4	♘f4
	14	g3	d5? (7)

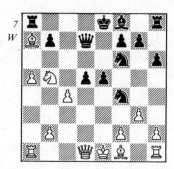

The final link in Black's mistaken plan. Why such a strong player as Panchenko should fail to sense danger here can only be explained by his reluctance to acquiesce in the worse position after 14 ... ♘e6 15 ♗g2, or 14 ... ♕c6 15 gf ♖xa7 16 ♘xa7 ♕xh1 17 ♕a4+ ♘d7 18 0-0-0 ♕xh2 19 fe. After all, White's next move, which essentially decides the outcome of the game, is not at all hard to foresee.

	15	♕a4!

Probably Chekhov didn't even bother to spend any time on the variations after 15 gf ♗b4+ 16 ♔e2 – when Panchenko would have achieved what he had been aiming for from the first moves of the game.

	15	...	♘e6
	16	♗g2	♖c8

16 ... d4 loses to 17 ♘xb7.

17	cd	♘c5
18	♗xc5	♗xc5
19	0-0	0-0
20	d6	

White emerges with an advanced passed pawn to the good. Now he threatens to strengthen his position still more with 21 b4!

| 20 | ... | ♘g4 |

A last desperate try.

| 21 | ♘a7! | |

Not wishing to make any concessions to his opponent, even psychological ones; but then, after 21 h3 ♘xf2 22 ♖xf2 ♕f5 23 ♖f1 ♗xf2+ 24 ♖xf2 ♖c1+ 25 ♖f1 ♖xf1+ 26 ♗xf1 ♕g5 27 ♕b3, White would likewise retain all the winning chances.

| 21 | ... | ♗xf2+ |

Or 21 ... ♕xa4 22 ♖xa4 ♗xa7 23 ♖xg4 ♖c2 24 ♖b4 ♗c5 25 ♖xb7 ♗xd6 26 ♗d5.

22	♖xf2	♖c1+
23	♗f1	♕xa4
24	♖xa4	♘xf2
25	♔xf2	♖d8
26	♖c4!	

The entire game, including its technical part, is conducted by Chekhov on a very high level. 26 ♘b5 ♖c2+ was clearly weaker. 26 ... ♖xc4 27 ♗xc4 ♖xd6 28 ♔e3 ♔f8 29 ♘c8! ♖d1 30 ♘b6 ♖b1 31 ♗d5 ♖xb2 32 ♗xb7 ♖b5 33 a6 ♖xb6 34 a7 ♖b3+ 35 ♔e4 ♖a3 36 a8♕+ ♖xa8 37 ♗xa8 f6 38 ♔f5 ♔f7 39 ♗d5+ ♔e7 40 ♔g6 ♔d6 41

♗e4 1-0

Playing to complicate the position is an extreme expedient, which a player should only resort to when he cannot find a clear and precise plan.

                                    Alekhine

Korsunsky-Yusupov
Baku 1979
Petroff Defence

1	e4	e5
2	♘f3	♘f6
3	♘xe5	d6
4	♘f3	♘xe4
5	d4	d5
6	♗d3	♗e7

The other playable continuation, 6 ... ♗d6, leaves White with somewhat the better game after 7 0-0 0-0 8 c4 ♘f6 (or 8 ... c6) 9 ♘c3 dc 10 ♗xc4 ♗g4.

| 7 | 0-0 | ♘c6 |
| 8 | ♖e1 | ♗g4 |

Robert Byrne recommends 8 ... ♗f5!? and considers that after 9 ♘c3 ♘xc3 10 bc ♗xd3 11 ♕xd3 0-0 12 ♖b1 Black's position is quite promising.

| 9 | c4 | |

The most active continuation, although many players prefer the more modest-looking 9 c3 after which, in view of the threatened 10 ♕b3, Black has to seek equality by means of a pawn sacrifice: 9 ... f5 10 ♕b3 0-0 11 ♘bd2 ♔h8 12

♕xb7 ♖f6 13 ♕b3 ♖g6 14 ♗e2 ♕d6 15 ♘f1 f4 16 ♘3d2 ♘xf2! 17 ♗xg4 ♖xg4 18 ♖xe7 ♘h3+ 19 ♔h1 ♘f2+ ½-½ Tukmakov-Dvoretsky, Odessa 1974.

9 ...   ♘f6

In Chigorin-Schiffers, St Petersburg 1879, White obtained the advantage after 9 ... ♗xf3 (9 ... ♘xd4? 10 ♗xe4 de 11 ♕xd4) 10 ♕f3 ♘xd4 11 ♕e3 ♘f5 12 ♕h3 ♘fd6 13 cd ♘f6 14 ♗g5.

10	**cd**	**♘xd5**
11	**♘c3**	**0-0**
12	**♗e4**	**♗e6!?**

12 ... ♗b4!? is frowned on by the books, which quote analysis by Keres starting with 13 ♘xd5 ♗xe1 14 ♕xe1.

Indeed, after 14 ... f5 15 ♗g5 ♕d6? 16 ♘e7+ ♘xe7 17 ♗xe7, White wins. However, by playing 15 ... ♕d7! (pointed out by A. Yuneyev), Black obtains the advantage. For example: 16 ♘e7+ ♘xe7 17 ♗xe7 fe, or 17 ♘e5 ♕xd4! 18 ♘xg4 ♘g6! Alternatively, 16 ♗c2 ♗xf3 17 gf ♘xd4 18 ♕d1 c5. Obviously, instead of 13 ♘xd5? White has to choose the more modest continuation 13 ♗d2.

As to the variation 12 ... ♘f6 13 d5 ♘b4 14 a3 ♘xe4 15 ♖xe4 16 ♗xf3 16 ♕xf3 ♘a6 17 b4, the ensuing position is in White's favour.

13	**♕c2**	**h6**

After mature reflection, Yusupov refrains from a continuation recommended by some works of theory – 13 ... f5?! Indeed, 14 ♗d3 ♘db4 15 ♕e2 ♘xd3 16 ♕xe6+ ♔h8 17 ♖d1 gives White the better game.

14 ♗f5?!

It looks as though the exchange of white-squared bishops might secure White some initiative in the coming middlegame, but that is not the case. 14 a3, with 15 ♘e4 to follow, was more in keeping with the position.

14	**...**	**♘cb4**
15	**♕b1**	**♗xf5**
16	**♕xf5**	**♗f6**
17	**♘e4?!**	

Korsunsky feels an obligation to punish his opponent for his 13th move (13 ... h6 instead of 13 ... f5). But in vain – the position demanded urgent prophylactic measures, not headstrong attack. With 17 ♗d2, White could still have maintained the balance.

17	**...**	**♕c8!**
18	**♕h5**	**c6**
19	**♗xh6?!**	

White did not play his last two moves in order to make do with the worse position after 19 ♖d1. However, in sacrificing his bishop he failed to evaluate all the consequences, confining his calculations to the crude variation 19 ... gh? 20 ♘xf6+ ♘xf6 21 ♕xh6 after which there is no defence against the terrible threat of 22 ♖e5. The consequences of White's omission are immediately felt.

19	...	♘c2!
20	♘e5	

No other way of strengthening the attack is to be found. On 20 ♘d6 ♕d7 21 ♘f5 (threatening 22 ♗xg7), Black plays 21 ... g6, while 20 ♘xf6+ ♘xf6 21 ♕g5 is met by 21 ... ♕g4.

20	...	♘xe1
21	♘g4	

Setting a transparent trap: 21 ... ♘c2? 22 ♘gxf6+ ♘xf6 23 ♕g5 ♘e8 24 ♘f6+ ♔h8 25 ♗xg7+ ♘xg7 26 ♕h6 mate.

21	...	♗xd4!

Very coolly played. The flimsiness of White's designs is further underlined by another possibility of defence: 22 ... ♕e6 23 ♖xe1 ♖fe8! 24 h3 ♗xd4, and White has no compensation for the exchange.

22	♖d1	♗xb2
23	♖xd5	cd
24	♗xg7 (8)	

Now 24 ... ♗xg7? can be met by 25 ♘ef6+ ♗xf6 26 ♘xf6+ ♔g7 27 ♕g5+ ♔h8 28 ♕h6 mate.

If Black had wanted, he could have extinguished the last flickers of White's attack even sooner — namely, by 22 ... ♘c2. But Black has calculated everything precisely, and now springs an unpleasant surprise on his opponent.

24	...	♘f3+!!

Prepared long in advance, this blow enables the queen to join in the defence with gain of tempo, after which nothing remains of White's attack but a few checks.

25	gf	♕c1+
26	♔g2	♗xg7
27	♘ef6+	♗xf6
28	♘xf6+	♔g7
29	♕e5	♖g8!

Now it's Black's turn to aim at his opponent's king.

30	♘g4+	♔f8
31	♕d6+	♔e8
32	♕e5+	♔d7
33	♕f5+	♔c6
	0-1	

Harmonious co-operation of the pieces and combinations

Vaisman-Shteinberg
Harkov 1974
Pirc Defence

1	d4	g6
2	e4	♗g7
3	♘f3	d6

4	c3	♘f6
5	♘bd2	0-0
6	♗e2	♘c6
7	0-0	e5
8	de	de

This whole variation is a rarity in competitions. And in opening books, Black's last move is not even considered. The recommended line is 8 ... ♘xe5 9 ♘xe5 de 10 ♕c2 ♗h6 11 ♖d1 ♕e7 with equality, Fuchs-Matulović, Kapfenberg 1970.

9	♕c2	♕e7
10	a4	♘h5
11	♖e1?	

White wants a quiet life without weakening himself and declines to play 11 g3, which would keep the black knight on its unattractive square. However, in a game of chess you have to be constantly conceding some points in order to gain others. A player's calibre is shown by his ability to secure an advantage (even just a microscopic one) from that kind of 'bargain'. The accumulation of such advantages should lead to a win.

A dislike for giving anything away hampers the imagination and encourages a policy of marking time, where play for the win is replaced by waiting for mistakes from the opponent. Such a course very often leads to loss of the initiative and to the eventual formation of weaknesses in your own camp when parrying the opponent's threats.

11	...	♘f4
12	♗f1	♗g4!
13	h3	

He has to stem the kingside initiative that is taking shape for Black (13 ... ♕f6 and 14 ... ♘h3+).

13	...	♗e6
14	♔h2	♕c5!

At first sight this looks like a waste of time, but in fact it initiates a deeply calculated combinative attack.

15	♘b3 *(9)*	

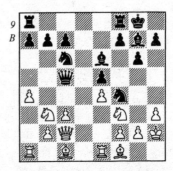

15	...	♘b4!

The point of Black's last move. Of course not 15 ... ♗xb3 16 ♕xb3 ♕xf2?? 17 ♗e3 and White wins.

16	♕d1	♕xf2
17	♗xf4	ef
18	cb	♖ad8!
19	♘bd2	♗xh3
20	♕e2	♕g3+
21	♔h1	

As a result of the forced line of play, Black has obtained two pawns and a dangerous attack for his piece. Here White couldn't retreat his king to g1 because of 21 ... ♗g4, when there is no defence against 22 ... ♗d4+. For example: 21 ♕c4 ♖xd2! 22 ♘xd2 ♖d8 (but not 22 ... f3? 23 ♘xf3 ♗xf3 24 ♖e3 and White comes out a rook up), or 21 ♕f2 ♕xf2+ 22 ♔xf2 ♖xd2+ 23 ♘xd2 ♗d4+.

21	...	♗g4
22	e5	♖fe8
23	♕c4?	(10)

It was essential to defend with 23 ♘e4, although after 23 ... ♗xf3 24 ♕xf3 ♕xf3 25 gf ♗xe5 Black probably stands better in view of White's pawn weaknesses.

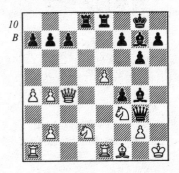

10
B

23   ...   ♖xd2!

This forced sacrifice (the threat was 24 ♘e4, winning Black's queen) puts White in a critical position again.

24   ♘xd2   ♖xe5?!

In this tense situation Shteinberg misses the strongest continuation

– 24 ... ♗xe5! and now:

a) 25 ♖xe5 ♖xe5 26 ♖a3 ♕f2 27 ♘f3 ♖h5+ 28 ♘h2 f3 and there is no defence against 29 ... ♕g3.

b) 25 ♕d3 ♕h4+ 26 ♔g1 ♖d8 27 ♖xe5 ♖xd3 28 ♖e8+ (or 28 ♗xd3 ♕d8) 28 ... ♔g7 29 ♗xd3 f3 with decisive threats.

c) 25 ♘f3 ♗xf3 26 gf ♕xf3+ 27 ♔g2 ♕h5+ 28 ♔g1 f3 winning a piece.

| 25 | ♖xe5 | ♗xe5 |
| 26 | ♕d3? | |

This loses outright, whereas 26 ♖a3! would have given saving chances: 26 ... f3 27 ♘xf3 ♗xf3 28 ♔g1! (but not 28 ♕xf7+? ♔xf7 29 ♖xf3+ ♕xf3 30 gf ♗xb2 with a won endgame for Black) 28 ... ♕h2+ 29 ♔f2 ♗c6 30 ♖h3 ♕f4+ and Black will hardly be able to realise his advantage (analysis by A. Grinfeld).

26	...	♕h4+
27	♔g1	f3
28	♘xf3	♗xf3
	0-1	

Mastery of the art of combination, the ability in any given situation to find the most telling move, leading quickly to fulfilment of the plan that you have conceived – this is higher than any principles, or rather it is the only chess principle that can be formulated as such.

Chigorin

Dieks-Marjanović
World Junior Ch., Manila 1974
Sicilian Defence

1	e4	c5
2	♘f3	e6
3	d4	cd
4	♘xd4	♘c6
5	♘b5	d6
6	c4	a6
7	♘5c3	♘f6
8	♗e2	♗e7
9	0-0	0-0
10	♗e3	♕c7?!

A more energetic line is 10 ... ♖b8 11 ♘d2 (after 11 ♕d2?! b5! 12 cb ab 13 ♗xb5 ♘xe4 Black seems to have the better prospects) 11 ... ♖e8 12 a3 ♘d7 13 b4 b6 with equality according to the *Encyclopaedia of Chess Openings* (ECO).

11	♘a3	b6
12	♕e1	♗b7
13	♖d1?!	

Both sides are committing inaccuracies in the opening. A more logical reply to Black's 12th move seems to be 13 ♖c1! and a set-up with f3, ♕f2 and ♘d5 (indicated by Marjanović).

13	...	♖ab8
14	f3	♖fd8
15	♕f2	♗a8
16	♖d2	♘b4
17	♖fd1	d5
18	cd	ed
19	e5?	

This is refuted by an original combination. White had to seek equality in further exchanges: 19 ed ♘fxd5 20 ♘xd5 ♘xd5 21 ♗d4.

19	...	♕xe5
20	♗xb6 *(11)*	

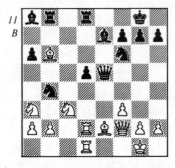

20	...	♖xb6!

A precisely calculated combination, the theme of which is the unfortunate placing of White's king and queen on the g1-a7 diagonal.

21	♕xb6	♘d7
22	♕a5	

Clearly the only move.

22	...	♖b8
23	♘c2	

There is no other way to save the queen from the threatened 23 ... ♗d8 and 24 ... ♘c5.

23	...	♗g5
24	♘xb4	♗xd2
25	♗f1	

Or 25 ♗xa6? ♗e3+ 26 ♔h1 ♗b6 and 27 ... ♗c7; or 25 ♘xa6? ♗xc3 and 26 ... ♕xe2 (Marjanović).

25	...	♗e3+
26	♔h1	♗b6
27	♕xa6	♗c7

28	g3	d4
29	♗e2	♘f8

By this time, 'all roads lead to Rome'. All White's minor pieces are now *en prise*.

30	♕c4	dc
31	bc	♖e8
32	♖d2	♗xf3+!

0-1

Spassky-Avtonomov
Leningrad Junior Ch 1949
Queen's Gambit Accepted

1	d4	d5
2	c4	dc
3	♘f3	♘f6
4	e3	c5
5	♗xc4	e6
6	0-0	a6
7	♕e2	b5
8	♗b3	♘c6
9	♘c3	cd?

Exchanging at this point leads to a bad position. He should have continued 9 ... ♗b7 10 ♖d1 ♕c7 11 d5! ed 12 ♘xd5 ♘xd5 13 ♗xd5 ♗e7 followed by kingside castling.

10	♖d1	♗b7
11	ed	♘b4 (12)

Black attempts to blockade the d-pawn with a piece. If he succeeded in this, his game would be perfectly satisfactory. But the position of the white queen and the black king on the same file creates combinative possibilities which Spassky utilises for an attack.

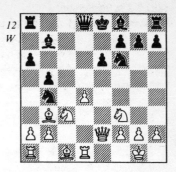

12	d5!

An elegant pawn sacrifice which leads to a forced win.

12	...	♘bxd5
13	♗g5	♗e7
14	♗xf6	gf

14 ... ♗xf6? loses a piece to 15 ♘xd5.

15	♘xd5	♗xd5
16	♗xd5	ed
17	♘d4	♔f8

He can't castle because of 18 ♘f5 winning his bishop, while 17 ... ♕d7 could be met by 18 ♖e1 ♖a7 19 ♖ac1 0-0 20 ♘c6.

18	♘f5	h5

18 ... ♖a7 fails to save him in view of 19 ♕e3 ♖d7 20 ♕h6+ ♔e8 21 ♘g7+.

19	♖xd5!	♕xd5
20	♕xe7+	♔g8
21	♕xf6	

1-0

The defender always faces a more difficult task than the attacker; the slightest false step may prove fatal to him.

Romanovsky

Demin-Spassky
Leningrad Schoolboys' Ch 1951
Sicilian Defence

1	e4	c5
2	♘f3	♘c6
3	d4	cd
4	♘xd4	g6
5	c4	♗g7
6	♗e3	♘h6

It isn't easy to break free from old attachments. Spassky used to play this difficult variation in his childhood, and although frowned on by chess theory it continued to attract him in maturer years.

7	♘c3	0-0
8	♗e2	d6
9	0-0	f5
10	ef	gf

10 ... ♗xd4 would be met, not by 11 ♗xd4? ♘xf5 with an excellent position for Black, but by 11 ♗xh6.

A different exchanging operation is also unattractive for Black: 10 ... ♘xd4 11 ♗xd4 ♗xd4 12 ♕xd4 ♘xf5 13 ♕d2 ♗d7 14 ♗f3 ♗c6 15 ♗d5+ and White is better, Tal-Kupreichik, Sochi 1970.

11	f4!	♗d7
12	♗f3!?	

The usual continuation in this position is 12 ♕d2 ♘g4 13 ♗xg4 fg 14 ♘d5 ♖c8 with some advantage to White (*ECO*). For

that reason, White's last move may look like a loss of tempo. In fact, though, it forms the first link in a plan for conquering the central squares, and happens to involve a hidden trap. If Black plays 12 ... ♘g4?! on the analogy of the normal line, then after 13 ♗xg4 fg, the position of White's queen on d1 (rather than d2) makes possible the retort 14 f5! This severely cramps Black's game, since taking the pawn sacrifice is dangerous: 14 ... ♘xd4 15 ♗xd4 ♖xf5! (15 ... ♗xf5? 16 ♗xg7 ♔xg7 17 ♖xf5 and White wins) 16 ♖xf5 ♗xf5 17 ♗xg7 ♔xg7 18 ♕d2 with a strong initiative; while on 14 ... ♕b6? the simple 15 ♘ce2! is highly unpleasant (15 f6? is a mistake because of 15 ... ♖xf6! but not 15 ... ♗xf6? 16 ♖xf6! ef 17 ♘f5 and 18 ♕g4+).

12	...	♔h8
13	♘ce2	e5

In spite of Black's central pawns, the advantage in the centre lies with White. He was threatening to gain control of all the key squares by the manoeuvre ♘e2-g3-h5, hence Black is compelled to stir up a tactical fight. But in the process the important point d6 is weakened and White's other knight will now head towards it.

14	♘b5	e4
15	♗h5	♗xb2
16	♖b1	♗g7

17	♘xd6	b6
18	c5	♕h4
19	♘g3	bc
20	♖b7	♗e6

20 ... ♖ad8 is very stongly answered either by 21 ♗xc5 or by 21 ♕d5! threatening 22 ♖xd7. On the other hand, 21 ♕a4? (with the same idea) would lose to 21 ... ♘e5! followed by 22 ... ♘g4.

21	♗xc5	♘g8

Black's queen and knight are out of action on the kingside. The attempt to bring them back into play is energetically refuted by White.

22	♗f7!	

The consequences of this powerful move had to be precisely analysed.

22	...	♘d8
23	♘dxf5	♗xf5
24	♘xf5	♕f6 *(13)*

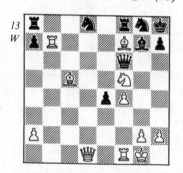

13
W

White's positional advantage is undeniable. Black's pieces are deprived of space and mobility, while White's rook and minor pieces dominate the enemy camp.

This circumstance is exploited by Demin with the aid of a deeply calculated combination on the deflection theme.

25	♗d4!	

With the tempting 25 ♗xf8? White could even lose after 25 ... ♗xf8 26 ♗xg8 ♘xb7 27 ♗d5 (27 ♕d5 ♗c5+ 28 ♔h1 ♖xg8) 27 ... ♖d8 28 ♘e3 ♗c5.

25	...	♕xf5
26	♗xg7+	♔xg7
27	♗e6+	♘xb7
28	♗xf5	♖xf5
29	♕g4+	♔f6
30	♖c1	

Black has more than enough material for the queen, but the disjointed actions of his pieces, scattered all round the board, make his position untenable. For example: 30 ... ♘e7 31 ♖c7 ♘d6 32 ♕h4+, or 30 ... ♘c5 31 ♕h4+ ♔e6 32 g4 ♖d5 33 ♕xh7 ♘f6 34 ♕c7! ♖g8 (34 ... ♖ad8? 35 f5+) 35 ♖xc5 ♖xg4+ 36 ♔f2 and White should win.

In time trouble Spassky played

30	...	♘d8?

and ceased resistance after

31	♕xg8	

1-0

Kozlov-Suleimanov
USSR Junior Team Ch, Erevan 1969
Scotch

1	e4	e5
2	♘f3	♘c6

3	d4	ed
4	♘xd4	♘f6
5	♘xc6	bc
6	e5	♕e7
7	♕e2	♘d5
8	c4	♗a6
9	♘d2	♘f4?

Of the three possibilities for moving the knight away, this is the worst. Black could have equalised by 9 ... ♘b4 10 ♘f3 c5! 11 a3 ♘c6 12 ♗d2 ♕e6. Now White gains the advantage in the centre.

10	♕e4	♘g6
11	f4	0-0-0

There is no alternative, for kingside castling would demand lengthy preparation, and in any case the white pawns on e5 and f4 would then cause Black a great deal of worry.

12	b3	f6
13	♗b2	♖e8
14	0-0-0	fe *(14)*

15 f5!

The signal for the attack! White masterfully exploits his space advantage for the regrouping of his forces.

15	...	♘f4
16	♘f3	d6
17	c5!	

The next stage in the plan White has initiated. He hasn't the slightest interest in 17 ♕xc6? ♗b7 when Black would stand no worse.

17	...	♗b7

Of course not 17 ... ♗xf1? 18 ♕xc6 ♔b8 (mate in two was threatened) 19 ♖hxf1 with powerful threats.

18	♕a4	♔b8
19	g3	♘d5 *(15)*

20 ♖xd5!

Giving the opponent no respite. By sacrificing the exchange, White shuts off Black's main forces on the kingside, from where they can only watch while their king perishes.

20	...	cd
21	c6	♗c8
22	♗a6	♔a8

There is no other defence.

23 ♘d4!

Blow follows blow. The knight cannot be taken, since after 23 ...

ed 24 ♗xd4 the point a7 is
indefensible.

23	...	♕g5+
24	♔b1	♕e3
25	♗b7+!	♔b8
26	♖d1	

26 ... ♕e4+ was threatened.

| 26 | ... | ♗e7 |
| 27 | ♕b5 | |

1-0

**Magerramov-Kasparov
Baku 1977**
Queen's Gambit Declined

1	♘f3	♘f6
2	d4	e6
3	c4	d5
4	♘c3	♗e7
5	♗g5	0-0
6	e3	h6
7	♗h4	b6
8	♕b3	♗b7
9	♗xf6	♗xf6
10	cd	ed
11	♖d1	c5!?

A new move. A similar idea has
been seen one move later, i.e. 12 ...
c5 after 11 ... ♖e8 12 ♗d3. The
insertion of these moves undoubtedly
benefits Black.

| 12 | dc | ♘d7 |
| 13 | c6?! | |

13 cb! looks more to the point.

| 13 | ... | ♗xc6 |
| 14 | ♘d4?! | |

What about 14 ♘xd5! ♘c5 15
♘xf6+ ♕xf6 16 ♕c3, forcing a
queen exchange (16 ... ♕e7 17 b4

♘e4 18 ♕xc6 ♕xb4+ 19 ♘d2
♖fd8 20 ♕c4; or 16 ... ♕g6 17
♘e5; or 16 ... ♕e6 17 ♘d4).

| 14 | ... | ♗xd4 |
| 15 | ♖xd4?! | |

This third inaccuracy in a row
throws away the game. By now
White should have been prepared
to settle for somewhat the worse
position after 15 ed.

15	...	♘c5
16	♕d1	♘e6
17	♖d2	d4!
18	ed	♖e8
19	f3 *(16)*	

Preparing an escape for the king
since he can't play 19 d5 ♘f4+ 20
♗e2 ♘xg2+ 21 ♔f1 ♗d7 22
♔xg2? ♕g5+ 23 ♔f1 ♗h3+ 24 ♔e1
♕g2 and Black wins (Kasparov).

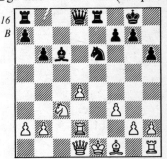

| 19 | ... | ♗xf3!! |

A most powerful continuation.

20	gf	♕h4+
21	♖f2	♘xd4+
22	♗e2	♘xf3+
23	♔f1	♕h3+
24	♖g2	♘h4
25	♖hg1	♖ad8

26 ♕e1

The position is lost for White. 26 ♕a4 could be met by 26 ... ♘f5! (preventing 27 ♕g4) 27 ♕f4 ♖d4 28 ♕f2 ♖d2 with the threat of 29 ... ♖8xe2 and 30 ... ♖d1+; or 28 ♕f3 ♘e3+ 29 ♔f2 ♕h4+ 30 ♕g3 ♕f6+ 31 ♗f3 (31 ♔e1 ♘c2 mate, or 31 ♕f3 ♖f4) 31 ... ♖d2+ 32 ♔e1 ♖xg2.

26	**...**	**♖d3!**
27	**♕f2**	**♘f3!** *(17)*

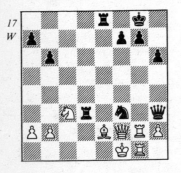

17
W

A picturesque position. White can only move his rook from g1 to h1 and back (28 ♘d1? ♖xd1+ and 29 ... ♘xh2 mate).

28	**♖h1**	**♔h8**
29	**♖g1**	**b5!**

0-1

Lputian-Kasparov
Tbilisi 1976
King's Indian

1	**d4**	**♘f6**
2	**c4**	**g6**
3	**♘c3**	**♗g7**
4	**e4**	**d6**

5	**f3**	**♘c6**
6	**♗e3**	**a6**
7	**♕d2**	**♖b8**
8	**♖b1**	**0-0**
9	**b4**	

In this position, which promises a complex, interesting struggle, White usually plays 9 ♘ge2 — supporting the central point d4 — and only afterwards begins a queenside offensive. Basically, with the immediate 9 b4 White has provoked Black's reply with its following pawn sacrifice.

9	**...**	**e5!**
10	**d5**	**♘d4**
11	**♘ge2**	**c5**
12	**dc**	**bc!**
13	**♘xd4**	**ed**
14	**♗xd4**	**♖e8!** *(18)*

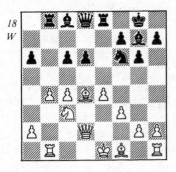

18
W

14 ... c5 15 bc ♘xe4 16 fe ♕h4+ looks very tempting, but after 17 ♔d1 ♖xb1+ 18 ♘xb1 ♕xe4 19 ♗xg7 ♕xb1+ 20 ♕c1 ♗g4+ 21 ♔d2 ♕xc1+ 22 ♔xc1 ♔xg7 23 cd ♖d8 24 c5 ♖c8 25 ♗xa6 ♖xc5+ 26 ♔b2 the complications culminate

in a favourable endgame for White. 14 ... ♖e8! confronts White with the complex task of finding the right path in a dangerous situation. Perhaps the correct solution was 15 ♗d3.

15	♗e2	c5!
16	bc	♘xe4
17	fe	♕h4+
18	g3	

18 ♗f2 would be followed by 18 ... ♗xc3 19 ♗xh4 ♖xb1+ 20 ♔f2 ♗xd2 21 ♖xb1 dc with a considerable advantage to Black. But no doubt that variation would have suited White better if he had foreseen what was in store for him.

| 18 | ... | ♖xb1+ |
| 19 | ♔f2 *(19)* | |

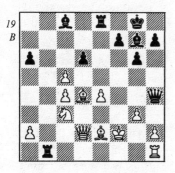

19	...	♖b2!!
20	gh	♖xd2
21	♗xg7	♔xg7
22	♔e3	♖c2
23	♔d3	♖xc3+!
24	♔xc3	dc

Black's combination has given

him a technically won endgame, in spite of the level material.

| 25 | ♗d3 | ♗b7 |
| 26 | ♖e1 | ♖e5 |

26 ... f5 27 e5 ♗e4 28 ♗xe4 ♖xe5 was also sufficient.

27	a4	f5
28	♖b1	♗xe4
29	♖b6	f4
30	♖xa6	f3
31	♗f1	♗f5
32	♖a7+	♔h6
33	♔d2	f2
34	♗e2	♗g4
35	♗d3	♖e1
36.	♖f7	♗f5
37	a5	♗xd3
38	♖xf2	♖f1
	0-1	

Notes by Kasparov

Ability to find the right strategic plan

Vilner-Minogina
Kiev 1979
Sicilian

1	e4	c5
2	♘f3	e6
3	♘c3	♘c6
4	d4	cd
5	♘xd4	d6
6	g3	♘f6
7	♗g2	♗d7
8	0-0	a6
9	♗e3	♗e7
10	♕e2	0-0
11	♖ad1	♕c7

12 f4

Vilner plays this line of the Sicilian frequently and has an excellent feel for all the subtleties of the coming middlegame. The immediate advance of the f-pawn is the strongest continuation against the move-order Black has chosen.

12	...	♖ac8
13	f5	b5
14	a3	♘xd4
15	♗xd4	♕c4
16	♖d3!	

With a possible kingside attack in view, there is of course no point in exchanging queens.

16	...	a5
17	g4	e5

Essential. The immediate 17 ... b4? would lose to 18 g5 bc 19 gf gf 20 ♕h5 etc., or 18 ...♘e8 19 f6 ♗d8 20 fg ♘xg7 21 ♗xg7 ♔xg7 22 ♕h5 e5 23 ♕h6+ ♔g8 24 ♘d5.

18	♗e3	b4
19	g5	bc
20	gf	♗xf6
21	b3	♕c7
22	a4! (20)	

The logical culmination of White's plan. Black's three pawn weaknesses plus White's strong pressure on the central d-file give compensation for the pawn sacrificed. Black must now play with extreme caution to avoid ending up in a lost position.

| 22 | ... | ♖b8 |

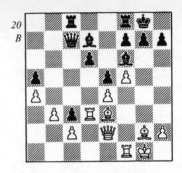

22 ... ♖fd8 could be met by 23 ♕f2 ♖b8 24 ♕g3 ♔h8 25 ♖fd1 ♗e8 26 ♗f2 ♖bc8 27 ♗e1, winning the pawn back with the better position.

23	♕d1	♖fd8
24	♖xd6	♗e7
25	♖d3	f6
26	♕g4?!	

A pointless move, though it doesn't actually spoil anything. 26 ♕f3! was stronger.

26	...	♗e8
27	♖fd1	♗c5
28	♕e2	♕b6
29	♗xc5	♕xc5+
30	♕f2	♕xf2+
31	♔xf2	♖xd3
32	♖xd3	♖c8!

Exploiting her chief trump for the defence: after 33 ... ♗f7, the threat of 34 ... ♗xb3 will stop White's rook from penetrating into the black camp.

33	♗f1	♗f7
34	♖d1	♔f8
35	♔e3	♔e7

36	♗b5	♔f8?

Allows White to exchange rooks, after which the pawn on c3 will fall, leaving Black with a lost game. The calm 36 ... ♖c7! would have maintained the balance, since no ways to strengthen White's position are to be seen. For example: 37 ♖g1 g5! 38 ♔d3 (after 38 fg ♗xg6, White's actions are hampered by the need to defend the e-pawn) 38 ... ♖c8 39 ♗c4 (39 h4 gh 40 ♖h1 ♖g8 41 ♖xh4 ♖g3+, or 41 ♔xc3 ♖g3+ 42 ♔b2 h3 43 ♗f1 ♗h5; in the last variation Black even stands better) 39 ... ♗xc4 40 bc ♖d8+ 41 ♔xc3 ♖d4, and again Black even has the better prospects.

37	♗a6	♖c7

It might appear that after 37 ... ♖c6 38 ♗b7 ♖c7 39 ♗d5 ♖d7 40 ♖d3 ♗xd5 41 ed ♔e7 42 ♔e4 ♔d6 43 ♖xc3 ♖c7!? 44 ♖xc7 ♔xc7 45 c3? ♔d6 46 b4 ab 47 cb g6, Black holds the draw. However, as E. Shekhtman has shown, it turns out that after 48 a5! gf+ 49 ♔xf5 ♔xd5 50 a6 ♔c6 51 b5+ ♔b6 52 ♔e4 ♔a7 53 ♔d5 ♔b6 54 ♔d6 e4 55 a7! ♔xa7 56 ♔c7 White will give mate. In addition, White can improve with 45 b4! ab 46 a5 and one of the passed pawns will queen.

38	♖d8+	♔e7
39	♖c8	♔d7
40	♖xc7+	♔xc7
41	♔d3	♗h5
42	♔xc3	♔b6
43	♗c4	♗f3
44	♔d3	g6
45	♔e3?	

Missing the win which could have been achieved by 45 ♗g8! gf 46 ♗xh7 fe+ 47 ♗xe4 ♗g4 48 ♗g6! ♗h3 49 ♔e4 ♔c5 50 ♗f5 ♗xf5+ 51 ♔xf5 ♔d4 52 h4 e4 53 ♔f4 containing Black's passed e-pawn. The verdict isn't altered by 46 ..♗xe4+ 47 ♔d2 when Black can't stop the advance of the white pawns.

45	...	♗d1
46	♔d2	♗f3
47	fg	hg
48	♔e3	♗d1
49	h4	

It isn't hard to see that the win has slipped away. For example: 49 ♔d2 ♗f3 50 ♗d3 ♔c5 51 c3 ♗g4 with 52 ... f5 to follow.

49	...	g5
50	♗e2	♗xc2
51	h5	♗xb3
52	♔d3	♔c5
53	♔c3	♗g8
54	♗g4	♗h7
55	♗f5	g4!

Forcing the draw.

56	♔d3	g3
57	♔e3	♗g8
58	h6	♔b4
59	h7	♗xh7
60	♗xh7	♔xa4

½-½

For four centuries there has been an extraordinary growth in the theory of the Ruy Lopez. And yet the basic question – the question of the best defence – has yet to be settled, an answer to it has still to be found to this day.

Bronstein

Diesen-Egmont
World Junior Ch., Groningen 1977
Ruy Lopez

1	e4	e5
2	♘f3	♘c6
3	♗b5	a6
4	♗a4	♘f6
5	0-0	♗e7
6	♖e1	b5
7	♗b3	0-0
8	d4	

This is a way to sidestep the Marshall Attack. Still, White now has to reckon with the possibility of 8 ... ♘xd4!? 9 ♗xf7+ ♖xf7 10 ♘xe5 ♖f8! 11 ♕xd4 c5 12 ♕d1 ♕c7 or 12 ... ♗b7!? when the initiative fully compensates Black for the pawn minus.

8	...	d6
9	c3	♗g4
10	♗e3	ed
11	cd	♘a5
12	♗c2	c5
13	♘bd2	

A line seen more often is 13 dc dc and only then 14 ♘bd2.

13	...	cd

14	♗xd4	♘c6
15	♗e3	d5
16	h3	

The continuation 16 ed ♘xd5 17 ♗xh7+ ♔xh7 18 ♕c2+ ♔g8 19 ♕xc6 ♗b4 20 ♗g5 f6 21 ♖e4 ♖c8 is clearly no good for White. An equal game results from 17 ♕b1 ♘f6 18 ♗e4.

16	...	♗h5
17	g4!	de

17 ... d4?! is dubious: 18 ♗f4 d3 19 ♗b1 ♗g6 20 ♕b3! and White wins a pawn (20 ♖e3 ♗c5 21 ♖xd3 ♕b6 22 ♕e2 ♖fe8 is not so good).

18	gh	ef
19	♕xf3!	(21)

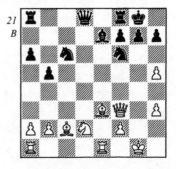

21
B

Not many players would have decided, several moves in advance, to accept a position with such a pawn structure. But Diesen has correctly weighed up the main factors: the great activity of White's pieces on the open files and diagonals and the unavoidable weakening of Black's castled position (after ... h7-h6). Incidentally, White had to calculate the variation 19 ... ♘d4? 20 ♗xd4 ♛xd4 21 ♘b3 ♛xb2 22 ♖e2 ♛a3 23 h6 g6 24 ♖ae1 ♖ae8 25 ♖xe7 and wins. Black would therefore have to play 21 ... ♛a7, but after 22 ♘a5! White's threats are very powerful. For example: 22 ... ♛c5 23 ♘c6 ♗d6 24 ♗b3 ♖ac8 25 ♖ac1 ♛g5+ (25 ... ♛xh5 26 ♛xh5 ♘xh5 27 ♘e7+ ♗xe7 28 ♖xc8 ♖xc8 29 ♖xe7 ♖f8 30 ♖a7 with a big endgame advantage) 26 ♔h1 ♘xh5 27 ♘e7+! ♗xe7 28 ♛xf7+! ♖xf7 29 ♖xc8+ ♗f8 30 ♖ee8 and White wins.

19	...	♘b4
20	♗b3	♘bd5
21	♗g5	h6
22	♗h4	♖e8
23	♖ad1	

White's central pressure is increasing; with his next manoeuvre, Black attempts to reduce it.

23	...	♖a7
24	♘e4	♖d7
25	♘g3!	

Thanks to the direct threat of 26 ♖xd5! ♘xd5 27 ♗xd5 ♖xd5 28 ♖xe7, White manages to bring his knight to the important f5 square with gain of tempo.

25	...	♘c7
26	♘f5	♗b4

Black has no useful moves. His position is lost.

| 27 | ♘xh6+! | |
| | 1-0 | |

A. Petrosian-Belyavsky
Riga 1973
King's Indian

1	d4	♘f6
2	c4	g6
3	♘c3	♗g7
4	e4	0-0
5	♗e3	d6
6	f3	e5
7	d5	♘h5
8	♛d2	f5
9	0-0-0	♘d7
10	♗d3	♘c5

A more reliable line is 10 ... fe 11 ♘xe4 ♘f4 12 ♗c2 ♘f6 13 ♘c3 b5!

| 11 | ♗c2 | a6?! |

Black handles the opening imprecisely. The attempt to open lines on the queenside with ... a7-a6 has been seen often enough, but without the insertion of 10 ... ♘c5. On the basis of analysis by Minev, ECO gives 10 ... a6 11 ♘ge2 b5 12 cb ♘f4 13 ♘xf4 ef 14 ♗xf4 fe 15 fe ♘c5 16 ♖hf1 ab 17 ♔b1! (17 ♗xb5? ♖xa2 is bad for White) with a small advantage. After the moves 10 ... ♘c5 11 ♗c2, Black should have pursued a different plan of action – fortifying the knight's position on c5 with 11 ... a5 – seeing that it is too late for 11 ... fe on account of 12 ♗xc5! dc 13 ♘xe4 when White's central advantage is undeniable.

Black's last move would have

chances of success if White were to opt for the stock plan of attacking with his g- and h-pawns. But in this kind of position with an advanced d-pawn, where White enjoys a space advantage on the queenside and hence more freedom of manoeuvre for his pieces in that sector, he often launches a pawn-storm in front of his own king. Carrying through a strategic plan of this kind is not simple, since the under-protected king position necessitates highly precise play. Petrosian, as will be seen from the following, acquitted himself of this difficult task brilliantly.

12   ♘ge2   b5 *(22)*

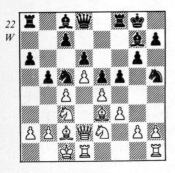

13   b4!

Forty-six minutes of precious time were used on this move which forms the first link in the attack against Black's queenside.

13   ...   ♘d7
14   cb

The obvious-looking 14 c5? would lead to unnecessary com-

plications: 14 ... a5 15 ♘xb5 ab 16 cd cd 17 ♘xd6 ♗a6! 18 ef ♗xe2 19 ♕xe2 ♖xa2 20 ♕c4 ♕a8, or 16 c6 ♘df6 17 ♕xb4 ♖xa2 18 ♘a3?! fe 19 ♔b1 ♖xc2 20 ♘xc2 ef 21 gf ♗h3! (21 ... ♗f5 would be answered by 22 ♕b7!) with numerous threats.

Of course these variations are not forced for White, but they graphically illustrate the kind of dangers that can arise in this sort of position.

14   ...   ab
15   ♔b2

From here until the end of the game Petrosian shows remarkable *sang-froid* in the way he parries his opponent's many tactical threats.

15   ...   ♗a6
16   ♘c1   ♕b8?

This tempting move was played almost without reflection; it finally wrecks Black's game which was difficult in any case. He had to decide on the immediate 16 ... ♘b6! which would have thwarted White's aim of bringing a knight to a5; then, with the opening of the c-file, Black could have obtained counter-chances after 17 ♗xb6 cb 18 ♗d3 ♕d7 19 g3? ♖ac8 20 ♕e2 ♘f4! Alternatively, 17 ♗d3 ♘a4+! 18 ♘xa4 ba 19 a3! (19 b5? ♕b8 20 ♕b4 ♘f4) 19 ... fe 20 fe ♘f6.

17   ♘b3   ♘b6
18   ♘a5   ♘c4+

19	♘xc4	bc
20	a3	♘f4?!

Again too nonchalantly played; now Black soon runs out of constructive moves. He had to try to start up some kingside play by more potent methods, without caring about material sacrifices: 20 ... fe 21 fe (it's inconvenient for a piece to recapture, since it will remain immobile for a long time in view of the threat to advance the black e-pawn) 21 ... ♖f4! planning the knight manoeuvre ... ♘h5-f6-g4.

| 21 | ♖a1 | ♘d3+ |

There doesn't seem to be any way for Black to improve his position; but after the move played, White's initiative on the queenside flares up with new strength.

| 22 | ♗xd3 | cd (23) |

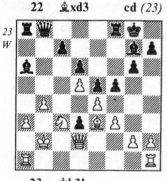

23
W

| 23 | ♔b3! |

All *à la* Steinitz! The king itself participates in White's operations, actively supporting the advance

of his pawns.

23	...	♖c8
24	a4	c6
25	dc	♖xc6
26	b5	d5

A desperate attempt to bring into play his black-squared bishop which all this time has been acting a miserable onlooker's role.

27	♘xd5	♗f8
28	♕xd3	♕d6
29	♔b2!	

Precisely played! White prepares exchanges in the c-file, and for this purpose he needs control of the third rank, particularly the a3 point. This is considerably stronger than the tempting 29 ♘f6+ ♔g7!

29	...	♖b8
30	♖hc1	♔h8
31	♖c3	♗b7
32	♖ac1	fe
33	fe	♖xc3
34	♖xc3	♗xd5
35	♗c5!	♕f6
36	♕xd5	♖d8
37	♕c6	♕f4

37 ... ♖d2+ would be met by 38 ♖c2!

38	♗xf8	♕xf8
39	♕c5	♕f4
40	♕c6	

The last few moves were made in time-trouble.

| 40 | ... | ♕d2+ |
| 41 | ♔a3 | h5 |

One fails to see what makes

Black play on.

42	♕f6+	♔h7
43	♖c7+	♔h6
44	♕g7+	♔g5
45	♕xe5+	♔h6
46	♕g7+	♔g5

47	♖c5+	♔h4
48	♕f6+	g5
49	♕xg5+!	
	1-0	

On 49 ... ♕xg5, White plays 50 g3+.

2 Typical Mistakes by Young Players

Hasty moves and, in consequence, blunders.

It is essential that every move should be checked, however obvious it may seem from a distance.

Capablanca

Every move should be checked – this advice is followed by all strong players. They solve this problem in different ways, but one rule has long been employed by many of them. Here is what Grandmaster Kotov has written about it: *'When you've finished analysing variations, you must first of all write down the proposed move on your scoresheet. The point is to do this before moving! I have observed a good many of my colleagues and have noticed that the majority of grandmasters will first write a move down and then play it on the board. Only a few do it the other way round.'*

Diesen-Halasz
Schilde 1973
Ruy Lopez

1	e4	e5
2	♘f3	♘c6
3	♗b5	a6
4	♗a4	d6
5	0-0	b5

A playable move, though seen less often than 5 ... ♗g4 6 h3 h5 with complex play.

6	♗b3	♘a5
7	d4	ed
8	♕xd4	

By transposition of moves we have reached a well-known position from the variation 4 ... b5 5 ♗b3 ♘a5 6 0-0 d6 7 d4 ed. Theoretical manuals give some preference to White's position after 8 ♘xd4. The move Diesen plays is hardly any stronger than the normal one. But it proves to have a wholly unexpected psychological effect.

8	...	c5? (24)

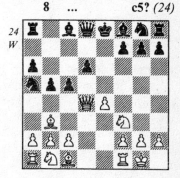

A crude error, characteristic of players who think dogmatically. The position which has been reached is very similar in type to one arising out of the Steinitz Deferred; and without stopping to think, Black tries to carry out the stock manoeuvre leading (so he imagines) to the win of a piece. The position *is* similar, but not entirely so since the knights are still on f3 and a5; and Mark Diesen, later to become World Junior Champion, immediately exploits this circumstance.

9 &xf7+ &xf7
10 ♕d5+ &e8

A forced retreat. On 10 ... &e6, White wins at once with 11 ♘g5+ ♕xg5 12 ♕xg5.

11 ♕xa8
1-0

Razuvayev-Kupreichik
USSR Students' Ch., Dubna 1970
English

1	c4	e5
2	♘c3	♘c6
3	♘f3	f5
4	d4	e4
5	&g5	

A more solid line is 5 ♘d2 ♘f6 (White has an excellent game after 5 ... ♘xd4 6 ♘dxe4) 6 e3, when White is playing the Steinitz variation of the French Defence with colours reversed and an extra tempo.

5	...	♘f6
6	d5?	

An ill-considered decision. The forced variation introduced by this move unexpectedly leads White to defeat. It was still not too late for 6 ♘d2!

6	...	ef
7	dc	fg
8	cd+??	*(25)*

In a note to his game with Smyslov at Groningen 1946, Botvinnik writes: *At this point, in working out the variation which follows, I came to the conclusion that it led to a won endgame with an extra pawn; and so, omitting to check over the variation again (every time my opponent played), I quickly made the moves I had planned. This was unpardonable negligence.*

Razuvayev devotes a great deal of time to chess. An experienced master who quickly achieved the grandmaster title, he was undoubtedly familiar with the advice of Botvinnik and Capablanca, and he alone can explain why on this particular day he didn't follow it. 8 &xg2 would have lost no more than a pawn, whereas now White is simply left with the unenviable choice of being a piece down or a rook down.

8 ... ♘xd7!!

The psychological shock of this unexpected stroke was evidently

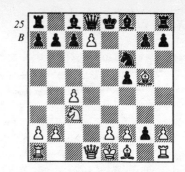

25
B

so great that Razuvayev played on for a few more moves.

9	♗xd8	gh♕
10	♗xc7	♕c6
11	♗g3	♗b4
12	♕b3	♗xc3+
13	♕xc3	0-0
14	e3	♘f6
15	♗e5	♗e6

0-1

Curiously enough, in 1971, in the USSR Ch. final, Doroshkevich fell into this very same trap in his game with Tukmakov.

Dolmatov-Lerner
Daugavpils 1978
Philidor's Defence

1	e4	e5
2	♘f3	d6
3	d4	ed
4	♘xd4	♘f6
5	♘c3	♗e7
6	♗e2	0-0
7	0-0	♖e8
8	f4	♗f8

9	♗f3	♘a6
10	♖e1	c6
11	♗e3	d5?!

Black has obtained the passive but solid position typical of this rarely seen variation. His last move is prompted by a wish to establish parity in the centre as soon as he can. But he ought not to have hurried. By increasing the pressure on the e-pawn with 11 ... ♘c5, he could have gained time to develop his pieces and achieve a satisfactory game. For example: 12 ♗f2 ♘e6 13 ♘xe6 ♗xe6 with 14 ... ♕a5 and 15 ... ♖ad8 to follow. Or 13 e5 de 14 fe ♘xd4 15 ♗xd4 ♘d7, with a view to 16 ... ♘c5, 16 ... ♘b6 or even 16 ... c5. Probably White does best with 13 ♕e2 ♘xd4 14 ♗xd4 ♗e6 15 ♖ad1 ♕c7 16 h3 ♖ad8 17 g4!? with the initiative.

12	e5	c5?

After 12 ... ♘d7! White has more space but that is all. It's hard to carry out the advance f4-f5, without which he can't possibly work up an initiative. And an attempt to exploit the temporary weakening of Black's castled position would be impracticable because of the unfavourable position of the white king's bishop. The move Lerner plays is a gross error, all the more surprising since in the previous game between the same opponents Dolmatov had blundered a piece away in the most elementary fashion. This very fact ought to have put Lerner on his guard (miracles don't happen twice running) and made him double-check the variation which was to lead him to defeat by force.

| 13 | ef | ♖xe3 |
| 14 | ♖xe3 | cd *(26)* |

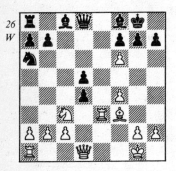

26
W

15   ♗xd5!

Undoubtedly Black had overlooked this reply after which he remains the exchange down with a shattered position. But Black's error becomes even more of a mystery when you realise that White also emerges with a won position from the other possible variation: 15 ♕xd4!? ♗c5 16 ♕d2 ♕xf6 17 ♔h1; or 16 ... ♕b6 17 ♘xd5 ♕xb2 18 ♘e7+ ♗xe7 19 ♖xe7 ♕xa1+ 20 ♖e1; or 16 ... d4 17 ♘e4.

15   ...   ♗f5

Black's position is hopeless. If he takes the rook or knight, 16 ♗xf7+ wins, while 15 ... ♕b6 is met by the simple. 16 ♘a4. Other moves of the white-squared bishop also lead to defeat: 15 ... ♗d7 16 ♕h5 g6 (16 ... ♗e8 17 ♖h3) 17 ♗xf7+ ♔xf7 (17 ... ♔h8 18 ♗xg6 h6 19 ♖e7) 18 ♕xh7+ ♔xf6 19 ♘d5+ ♔f5 20 ♖e5+ ♔g4 21 ♕h3 mate; or 15 ... ♗e6 16 ♖xe6 fe (16 ... dc 17 ♖xa6) 17 ♗xe6+ ♔h8 18 gf+ ♗xg7 19 ♘e4 ♕b6 20 ♗b3.

| 16 | ♖e5 | ♗g6 |
| 17 | fg | ♔xg7 |

Also after 17 ... ♗xg7 18 ♕xd4! ♗xe5 19 fe Black could resign with a clear conscience.

| 18 | ♘e4 | f6 |
| 19 | ♕xd4 | ♗xe4 |

If 19 ... fe, then 20 ♕xe5+ ♔h6 21 f5 or even 21 g4.

20   ♕xe4   ♘c5

Here too the capture of the rook leads to loss: 20 ... fe 21 ♕xe5+ ♕f6 (21 ... ♔g6 22 ♕e6+) 22 ♕xf6+ ♔xf6 23 ♗xb7.

21	♕f3	fe
22	♕g4+	♔h6
23	♖e1	♘d7
24	♔h1	♗c5
25	♖d1	♘f8
26	♗xb7	

1-0

Some useful practical advice is given by Kotov:
After each move, approach your evaluation of the position and your analysis of variations just as if the position were entirely new

to you. *Of course, the fact of your having seen this position in your mind's eye during the preceding moves will help you with your new calculations. But train yourself to prevent your former calculation from ever dominating your appraisal of the new situation.*

Learning openings without understanding the ideas.

The most thoroughly studied phase of the game is the opening. Quite often, talented young players equate ignorance of the openings with ignorance of 'theory', and therefore strive to memorise the numerous ramifications of the complex systems that are used in international tournaments.

However, '*it is not the mechanical study of variations devised by others that determines one's ability to solve the problems of the opening successfully*' (Romanovsky).

If a player learns variations without understanding the basic ideas of an opening and its characteristic type of middle-game, the result is that when he encounters something unexpected he loses confidence in himself, commits errors, defends himself weakly. Once in an unfamiliar situation, he is incapable of thinking independently, and racks his brains trying to remember the book line. In such cases, his alertness is abruptly diminished; this, as a rule, leads to mistakes and defeat. Obviously this sort of occurrence is what gave rise to the view that opening study is of small account in perfecting one's chess. This opinion, expressed in print as far back as the thirties, has since been repeated in various forms and has finally acquired the status of a dogma. Yet the opening is a very important part of the game. A mistake in the opening can do irreparable damage and lead to loss, while a well-played opening facilitates the conduct of the middle-game; the latter, after all, has its basis in the opening stage.

The main task when studying an opening is to understand the strategic essence of certain basic positions which determine the scheme of variations.

Kotov

A game from the USSR Junior Ch., Kaluga 1968
Sicilian

1	e4	c5
2	♘f3	d6
3	d4	cd
4	♘xd4	♘f6
5	♘c3	a6
6	♗g5	e6
7	f4	♛b6

Black chooses one of the

sharpest lines of the Najdorf Variation, the object of detailed analysis over the past two decades.

As we have said, games by young players reveal a penchant for fashionable variations. Unfortunately, though, instead of painstaking investigation of a position that arises out of a forced line of play, the contestant merely memorises the first ten to fifteen moves, which leads to irresolute play in the middlegame due to ignorance of the ideas typical of it.

The course of the present game shows White suffering from just this malady. It follows that at the first convenient opportunity, he ought to have sidestepped the forcing continuation. Such a possibility was available here in the move 8 ♘b3.

Yet White did not take the opportunity. How is this? Unfortunately it must be stated that now and again, even in tournaments on a very high level, you meet competitors who 'hope for the best' rather than prepare for the contest seriously. The one thing hard to understand is what mysterious force draws such players into a complex struggle in an opening they have hardly studied when there is no harm in employing some well-known classical system instead, thereby avoiding the possibility of ending up in an unfamiliar and generally disadvantageous position.

8	♕d2	♕xb2
9	♘b3	

Like 9 ♖b1, this move too has had its share of detailed analysis.

9	...	♘c6
10	♗e2	

Usually 10 ♗d3 is played here.

10	...	d5
11	♗xf6	gf
12	♘d1	

Playable, but if White had been sufficiently familiar with this position he would have given consideration to the continuation 12 ♘a4. There could follow 12 ... ♕a3 13 ♘b6 ♖b8 14 ed ♘a5! or even 13 ... ♘a5!? at once.

12	...	♕a3
13	ed	♘a5
14	0-0	♘xb3
15	cb	f5
16	♗f3	♗g7
17	♖c1	0-0
18	de?	

What is this? Disregard for well-known principles, tiredness, or a miscalculation? After 18 ♘c3 White would have a fully satisfactory position.

18	...	♗xe6
19	♘e3	

Even if the pawn on b7 could be taken, it would not have been worth developing the opponent's game and parting with the pride of White's position, the pawn on d5. But the b-pawn is immune, since after 19 ♗xb7 ♖ad8 20 ♕c2 ♕b4 and 21 ... ♖d2, the black pieces break through into White's camp.

19	...	♖ad8
20	♕f2	♕b4
21	♔h1	b5
22	♕g3	♖d3
23	♖fe1	♖fd8
24	♕g5	h6
25	♕h4	♕a5
26	♖c5	♕xa2
27	♘d5?!	*(27)*

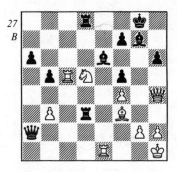

27
B

With many young players you often observe that while success causes elation, a setback will cause an abrupt loss of interest. Finding himself in a bad position after some bad play, White loses his taste for continuing the struggle and makes mistake after mistake.

In view of the weakness of his kingside, it would not have been easy for Black to exploit his advantage after 27 ♘xf5 ♗xf5 28

♖xf5 ♕xb3 29 ♕g4! The forced tactical line which White now initiates leads him to defeat. His last move is based on an interference motif – the rook on d8 is now *en prise*.

27	...	♖8xd5!
28	♗xd5	♗xd5
29	♕d8+	

A dual attack. Here White's calculations ended, but Black has seen further.

29	...	♔h7
30	♖xd5	♕d2!
	0-1	

A dual attack of rare elegance in reply. White loses a rook.

A game from the USSR Junior Team Ch., Lvov 1976
Sicilian

1	e4	c5
2	♘f3	d6
3	d4	cd
4	♘xd4	♘f6
5	♘c3	a6
6	♗g5	e6
7	f4	b5
8	e5	de
9	fe	♕c7
10	♕e2	♘fd7
11	0-0-0	♗b7
12	♕g4	

12 ♕h5 doesn't cause Black difficulties. The game Quinteros-Polugayevsky, Manila 1976, continued 12 ... g6 13 ♕h4 ♗g7 14 ♗e7 ♕xe5 15 ♗xb5 ♕h5, with

good prospects for Black.

| 12 | ... | ♕xe5 |
| 13 | ♗xb5 | |

13 ♗d3 is considered strongest, after which Black has to play very carefully: 13 ... h6! 14 ♗h4 g5 15 ♗g3 (another line to have been played is 15 ♘xe6 h5! 16 ♕xg5 ♗h6 17 ♖he1 fe! 18 ♗g6+ ♔f8 19 ♖f1+ ♕f6!! and Black wins, Boleslavsky-Kapengut, Minsk 1977) 15 ... ♕e3+ 16 ♔b1 h5 17 ♖he1 hg! 18 ♖xe3 ♘c5 19 ♘cxb5! ab 20 ♗xb5+ ♘bd7 21 b4 0-0-0 22 bc ♘xc5 with an unclear position (Polugayevsky).

| 13 | ... | ab |
| 14 | ♘cxb5?! | |

A dubious innovation. The familiar continuation is 14 ♖he1 h5! This last move is essential to relieve the point e6 from attack by the white queen, after which Black obtains a satisfactory position.

After 14 ♘cxb5, Black could repulse the attack with 14 ... f5 (recommended by Kimelfeld and M. Yudovich jun.), so as to free the f7 square for the king. For example: 15 ♘c7+ (obviously forced) 15 ... ♕xc7 16 ♘xe6 fg! 17 ♘xc7+ ♔f7 18 ♘xa8 ♗xa8 etc. But instead of appraising the new continuation by original thinking, Black fell back on his memory, and on the principle of analogy played:

| 14 | ... | h5? *(28)* |

This loses by force.

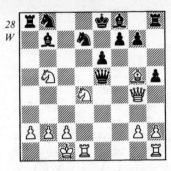

15	♘c7+!	♕xc7
16	♘xe6!	♕e5
17	♘c7+!	

In order to open up the e-file White has sacrificed two knights on c7. Now comes the showdown.

17	...	♕xc7
18	♕e2+	♘e5
19	♕xe5+!	♗e7
20	♕xc7	♗xg5+
21	♔b1	0-0
22	♕xb7	

and White won.

Lisenko-Zhiltsova — Ioseliani
Kishinyov 1976
Sicilian

1	e4	c5
2	♘f3	♘c6
3	d4	cd
4	♘xd4	♘f6
5	♘c3	d6
6	♗c4	e6
7	♗e3	♗e7
8	♕e2	a6
9	0-0-0	♕c7

10	♗b3	0-0
11	g4	♘d7
12	g5	♘c5
13	♖hg1	♗d7
14	♕h5	♖fc8
15	♖g3	g6
16	♕h6	♗f8
17	♕h4	♗e7 (29)

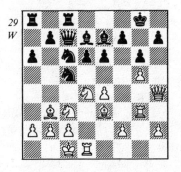

29
W

One of the contemporary standard positions. With 18 ♕h6 ♗f8 the game could be drawn by repetition.

18   f4?!

This move doesn't yet spoil anything, though a more accurate one, according to analysis by Nikitin and A. Ostapenko, is 18 ♘de2! which forces the immediate 18 ... h5! because of the threat of 19 ♘f4. (18 ... b5? 19 ♘f4! h5 20 ♘xh5 gh 21 ♕xh5 and White wins.) The main line of the analysis goes: 18 ... h5! 19 f4 b5 20 f5 ♘xb3+ 21 ab b4 22 ♘f4 bc 23 bc (with the impetuous 23 fg? White can even lose after 23 ... ♘e5 24 ♕xh5 cb+ 25 ♔d2 ♕xc2+ 26 ♔e1 ♕xd1+ 27 ♕xd1 ♖c1 28 ♗xc1

b1♕) 23 ... ♕a5 24 fg fg! 25 ♘xg6 ♔g7 26 ♘xe7 ♘xe7 27 ♗d4+ e5 28 g6 ♘g8! With an extra piece Black should beat off the attack.

18   ...   b5
19   ♘xc6?!

This exchange, a colourless move from every point of view, forcefully illustrates the enormous gulf between playing an opening variation learnt by heart and playing the ensuing middle-game. In one and the same game we can observe masterly conduct of the opening over a stretch of 15 to 18 moves, and, after that, helpless thrusts with the pieces to create one-move threats. Admittedly, by playing 18 f4?! and declining the draw, White was setting herself no easy task. It is too late now for 19 ♘de2? with the aim of sacrificing the knight on h5 after 19 ... b4 20 ♖h3 h5 21 ♘g3. The white king too is in danger and Black launches a mating attack first: 21 ... bc 22 ♘xh5 ♘xb3+ 23 ab cb+ 24 ♔xb2 ♘a5 etc.

19 f5? also loses in view of 19 ... ♘xb3+ 20 ab b4! (but not 20 ... ♘xd4? 21 ♗xd4 e5 22 ♖d2 ed 23 ♘d5 ♕d8 24 ♖h3 h5 25 ♘f6+ ♗xf6 26 gf with definite compensation for the piece sacrificed). However, the immediate 19 ♘f5!? doesn't look bad; one possibility is 19 ... ef 20 ♘d5 ♘xb3+ 21 ab ♕d8 22 e5 de (or 22 ... ♗e6 23 ed

♗d5 24 de ♘xe7 25 ♗d4 h5 26 gh ♔h7 27 ♗f6 with good prospects of regaining the piece or giving mate) 23 ♘f6+ ♗xf6 24 gf ♘b8 25 ♖h3 h5 26 ♕g5 ♕f8 27 ♖xh5 ♗e6 28 ♗c5! ♖xc5 29 ♖d8 and White wins.

19	...	♕xc6
20	♗d4	

This is the 'point' of the preceding move — White threatens mate with 21 ♕xh7+.

20	...	h5!
21	♖d2	b4

The superficiality of White's play is brought out further by the fact that Black could simply have taken the central pawn here. But the move played is stronger.

22 ♗d5 *(30)*

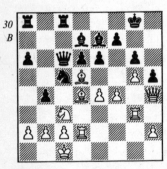

22	...	bc!

The quickest way to achieve the aim. With a material plus, Black obtains an overwhelming attack, which the thirteen-year-old girl carries through impeccably.

| 23 | ♗xc6 | cd+ |

24	♔xd2	♗xc6
25	♗xc5	dc
26	f5	♖d8+
27	♔c1	ef
28	ef	♖d4!
29	♕h3	♖ad8
30	b3	♗d7
31	♕f1	♗xf5
32	♕xa6	♖d2
33	♖c3	♗xg5
34	♔b2	♖2d6

0-1

Vladimirov-Kochiev
Young Masters', Lvov 1975
Sicilian

1	e4	c5
2	♘f3	e6
3	d4	cd
4	♘xd4	♘c6
5	♘c3	d6
6	♗c4	♘f6
7	♗e3	♗e7
8	♕e2	0-0
9	0-0-0	♗d7
10	♖hg1?	

As we saw from the previous example, in the Sozin Variation both attack and defence demand exceptional precision. One wasted tempo may lead to disaster. The move 9 ... ♗d7 is relatively little studied. Its aim consists in organising a pawn attack on the queenside as quickly as possible. After the correct 10 ♗b3! Black cannot play 10 ... ♘a5? since this would renounce the option of capturing on d4, and White would have the unpleasant reply 11 g4! at his disposal. 10 ... ♖c8 is also inadvisable because of 11 ♘db5. There remains the attempt to solve the problems of the position by 10 ... ♕b8 11 g4 ♘xd4 12 ♗xd4 b5! (but not 12 ... e5? on account of 13 ♗xe5 de 14 g5, gaining control of the central point d5) 13 g5 ♘e8 14 ♖dg1 b4 with complex play.

White's last move is borrowed from the variation 9 ... a6 10 ♗b3 ♕c7 11 ♖hg1. In that line it is justified since it prepares 12 g4. In this position, however, the move fails in its aim and is the initial cause of White's rapid defeat.

10   ...   ♖c8!

In contrast to his opponent, Kochiev avoids routine moves and plays in a constructive way. Now 11 ♘db5 can be met by 11 ... ♘e5 12 ♗b3 ♗xb5 13 ♕xb5 ♖xc3! 14 bc ♘xe4 15 ♗d4 ♕c7 with a good game for Black.

11   ♗b3   ♘a5
12   ♘db5

The planned 12 g4? has to be abandoned because of 12 ... ♖xc3! 13 bc ♘xe4 when White is left with a battered position. It must be acknowledged, then, that 10 ♖g1 has proved an unnecessary loss of tempo.

12   ...   ♘xb3+
13   ab   ♕a5! (31)

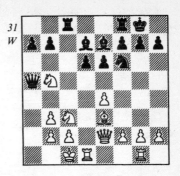

14   f3

The pawn on d6 turns out to be invulnerable: 14 ♘xd6 ♖xc3 15 bc ♗xd6 16 ♖xd6 ♕a3+ and Black wins.

14   ...   a6
15   ♘d4   g6!
16   ♕d3   e5
17   ♘de2   d5!

It is becoming clear that Black has gained full possession of the initiative, which grows into an irresistible attack.

18   ed

18 ♘xd5 is no better: 18 ... ♘xd5 19 ♕xd5 ♕a1+ and 20 ... ♕xb2.

18   ...   ♗f5
19   ♘e4   ♕a1+
20   ♔d2   ♕xb2

0-1

White resigns in view of the threatened 21 ... ♗b4+.

Quite often, 'theoretical' is synonymous with 'hackneyed'. For what is the 'theoretical' in chess, if not the material found in textbooks, which you try to copy whenever you cannot think up something stronger, or equally strong yet original?

Chigorin

Zagorskaya-Goikhenberg
USSR Junior Ch., Kapsukas 1977
Sicilian

1	e4	c5
2	♘f3	♘c6
3	d4	cd
4	♘xd4	g6
5	♘c3	♗g7
6	♗e3	♘f6

If you look at what openings are played in junior tournaments, especially by girls, you are immediately struck by the abundance of 'Dragons', which occur with astonishing consistency in virtually every round.

The reason why the study of the Dragon Variation is so widespread is, of course, that it is highly convenient for chess trainers. Not much effort is required to reduce the strategic ideas of this variation to a single one: White conducts a pawn-storm against Black's castled position on the kingside, while Black counterattacks with pieces (sometimes with an exchange sacrifice on c3) against White's castled position on the queenside. The fact that this is only one drop in the boundless ocean of chess

ideas causes few of these trainers any concern. Instead of a wide outlook, the pupils acquire a narrow specialisation which fetters their imagination.

7	f3?!

An · inaccuracy, after which Black could have obtained a good game with 7 ... 0-0 8 ♕d2 (8 g4? is even worse: 8 ... ♕b6 9 ♘cb5 a6 10 ♘f5 ♕d8 11 ♘xg7 ab 12 g5 ♘xe4! and White has a shattered position, Szczepanec-Gawlikowski, Poland 1954) 8 ...d5 9 ♘xc6 bc 10 ed ♘xd5 11 ♗d4 e5 12 ♗c5 ♘xc3 13 ♗xf8 ♕xf8 and Black obtains a strong attack, Krnić-Velimirović, Yugoslavia 1971.

7	...	♕a5?
8	♗c4?	

A sorry impression is made by such play, in which recollection is substituted for understanding. Such, unfortunately, is the fate of many able girls, through the fault of their trainers who cripple their independent thought by cramming them with opening variations and setting forth hard and fast dogmas. Instead of trying to exploit an inaccuracy or a wrong move-order on the opponent's part, such players will themselves acquiesce in the transposition, so as to direct the play back into familiar channels. It was on these very grounds that White played her last move, instead 8 ♘b3! after which Black

would have had to return the
queen to d8. One other thing
worth noting is that the position
after 8 ♗c4? is known to theory,
but is lost for White. Zagorskaya
was evidently unaware of this.

8	...	♛b4
9	♗b3?	

White could have got off with
merely the worse position after 9
♘xc6 ♛xc4 10 ♘e5 ♛c7 11 ♘d3
d6 12 ♛d2 0-0 13 0-0 ♗e6, and
Black achieves ... d6-d5.

9	...	♘xe4!
10	♘xc6	♗xc3+
11	bc	♛xc3+
12	♔e2	dc

All this has been known since
the game Gurgenidze-A. Geller,
Erevan 1959.

13	♗d4?	

She had to seek practical
chances in the line 13 ♛g1 ♘f6 14
♗d4.

13	...	e5!
14	♗e3	♗f5

14 ... 0-0 was simpler.

15	♛g1	♘f6
16	♗d2	♛d4
17	♗e3	♛b2?

We quite often come across
such profoundly mistaken decisions
when one of the players, possessing
a material and positional advantage,
doesn't want to give anything
back at any price.

Black grudges White the a-
pawn, and ignores the fact that

after the natural 17 ... ♛d6! 18
♗xa7 ♘d5, she would keep one of
the two extra pawns while wresting
the incipient initiative from White's
hands and unleashing her pieces
against the opposing king, which
of course is far more important
than a pawn.

18	♖b1	♛a3
19	g4	♗d7
20	♛g3	♛e7
21	♔f2!?	(32)

A felicitous 'blunder', after
which the situation on the board is
unexpectedly transformed.

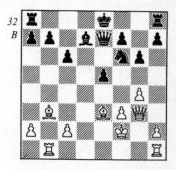

21	...	♗xg4?

It was imperative to forestall
the pin of the knight by playing 21
... ♘d5.

22	♔g2	♗d7

On 22 ... ♗e6, White wins with
23 ♗g5 ♗xb3 24 ♛h4, but as the
game continuation will show, a
stronger move was 22 ... ♗f5.

23	♗g5	♛d6?

It's interesting to survey the
stages by which Black has managed

to land herself in a lost position. The only way to continue the game was 23 ... ♘h5! 24 ♗xe7 ♘xg3 25 ♗f6 ♘h5! 26 ♖xh8 f6 27 ♖he1 0-0-0 28 ♗xf6 ♘xf6 29 ♖xe5. With the bishop on f5 Black would then stand no worse, but even with the bishop placed on d7 White's win would be made very difficult by the pawn weaknesses on both wings.

24   ♖he1?

There was an immediate win with 24 ♖hd1 ♘d5 25 c4 ♘f4+ 26 ♕xf4!, whereas, after the move played, Black has a saving resource: 24 ... 0-0-0! 25 ♖bd1 (25 ♕xe5 ♕xe5 26 ♖xe5 ♘d5 27 ♗xd8 ♖xd8 would lead to an ending with equal chances) 25 ... ♘d5! 26 ♗xd8 ♖xd8 27 c4 ♘f4+ and White cannot continue 28 ♕xf4? because of 28 ... ♕xd1 and Black wins. But the game takes a different course.

24   ...   ♘d5
25   ♗xd5   cd
26   ♖xe5+   ♔f8

With 26 ... ♗e6 27 ♖xe6+ ♕xe6 28 ♖e1 0-0, resistance could merely have been lengthened.

27   ♖e8+!
1-0

Reliance on general principles without a concrete plan.

Acquainting ourselves with the methods of play of the great masters, we cannot and should not imitate them by copying their precepts blindly and unthinkingly. We cannot because we shall never be in a position to repeat, in every instance, the psychological process which gave rise to this or that manner of conducting a game. We should not because if we did, then for us chess would be transformed from a game into a gruelling and pointless application of the memory.

C. Torre

A creatively thinking chessplayer, selecting the strongest continuation from a multitude of possibilities, is guided by his positional judgement. All the same, his train of thought will receive an imprint from the pattern inevitably formed by his analysis of similar positions in previous games by himself and others. This is not to be complained at, since studying the heritage of the past is an essential means to improvement. As usual, however, there is a reverse side to the coin. Material that has been inadequately worked through will settle in the memory not in the form of a finished whole but in the shape of isolated, disconnected fragments. In that case, very slight differences in position may go unnoticed, and routine play will almost invariably produce a negative result. This can be avoided if knowledge of the strategic principles is supported by precise calculation.

Characterising Fischer's play, Botvinnik has written:
The plans in his games are built on archetypal strategic precepts which he has absorbed during years of intensive creative work. With Fischer, these precepts are so thoroughly digested that there are many positions which he plays automatically, particularly those where what is demanded of the player is not so much profound intuition as the exact calculation of variations.

Vilner-Kochnyeva
Dnepropetrovsk 1978
Sicilian

1	e4	c5
2	♘f3	♘c6
3	d4	cd
4	♘xd4	♘f6
5	♘c3	d6
6	g3	

An all-purpose system for meeting the Sicilian. White can successfully fianchetto the king's bishop whatever move-order Black chooses. For example:

a) 5 ... e6 6 g3 d5 7 ed ♘xd5 8 ♘xc6 bc 9 ♗g2 and White's position is preferable.

b) 2 ... d6 3 d4 cd 4 ♘xd4 ♘f6 5 ♘c3 a6 6 g3 e5 7 ♘de2 ♗e6 8 ♗g2 ♗e7 9 0-0 ♘bd7 10 h3 b5 11 a4 b4

12 ♘d5 ♘xd5 13 ed ♗f5 14 f4 ♕c7 15 c3 bc 16 ♘xc3 and White has good prospects on both wings, Boleslavsky-Ciocaltea, Bucharest 1953.

6	...	e6

Or 6 ... e5 7 ♘de2 ♗g4 8 ♗g2 ♘d4 9 0-0 ♖c8 10 h3! ♗xe2 11 ♘xe2 ♘xc2 12 ♖b1 ♗e7 (if 12 ... ♘b4, then 13 ♕b3 winning the pawn back with the better game) 13 ♗d2 0-0 14 ♗c3 b5 15 ♖c1 ♘d4 16 ♘xd4 ed 17 ♕xd4 and White's advantage is undeniable, Boleslavsky-Shagalovich, Minsk 1955. An even worse line for Black is 6 ... ♗g4?! 7 f3 ♘xd4 8 ♕xd4! ♗xf3 9 ♗b5+ ♘d7 10 0-0 ♗h5 11 e5! with a winning attack.

7	♗g2	♗d7

Strongest. After 7 ... ♗e7 8 0-0 a6 9 ♗e3 0-0 10 ♕e2 ♕c7 11 ♖ad1 ♘a5 12 f4 ♘c4 13 ♗c1 ♖b8 14 g4 b5 15 g5 ♘d7 16 a3! ♘xa3 17 ♖d3, White threatens to bring the queen and rook across to the h-file. Black can avoid this variation by selecting a different move-order at an earlier stage of the game: 4 ... e6 5 ♘c3 a6 6 g3 ♕c7 7 ♗g2 ♘f6 8 0-0 ♗e7. Now White can't play 9 ♗e3? because of 9 ... ♘a5 and Black forestalls the important manoeuvre 10 ♕e2 and 11 ♖d1. Therefore White should adopt a plan introduced by 9 ♖e1!

There can follow:

a) 9 ... d6 10 ♘xc6 bc 11 e5 de 12 ♖xe5! 0-0 13 ♗f4 ♕b7 (13 ... ♗d6? loses a pawn to 14 ♖xe6) 14 ♘a4 and Black has serious weaknesses on the queenside, Keres-Johansson, Stockholm 1966.

b) 9 ... 0-0 10 ♘xc6 dc 11 e5 ♘d5 12 ♗d2 ♖d8 13 ♕h5 ♘b4 14 ♗f4 ♘xc2 15 ♘e4, and in view of White's threat of 16 ♘f6+, Black has a difficult defence ahead of him.

In Zvorykina-Zatulovskaya, Moscow 1958, Black attempted to neutralise the effect of the fianchettoed bishop by developing her own bishop on the long diagonal. After 2 ... e6 3 d4 cd 4 ♘xd4 a6 5 ♘c3 ♕c7 6 g3 b5 7 ♗g2 ♗b7 8 0-0 ♘f6 9 ♕e2 ♘c6 10 ♘xc6 ♕xc6 11 ♘d5! ♖c8 White could have obtained a big advantage with 12 ♗g5!

8	0-0	♗e7
9	♗e3	0-0
10	♕e2	♘xd4
11	♗xd4	♗c6

The books assess this position as equal. A game Klovan-Kirillov, Riga 1967, continued 12 ♖fd1 ♕a5 13 a3 ♖fd8 and Black had no difficulties. Thirteen-year-old Ira Vilner chooses a more logical continuation:

12	♖ad1!	♕a5
13	f4	♖fd8
14	f5	e5

15	♗e3	d5 *(33)*

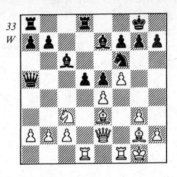

33
W

Many chessplayers, even of a high calibre, will assert, half jokingly and half seriously, that a difficult labour of analysis can be replaced by intuition. 'I played this move in a flash – it was obvious it couldn't be bad' is the sort of thing we often hear in a post-mortem.

Criticising such a policy is not simple – not after is has just been successful! One ought nonetheless to voice some doubt about the correctness of this 'method', which may grow into a regular habit of substituting considerations of a general kind for the analysis of concrete variations. We have here a case in point. Instead of appraising the state of the struggle on the basis of precise calculation, Black makes a move which, on general considerations, is wholly in the spirit of the position – a flank attack is countered by a break in the centre. Yet in chess there are no axioms. And for this dogmatic approach to the game Black has to play a high price. A stronger line was 15 ... b5 16 a3 b4 17 ab ♕xb4 18 ♗c1.

16	ed	♘xd5
17	♗xd5	♗xd5
18	f6!	gf

The game can't be saved. 18 ... ♗xf6 loses a piece to 19 b4. Black also loses after 18 ... ♗f8 19 ♘xd5 ♖xd5 20 fg ♗xg7 21 ♕f3 or 18 ... ♗c5 19 b4! ♗xb4 20 ♕g4 ♗f8 21 fg ♗c5 22 ♘xd5 ♖xd5 23 ♕f3 ♗xe3+ 24 ♔h1!

19	b4!	♗xb4
20	♘xd5	♖xd5
21	♖xd5	♕xd5
22	♕g4+	♔h8
23	♕xb4	

and Black **resigned** a few moves later.

Howell-Saeed
World Cadet Ch., Guayaquil 1982
French

1	e4	e6
2	d4	d5
3	♘d2	♘c6
4	♘gf3	♘f6
5	e5	♘d7
6	♗d3	f6
7	♘g5	♘dxe5

In Chiburdanidze-Zatulovskaya, Tbilisi 1976, Black went astray at once: 7 ... fg? 8 ♕h5+ g6 9 ♗xg6+ hg 10 ♕xg6+ ♔e7 11 ♘e4!

♗h6 12 ♗xg5+ ♗xg5 13 ♕g7+ ♔e8 14 ♕xh8+ ♘f8 15 ♕h5+ ♔d7 16 ♘c5+ with a big advantage to White.

8	de	fg
9	♕h5+	g6
10	♗xg6+	♔d7
11	f4	gf
12	♗d3	♕e8!

A new move. The familiar continuation is 12 ... ♘b4.

13 ♕xe8+

In this game White has chosen a sharp opening variation in the evident hope of outplaying his opponent in a tactical fight. Most likely the queen exchange was unwelcome to him, yet the position that has arisen is such that without serious risk this exchange is not to be avoided.

After 13 ♕g5 ♘b4! 14 ♘f3 (or 14 ♕xf4 ♘xd3+ 15 cd ♕g6) 14 ... ♘xd3+ 15 cd ♗b4+, or 13 ♕e2 ♘d4 14 ♕f2 ♗c5 15 ♕xf4 ♕h5! Black's advantage cannot be doubted.

13	...	♔xe8
14	♘f3	♘b4
15	♗xf4	c5
16	♔d2	♘xd3
17	cd	b6
18	♖hf1?	

We have here an opportunity to observe how White's moves, dictated by general precepts without being integrated into a concrete plan, are opposed to Black's play in which defence and attack contribute to an overall design. The position demanded 18 d4!

18	...	a5
19	♖f2	♖a7
20	g4?	

Though the circumstances are now less favourable, it was still not too late for 20 d4. White's premature activity results in the creation of further weaknesses.

| 20 | ... | ♖g8 |
| 21 | ♖g1?! | |

21 h3 was relatively better.

21	...	♖f7
22	♘e1	♗h6
23	g5 (34)	

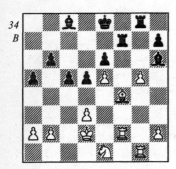

| 23 | ... | ♖xg5! |

An unexpected retort! Of course not 23 ... ♗xg5? on account of 24 ♔e2.

24	♗xg5	♖xf2+
25	♔e3	♖xh2
26	♗xh6	d4+!
27	♔f4	♖xh6

So Black has emerged with two extra pawns. Despite the futility of resistance, the finish is quite notable.

28	♖g7	♖h2
29	♘f3	♖xb2
30	♘g5	♖xa2
31	♖a7	♖f2+
32	♔g3	♖e2
33	♘e4	♖xe4!
34	de	♗d7
35	♔f2	c4
36	♔e2	a4

0-1

Ubilava-Timoshchenko
USSR Young Masters' Ch
Chelyabinsk 1974
Sicilian

1	e4	c5
2	♘f3	♘c6
3	♗b5	e6
4	0-0	♘ge7
5	♘c3	a6
6	♗xc6	♘xc6
7	d4	cd
8	♘xd4	d6
9	♘xc6	bc
10	♕h5?!	

A dubious innovation compared with the normal 10 ♕g4.

| 10 | ... | g6?! |

Playing according to routine. But the point is that, whereas after 10 ♕g4 Black has to play 10 ... ♕f6 or 10 ... g6, in the present case he can dispense with these moves and develop his bishop on e7. Even then, of course, White would remain with a lead in development. But this, as we know, is of importance mainly in open positions. Here, even though he would have only one piece developed, Black's position would not at all be worse. He would have no weak points on which White's pieces could establish themselves. The black pawns in the centre would look very impressive. Also, if occasion arose, the two bishops could demonstrate their power, since they are not inhibited by blocked pawn chains. Despite this, Black has decided to travel on well-worn paths and to bring the game back to a familiar position.

11 ♕h3 ♖b8?!

Incomprehensible neglect of basic development principles. An interesting struggle results from 11 ... e5 12 ♕g3 (or 12 ♕d3 a5 13 ♖d1 ♗a6 14 ♕d2 ♕c7 and 15 ... ♖d8) 12 ... ♗g7 13 f4 0-0! 14 f5 d5 with a good game.

Instead of 13 ... 0-0, a tempting line is 13 ... ef 14 ♗xf4 ♕b6+ 15 ♔h1 ♕xb2 16 e5?! 0-0 17 ♖ab1 ♕xc2 18 ♖bc1 ♕f5 19 ed ♗e6 20 ♗h6 ♗xh6! 21 ♖xf5 ♗xf5 22 ♖f1 ♗g7 and Black's position is no worse. However, 16 ♘a4 gives White an irresistible attack. For example, 16 ... ♕b5 (or 16 ... ♕xc2) 17 ♗xd6 ♕xa4 (Black can't save himself with 17 ... ♗xa1 18 ♖xa1 ♗e6 19 ♘c5 ♖d8 20 ♕e5 or

18 ...♕xa4 19 ♕e5+ ♗e6 20 ♕f6) 18 ♕h4 f6 19 ♖xf6 etc.

12 ♖d1 ♗g7
13 ♕g3 ♗e5? *(35)*

Leads to defeat. He had to decide on 13 ... e5, although after 14 b3! Black's position does not inspire confidence. For example: 14 ... ♖b7 15 ♗a3 ♖d7 16 ♖d3 0-0 17 ♖ad1 c5 18 ♘d5 and if 18 ... ♕a5?! then 19 b4! cb 20 ♗xb4 ♕xa2 21 ♗xd6! with a clear advantage.

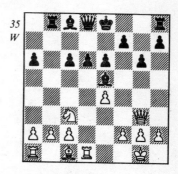

35
W

14 ♕xe5!!

Unexpected and very strong. White's combination is based on the theme of shutting the black pieces out of play. Black's king and king's rook remain silent onlookers for the rest of the game.

14 ... de
15 ♖xd8+ ♔xd8
16 ♗g5+ ♔e8

16 ... ♔c7? loses to 17 ♗f6 and 18 ♗xe5+.

17 ♗f6 ♖g8
18 ♖d1 ♗d7

19 ♘a4   ♖b4

Black is helpless. 19 ... c5 could be met by 20 ♘xc5 ♗b5 21 a4, and after driving the black bishop off the diagonal f1-a6, White takes the pawn on a6 and follows with a knight check on c7.

20 ♘c5   ♖d4
21 ♖xd4   ed
22 h4!

Anticipating 22 ... g5 which would now be answered by 23 h5!

22 ...   e5
23 f3   ♗e6
24 b3   a5
25 g4   h5
26 g5   ♗h3
27 ♔f2

The intervention of White's king quickly settles the issue.

27 ...   ♖f8
28 ♔e2   ♖g8
29 a4   ♖f8
30 b4   ab
31 a5   ♗c8
32 ♔d3   ♖g8
33 ♔c4

1-0

Underestimating the opponent's combinative chances

**Garbarino-Short
World Junior Ch.,
Copenhagen 1982**
French

1 e4   ˙e6
2 d4   d5

3 ♘d2   ♘c6
4 ♘gf3   ♘f6
5 e5   ♘d7
6 ♗e2   f6
7 ef   ♛xf6
8 ♘f1   ♗d6
9 ♘e3   0-0
10 0-0   ♛g6
11 c4

Another line to have been seen is 11 g3 ♘f6 12 ♘h4 ♛e8 13 f4 ♘e7 14 ♘g4 ♘e4 15 ♘f3 c5 16 ♗d3 ♘f5 17 c3 with a slight advantage to White, Velimirović-Vaganian, Rio de Janeiro 1979.

11 ...   ♘f6
12 g3   ♗d7
13 b3?

It's perfectly obvious that the weak point in Black's position is the e5 square and that White ought to bend his efforts towards seizing it. This could have been achieved by 13 c5 ♗e7 14 ♗b5, when Black cannot prevent White from posting a knight on e5 and following with f2-f4.

13 ...   ♖ae8
14 ♗b2   ♘e4
15 ♘e5   ♘xe5
16 de   ♗c5

It is becoming clear that White has achieved nothing with his last few moves. As a result of his planless play, the gaping 'hole' on e5 has now been plugged by a white pawn and the activity of the black pieces has abruptly increased.

17 ♗h5?? (36)

White had two threats – to take the pawn on d5, or to win the exchange. Yet with his last move Black ignored both of them, thus obliging White to evaluate very carefully the forced continuation he was choosing. But this he did not do. After 17 ♗d4! ♗xd4 18 ♕xd4 c5 20 ♕d1! ♘c3 21 ♗h5 ♘xd1 22 ♗xg6 hg 22 ♖axd1 d4 23 ♘c2 g5, Black's position is of course better, but there would still have been a prolonged struggle ahead. Now, White's position collapses in a few moves.

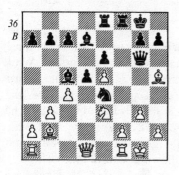

36
B

17 ... ♘xf2
18 ♖xf2

He also loses with 18 ♗xg6 ♘xd1 19 ♗xe8 ♖xf1+ 20 ♔xf1 ♘xe3+ 21 ♔e2 ♗xe8 22 b4 ♘xc4 etc.

18 ... ♕e4
19 ♘g4 ♖xf2
20 ♘xf2 ♖f8
0-1

Belyavsky-Kupreichik
Young Masters' Tournament,
Riga 1973
Sicilian

1	e4	c5
2	♘f3	d6
3	d4	cd
4	♘xd4	♘f6
5	♘c3	g6
6	♗e2	♗g7
7	f4?!	

The well-tried moves 7 ♗e3 and 7 0-0 are better. After the premature text move, Black has a simple possibility for obtaining an equal game.

7	...	0-0
8	0-0	♕b6
9	♗e3	♕xb2?!

9 ... ♘c6 is sounder, leading to a theoretical position in which White has no chance of gaining the advantage and must play very carefully to avoid ending up in a bad position. For example: 10 e5 de 11 fe ♘xe5 12 ♘f5 ♕xb2 13 ♘xe7+ ♔h8 14 ♗d4 ♕b4 (14 ... ♕a3 is also playable) 15 ♗xe5! (other continuations are worse: 15 ♘cd5 ♘xd5 16 ♘xd5 ♕xd4! 17 ♕xd4 ♘f3+, or 15 ♘xc8 ♖axc8 16 ♗xe5 ♖fd8 17 ♗xf6 ♗xf6! In this last variation 15 ... ♖d8 is also good for Black) 15 ... ♕xe7 16 ♕d4 ♘h5 (*ECO*), and it remains for White to prove that he has compensation for the pawn minus.

A stronger line, probably, is 10 ♕d3! ♘g4! 11 ♗xg4 ♗xd4 12 ♗xd4 ♕xd4+ 13 ♕xd4 ♘xd4 14 ♗d1 with equality.

| | 10 | ♕d3 | ♕b4? *(37)* |

37
W

10 ... ♘c6 11 ♖ab1 ♕a3 12 ♘xc6 bc 13 ♘d5 would have led to an equal position.However, in a game Wach-Olej, Poland 1973, White obtained some advantage by 11 a3?! ♘xe4 12 ♘xc6 ♘xc3 13 ♘xe7+ ♔h8 14 ♗f3 ♖e8? 15 ♘xc8 ♖axc8 16 ♗xa7! d5! 17 ♔h1. Probably Belyavsky was acquainted with this game and was trying to draw his opponent along the same path. But it appears he had not managed to carry through a really thorough analysis, since the general verdict pronounced on the variation by *ECO* on the basis of the Wach-Olej game is erroneous. As A. Yuneyev has shown, after 14 ... ♗d7! (instead of 14 ... ♖e8?) it is Black, not White, who gains a clear advantage. For example: 15 ♗d4? ♘e2+ 16 ♕xe2 ♕xd4+, or 15 ♕xd6 ♖ad8 16 ♕b4 ♕xb4 17

ab ♖fe8 18 ♗c5 b6.

Quite likely Kupreichik knew nothing of this and in making his 10th move was simply trying to avoid a drawish variation. But, to his misfortune, he had underestimated the tactical possibilities latent in the position. A forcing line of play now begins in which Black no longer has the power to alter anything.

11	e5	de
12	fe	♘g4
13	♗xg4	♗xg4
14	♖f4	♗d7
15	♘d5	♕a5
16	♘xe7+	♔h8
17	e6!	

This fearsome blow by a modest little pawn settles the outcome of the game. Acceptance of the sacrifice leads to immediate disaster: 17 ... ♗xe6 18 ♘xe6 fe 19 ♖h4! ♗xa1. 20 ♖xh7+ and mate in two.

17	...	♕d8
18	♖af1	♕xe7
19	♖xf7!	♖xf7
20	♖xf7	♕e8
21	♘f5!	

Belyavsky concludes the struggle very impressively.

21	...	gf
22	♗d4	♕xe6
23	♖f8+	♕g8
24	♖xg8+	♔xg8
25	♕g3	♔f7
26	♕xg7+	
		1-0

*There is a widespread notion
that the faculty of devising
combinations in chess cannot
be acquired but depends rather
on an inborn power of calculation
and imagination. Every experienced
player, however, knows that this
general opinion is erroneous
and that most combinations,
indeed, practically all of them,
are devised by recalling known
elements ....*

Réti

Umansky-Kärner
USSR Junior Ch,
Kaluga 1968
Queen's Gambit

1	d4	d5
2	c4	e6
3	♘c3	♘f6
4	♘f3	♗e7
5	♗f4	

Played in order to avoid well-studied variations. 5 ♗g5 is better, since it is then harder for Black to free his game by carrying out 5 ... c5.

5	...	c6

This attempt to channel the game back to the familiar strategic ideas of the Slav Defence gradually leads to an inferior position for Black. He could have rid himself of all difficulties by 5 ... c5! 6 dc ♗xc5 7 cd ♘xd5 8 ♘xd5 ed or 6 e3 cd 7 ed 0-0.

6	e3	0-0

7	♗d3	dc
8	♗xc4	b5
9	♗d3	a6
10	0-0	♗b7

Black is afraid to play 10 ... ♘bd7 because of 11 ♘e4 c5 12 ♘d6, exchanging one of his bishops. But if he had forced himself to examine this variation a little further he would have concluded that after 12 ... ♕b6! 13 ♘xc8 ♖axc8 the state of affairs is not at all bad for him, whereas after the move played he lands in a difficult position.

11	♘e4!	♘xe4
12	♗xe4	♘d7
13	♖c1	♖c8
14	♘e5	♘xe5
15	♗xe5	♕d7

All this time a dogged struggle around the advance ... c6-c5 has been in progress. Black has been preparing it, White has been striving to prevent it. It has now become clear that by simple means this move is impossible to stop and so White discovers a resource which does credit to his ingenuity. Under the disguise of trying to use his major pieces to seize the file that is about to be opened, White prepares a deeply calculated combination.

16	♖c3!	

Threatening to blockade Black's queen's wing after 17 ♕c2.

16	...	c5 *(38)*

17	♗xh7+!!	♔xh7
18	♕h5+	♔g8
19	♗xg7!	♔xg7
20	♕g4+	♔f6

If he went to the h-file, Black would be mated after 21 e4. The same kind of double bishop sacrifice (against a castled position on the kingside), exposing the opponent's king to a decisive queen and rook attack, has been seen a number of times in grandmaster practice.

It was first carried out in the game Lasker-Bauer, Amsterdam 1889, and afterwards in Nimzowitsch-Tarrasch, St Petersburg 1914, and Alekhine-Drewitt, Portsmouth 1923. We are now witnessing the combination being played, in an even more complex situation, in a schoolboys' tournament. The next stage of the game is characterised by the excellent play on both sides, in attack and in defence, in the midst of the tactical complexities that have arisen.

| 21 | e4 | ♗xe4 |

22	♕xe4	♕xd4
23	♖f3+	♔g7
24	♖g3+	♗g5!

Black finds the only moves to defend. 24 ... ♔f6? loses to 25 ♕f3+ ♔e5 26 ♖e1+ and 27 ♖d1, while 24 ... ♔h6 fails against 25 ♖h3+ ♔g7 (25 ... ♔g5 26 ♕f3) 26 ♕h7+ ♔f6 27 ♖f3+ ♔e5 28 ♖e1+ ♔d5 29 ♖d3.

| 25 | ♕f3! |

Of course not 25 ♖xg5+? ♔f6, when White is forced to exchange queens and go into a lost ending.

| 25 | ... | f6 |

25 ... ♔g6 may have been stronger.

26	♖d1	♕c4
27	♖d7+	♔g6

27 ... ♔g8? is decisively answered by 28 h4! ♕xh4 29 ♖h3 ♕f4 30 ♕h5 ♕c1+ 31 ♔h2 ♕f4+ 32 ♖g3 ♕f5 33 f4!

| 28 | ♖g4 |

Possibly the first inaccuracy in the conduct of the attack. A quicker way was 28 h4! ♕c1+ (28 ... ♕xh4 29 ♖h3 or 28 ... ♖h8 29 ♖xg5+!) 29 ♔h2 ♖h8 30 ♕e4+.

28	...	♕c1+
29	♖d1	♕c2
30	h4	♖cd8
31	♖e1	♕d3
32	♕c6	♔h5
33	♖1e4	♕d5

33 ... ♕d1+ 34 ♔h2 ♕xg4 35 ♖xg4 ♔xg4 loses to 36 ♕f3+ ♔xh4 37 ♕h3 mate.

34	♕c7	♖d7
35	♕g3	♗h6

With his exposed king Black shows astonishing sang-froid in defence. White should nevertheless win, in spite of being a piece down; his threats are too numerous.

36	♔h2	♕f5

The queen can't leave the fifth rank on account of 37 ♖e5+!

37	♕h3!

Lurking in ambush and threatening to finish the game with 38 ♖g5+! and 39 g4+!

37	...	♕xf2
38	♖g5+	fg
39	hg+	♔xg5
40	♕g4+	

1-0

On 40 ... ♔f6, White mates in two moves.

Kudishevich-V. Agzamov
USSR Junior Ch., Kaluga 1968
Ruy Lopez

1	e4	e5
2	♘f3	♘c6
3	♗b5	a6
4	♗a4	♘f6
5	0-0	♗e7
6	♖e1	b5
7	♗b3	d6
8	c3	0-0
9	d4	♗g4
10	♗e3	♘a5

More usually 10 ...ed 11 cd is played and only then 11 ... ♘a5. The move played could have been answered by 11 de ♗xf3 (not 11 ... ♘xb3? 12 ef! ♘xa1 13 fe and White emerges with two pieces for a rook) 12 ♕xf3 de 13 ♗c2 ♘c4 14 ♗c1 with a slight advantage in the shape of the bishop-pair.

11	♗c2	♘c4

Black neglects the opportunity to equalise with 11 ... d5.

12	♗c1	ed
13	cd	♘d7

By transposition, a theoretical position has been reached in which the usual continuation is 13 ... c5, attacking the white centre.

14	b3	♘a5
15	♘c3	

With a black pawn on c5, this active knight move would be impossible. White would have to make do with the decidedly more modest development of this piece on d2.

15	...	♗f6
16	♘d5	c5 (39)

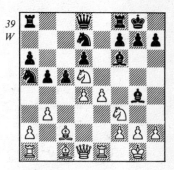

17	e5!

A deeply calculated combination,

the theme of which is the lack of protection for the point h7.

17	...	de
18	de	♘xe5
19	♖xe5!	♗xf3

19 ... ♗xe5 is even worse on account of 20 ♕d3 g6 21 ♘xe5.

20	♕d3!	g6
21	♘xf6+	♕xf6
22	♗b2	♗b7
23	♖b1	c4
24	♕h3	c3

This pawn sacrifice alters nothing. The ten-move combination is crowned by an attractive mating finish.

25	♗xc3	♕c6
26	♕xh7+!	
	1-0	

A game is lost because at some point the defender finds it impossible to match his opponent in the speed of regrouping his forces.

Nimzowitsch

Christiansen-Seirawan
USA 1978
Pirc

1	♘f3	g6
2	e4	♗g7
3	d4	d6
4	♘c3	♘f6
5	♗e2	0-0
6	0-0	♘c6

This came into fashion following Karpov-Pfleger, London 1977,

even though in that game White obtained some advantage. The idea of the move is not new and has been employed before in some variations of the Grünfeld Defence. Black provokes the advance of the central pawn, so that after the inevitable undermining move ... c7-c6 he can tie White's pieces down to the defence of it, or, if the occasion arises, open up the c-file for operations on the queenside.

7	d5	♘b8
8	♗g5	c6
9	♕d2	♕c7
10	♖ad1	♘bd7
11	♖fe1	a5
12	♗f1?!	

With a single imprecise move you can spoil any position. After 12 a4! ♘c5 13 ♗f1 ♗g4 14 ♕f4, with his better development and his space advantage, White could have stopped Black from showing any initiative on either wing.

12	...	a4
13	a3	♖e8
14	h3	♘b6
15	♗h6	cd
16	♗xg7	♔xg7
17	ed?	

Too nonchalantly played. 17 ♘xd5 was better so as to have the chance of pushing the c-pawn after the exchange of knights.

| 17 | ... | ♗d7 |
| 18 | ♖e3 | |

There's no other way to defend

the pawn on d5.

18	...	♖a5
19	♖d3	♘c4
20	♕c1	♖c5
21	♘g5!?	

He isn't going to end up playing 21 ♕a1 ... ! Having landed himself in a bad position, Christiansen as usual starts searching ingeniously for tactical chances.

21	...	♘xa3
22	♖d4!	h6
23	♘ge4	♘xe4
24	♖xe4	♘c4
25	♖dd4	♘b6?!

By excellently conducting his strategic operations on the queenside Black has won a pawn. At this point, however, he shows unnecessary haste. The move played may seem very menacing. For one thing, Black increases the pressure on the d5 pawn, and ties White's pieces to defence. For another thing he aims to complete the destruction of White's queenside with the advance ... a4-a3. Despite this, the retreat with the knight must be considered faulty. Seirawan ought to have borne in mind that three of his pieces — queen, rook and knight — are now completely shut off from the defence of the kingside. This is why 25 ... b5! was the move to take Black slowly but surely along the path to victory; in case of need, the knight could then immediately join in the defence

via e5.

26	♖h4	♖h8

The weak side of Black's position is illustrated by the variation 26 ... g5? 27 ♖xh6 ♔xh6 28 ♖h4+ ♔g6 29 ♗d3+ ♗f5 (29 ... f5 30 ♖g4!) 30 ♕d1 gh 31 ♕g4+ ♔h6 32 ♕xf5 and there is no stopping mate (Christiansen).

27	♕a1	♖a8?!

White's wily schemes would scarcely have turned out well had Black played 27 ... ♗f5! here.

28	♗d3	g5?? *(40)*

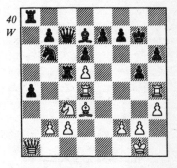

Seirawan shows astonishing carelessness. Already in the note to move 26, we saw the white bishop swiftly transformed from an inactive piece into a powerful fighting unit. But in that position the bishop was still on f1, whereas here it is already on d3 aiming unmistakably at the black king. 28 ... a3 looked tempting, but after 29 ♘e4 a2 a masked battery takes effect – 30 b4! and White wins. The sole but adequate defence was

to move the rook back with 28 ...
罝h8! But then we all know how
hard it is to realise your own
mistake.

    29   罝xh6!!

This hidden combinative idea
had escaped Black's notice.

    29   ...   🖒xh6

    30   罝h4+!!

This second rook sacrifice
which cannot be accepted (30 ...
gh 31 豐c1+ 🖒h5 32 豐d1+ 🖒h6 33
豐d2+ etc.) settles matters once
and for all.

    30   ...   🖒g7

    31   罝h7+   🖒f6

After 31 ... 🖒f8 the arrival of the
queen by 32 豐d1 and 33 豐h5 is
decisive. Not one of Black's pieces
can come to the defence of the
king in time.

    32   罝h6+   🖒g7

    33   罝h7+   🖒f6

Short of time, White repeats
moves.

    34   🖒e4+   🖒g6

Or 34 ... 🖒e5 35 b4+ 🖒xd5
36 bc dc 37 🖒xg5 c4 (37 ...
豐e5 38 奡e4+) 38 奡e4+ 🖒c5 39
罝h5 f5 40 奡xf5 奡xf5 41 🖒e4+
🖒d5 42 罝xf5+ 🖒xe4 43 g4! and
mates.

    35   豐d1   g4

After 35 ... 🖒xh7 36 豐h5+ 🖒g7
37 豐xg5+ 🖒f8 38 豐h6+ 🖒g8 39
🖒f6+ White forces mate.

    36   豐d2   罝xd5

    37   豐h6+   🖒f5

    38   罝xf7+

In the time-scramble White
overlooks a mate in three: 38
🖒xd6+ 🖒e5 39 🖒xf7+ 🖒d4 40
豐e3 mate.

    38   ...   🖒e5

    39   豐g7+   🖒e6

    40   罝f6+

Again White's tottering flag
stops him from giving mate, this
time in two moves: 40 罝xe7+ 🖒f5
41 豐g5 mate.

    40   ...   🖒e5

    41   罝xd6+   🖒f4

    42   g3+

                  1-0

Disparity between aggressive and defensive ability.

A serious brake on the achievements of young players is an
unwillingness – and consequently
an inability – to conduct a
painstaking defence over a long
stretch of time.

*. . . And this, of course, is an
immense defect. Essentially, all
modes of struggle in chess are
of equal value, which means they
should hold just as much attraction
provided they are given creative
substance. What difference does it
make if you repulse your opponent's
offensive by exact, correct play
and by this means gain a well-
merited victory? But unwillingness
goes hand in hand with inability.*

Learning to do what you don't like is not so simple.

Romanovsky

Kasparov-Yurtayev
USSR Junior Ch., Vilnius 1975
Sicilian

1	e4	c5
2	♘f3	♘c6
3	d4	cd
4	♘xd4	g6
5	c4	♗g7
6	♗e3	♘f6
7	♘c3	♘g4
8	♕xg4	♘xd4
9	♕d1	♘e6
10	♕d2	♕a5
11	♖c1	b6
12	♗e2?!	

12 ♗d3 ♗b7 13 0-0 with some advantage to White was preferable. Complications now arise which evidently had been well analysed by Yurtayev but were largely unfamiliar to Kasparov. From the very opening stage, then, the players were playing under unequal conditions, a fact which ultimately determines the outcome of the struggle.

12	...	♗b7
13	f3	f5
14	ef	gf
15	0-0	♖g8
16	♖fd1	d6
17	a3	f4
18	♗xf4	♗d4+?!
19	♔h1	

19 ♗e3? is unplayable because of 19 ... ♕g5.

19	...	♕f5

All this has been known for a long time and was published in an article by Kapengut, who in answer to 20 ♗e3 recommends the rook sacrifice 20 ... ♖xg2?! Moiseyev disagrees, regarding this sacrifice as dubious. He gives the following variation to support his view: 21 ♔xg2 ♕g4+ 22 ♔h1! ♗xf3+ 23 ♗xf3 ♕xf3+ 24 ♕g2 ♕xg2+ 25 ♔xg2 ♗xe3 26 ♖c2 and 26 ... ♘d4? fails against 27 ♖xd4 ♗xd4 28 ♘b5.

20	♘d5?!	

This is undoubtedly inferior to 20 ♗e3.

20	...	♗xd5
21	cd	♘xf4
22	♗b5+	♔f8
23	♕xd4	♖xg2 (41)

41
W

24	♗d7?	

Naively counting on winning after 24 ... ♕g5? 25 ♕h8+ ♔f7 26 ♕xh7+ ♔f6 27 ♖e1 ♖e2 (27 ...

♘xd5? 28 ♖e6 mate, or 27 ...
♕xd5 28 ♕h6+) 28 ♖g1 ♖g2 29
♗h3 ♘xh3 30 ♕xh3 ♖xg1+ 31
♖xg1 ♕xd5 32 ♕h6+ ♔f7 33
♕g6+ ♔f8 34 ♕g7+ ♔e8 35
♕g8+.

However, the nature of the position required White to put aside the thought of fighting for the initiative and go over to careful defence with 24 ♗f1.

While possessing an excellent command of the methods of attack, and not shunning active defence, Kasparov has never liked defending passively in positions where there is no scope for his creative imagination and he has to repel his opponent's direct threats over a long period of time. In such positions his play has been below par, with disturbing oversights and errors.

	24	...	♖xh2+!

A combination White had overlooked, though it is not complicated.

25	♔xh2	♕h5+
26	♔g3	♘e2+
27	♔f2	♘xd4
28	♖xd4	♕h2+
29	♔e3	♔g7

Black has sufficient material advantage for victory and he exploits it by accurate play.
30 ♖g4+ ♔h8 31 ♗e6 ♖f8 32 ♖cg1 h5 33 ♖g5 ♕f4+ 34 ♔d3 ♕xf3+ 35 ♔c2 ♕e2+ 36 ♔b3

♖f3+ 37 ♔a2 ♕c4+ 38 ♔b1 ♖f1+ and White **resigned** a few moves later.

A sacrifice must be appraised not only from the point of view of its correctness, but also, and most importantly, from the standpoint of how dangerous it is.

Spielmann

Taborov-Rohde
Schilde 1976
Catalan

1	♘f3	♘f6
2	g3	d5
3	♗g2	e6
4	0-0	♗e7
5	c4	dc
6	♕a4+	♘bd7
7	♕xc4	c5
8	d3	0-0
9	♘c3	a6?

An inaccuracy which lands Black in difficulties. The modest 9 ... b6 (Razuvayev) would have led to an even game, since in view of the awkward placing of his queen White couldn't have exploited the temporary weakening of the long diagonal.

10	♕b3!	♖a7

There's no other way to finish developing his queenside pieces.

11	♖d1	b5
12	a4	c4!?

Counterattack is the best means

of defence. The ingenious American doesn't want to acquiesce in the worse position after 12 ... b4?! 13 ♘b1 ♗b7 14 ♘bd2, so he sharpens the play without shrinking from material sacrifices.

13   dc   b4
14   ♗e3

It is not impossible that on 14 ♘b1!? Rohde would, true to his style, have set about analysing the consequences of the queen sacrifice 14 ... ♘c5 15 ♕c2 b3? 16 ♖xd8 ♖xd8 17 ♕c3 (after 17 ♕d2 ♖xd2 Black is no worse) 17 ... ♖d1+ 18 ♗f1 ♘ce4 19 ♕xb3 ♖xc1.

True enough, 20 ♕b8? ♖d7 21 ♕xc8+ ♖d8 22 ♕c7 ♖dd1 23 ♕xe7 ♖xf1+ 24 ♔g2 ♖xf2+ 25 ♔h3 g5 leads to a position where in spite of White's big material advantage Black has a very strong, indeed apparently winning, attack. However, 20 ♕e3! would leave without his queen or his attack either; therefore Black would have had to content himself with the prosaic 15 ... ♖d7 with some compensation for the lost pawn.

14   ...   ♕c7!

The rook has no convenient square to withdraw to. Moreover, after you have been psychologically prepared for a queen sacrifice, an exchange sacrifice seems a mere trifle.

15   ♗xa7   ♕xa7

16   ♘b1   ♘c5
17   ♕c2

Of course not 17 ♕xb4? because of 17 ... ♘d3!

17   ...   b3
18   ♕c1   ♘ce4
19   e3   ♘g4
20   ♘d4!?

On 20 ♖f1?! Black would have had to resort to further sacrifices in order to retain the initiative: 20 ... ♗c5 21 ♘d4 ♘exf2! 22 ♖xf2 ♖d8! This is the only move enabling him to fight on, whereas 22 ... e5? loses at once to 23 ♘c6 ♕b6 24 a5.

In answer to 22 ... ♖d8! White can add to his material gains: 23 ♘c6 ♗xe3!? 24 ♘xa7 ♗xc1 (42)

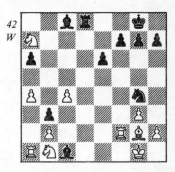

We have here an astonishing position in which, despite his extra rook, White has to think of taking drawing measures.

a) **25 ♘xc8?!** ♖d1+ 26 ♖f1! ♗e3+ 27 ♔h1 ♘f2+ with a draw.
b) **25 ♘c3** ♗e3 26 ♘xc8 ♗xf2+ 27 ♔f1 (27 ♔h1 ♖xc8) 27 ... ♖d2,

threatening ... ♘g4-e3 mate and ... ♘g4xh2 mate.

c) **25 ♖e2 ♖d1+ 26 ♗f1 ♗e3+ 27 ♖xe3 ♘xe3 28 ♔f2 ♘c2** and Black's position is preferable owing to the weakness of the pawn on b2.

d) **25 ♖f4 ♖d1+ 26 ♗f1 ♗xf4 27 gf ♘e3.** After 28 ♔f2 the chances are roughly equal.

e) **25 ♖f3? ♖d1+ 26 ♗f1 ♗b7.** In view of the threat of 27 ... ♗e3+ Black has a won position.

f) **25 ♘d2! ♗xd2 26 ♖xd2 ♖xd2 27 ♘xc8 ♘e3 28 ♗b7 (28 ♗e4 f5) 28 ... ♖xb2.** Despite White's extra piece the position is unclear.

We should mention that Black was under no compulsion to exchange queens. By continuing 23 ... ♕c7! (but not 23 ... ♕d7? 24 ♘xd8 ♗xe3 25 ♕xe3! ♘xe3 26 ♖d2) 24 ♘xd8 ♗xe3 25 ♕xe3 ♘xe3 26 ♘c3 ♕xd8 he would still have had a position with many chances.

Nor does White succeed in improving with 23 ♖e2?! e5 24 ♘c6 ♗xe3+ 25 ♖xe3 ♕xe3+ 26 ♕xe3 ♖d1+ or 24 ♘f3 ♗xe3+ 25 ♖xe3 ♘xe3 26 ♘c3 ♘g4+.

20	...	♘gxf2
21	♘c6	♕c5
22	♘xe7+	♕xe7
23	♘d2? *(43)*	

White aims to return the exchange and remain with an extra pawn after 23 ... ♘xd1? 24

♘xe4 f5 25 ♕xd1 fe 26 ♕d4, but overlooks his opponent's tactical rejoinder. He would have gained the advantage after 23 ♖d4 ♗b7 24 ♘c3 f5, when Black has insufficient compensation for the exchange.

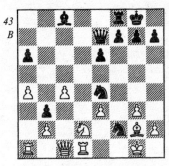

23	...	♘c5!
24	♖f1	♘fd3
25	♕c3	♕g5
26	♖f4?	

The second serious inaccuracy in the space of four moves. Already Black's position was at least no worse. White could have tried to maintain the balance with 26 ♘e4 ♕xe3+ 27 ♘f2 ♖d8 28 ♖ae1 ♕g5 29 ♖d1. Missing this opportunity, he returns the exchange and afterwards fails to save the game.

It would be possible for a player to be content with identifying his own mistakes. Yet it is very important to clarify whether their causes are accidental or follow a pattern. Here is what Rudolf

Spielmann writes in a similar context:

In practical play, the effect which attacking has on the morale plays a very major role, and is especially noticeable following a sacrifice. For this fact there are both chessplaying reasons and psychological reasons. The attacker usually has more pieces ready to hand, he enjoys spatial freedom and the possibility of carrying out various regroupings and manoeuvres at lightning speed. He can therefore pursue a number of subsidiary aims in addition to the main objective.

The defender's efforts are concentrated on understanding his opponent's plans, or often merely guessing at them. In favourable circumstances he can probe for some weakness in the enemy front. Carrying out these tasks requires considerably more precision and strength than attacking; hence the strain often leads to a weakening of the player's resistance, either as a result of the excessive difficulty of the task or because he loses confidence in his position .

| 26 | ... | e5! |

A good deal stronger, of course, than capturing at once.

| 27 | ♖f3 | |

Not 27 ♘e4? ♘xf4 28 ♘xg5 ♘e2+.

27	...	♗g4
28	♘e4	♘xe4
29	♕xd3	♗xf3
30	♗xf3	♘c5

The situation has been clarified. With material equality, Black has retained much the better position and proceeds to win by technique.

31	♕c3	e4
32	♗e2	♖d8
33	♖d1	♘d3
34	♕d2	h5
35	♔g2	

White is helpless. He has no adequate defence against the further advance of the black rook's pawn.

35 ... ♘f4+! 36 ef ♖xd2 37 fg ♖xe2+ 38 ♔h3 ♖xb2 39 ♖e1 ♖c2 40 ♖xe4 b2 41 ♖e8+ ♔h7 42 ♖b8 ♔g6 43 c5 ♔xg5 44 c6 f6 45 c7 ♖xc7 46 ♖xb2 ♖c4 47 ♖a2 ♔f5 48 ♔g2 ♔e4 49 ♖e2+ ♔d5 50 ♖e7 g5 51 ♖h7 ♖c2+ 52 ♔f3 ♖xh2 53 ♖d7+ ♔e5 54 ♖a7 g4+ 55 ♔e3 ♖g2 56 ♖xa6 ♖xg3+ 57 ♔f2 ♖f3+ 58 ♔g2 h4 0-1

Kochiev-Tukmakov
Odessa 1972
Sicilian

1	e4	c5
2	♘f3	d6
3	d4	cd
4	♘xd4	♘f6
5	♘c3	e6
6	g4	a6
7	g5	♘fd7
8	♗e3	b5
9	f4	♗b7

10   f5?!

10 ♗g2!? is more solid. With his last move White had to take into account the consequences of 10 ... b4 which forces him to sacrifice a piece.

10   ...   b4
11   fe

A worse alternative was 11 ♘xe6 fe 12 ♕h5+ g6 13 fg ♗g7 14 ♗d4 ♗xd4 15 g7+ ♔e7 16 gh♕ ♕xh8 when Black repels the attack and keeps his material plus.

11   ...   bc
12   ef+!   ♔xf7
13   ♕g4?!

White played more strongly in Belyavsky-Tal, Sukhumi 1972: 13 ♗c4+ ♔e8 14 0-0 ♘e5 15 ♕e2 (Gufeld recommends 15 ♘e6!?) 15 ... ♘bc6 16 ♖f5 ♕e7 with unclear play.

13   ...   ♕e7
14   ♗g2   ♘e5
15   0-0+   ♔e8
16   ♕g3   ♘bc6
17   bc   g6

Assessing this position, one has to prefer Black. He has kept his extra piece and fortified himself in the centre. However, White has retained the initiative, and the position with numerous weaknesses on both sides demands precise defence on Black's part.

18   ♖f6   ♘d8
19   ♗h3   ♗g7?! *(44)*

It's hard to condemn Black for

making this obvious-looking move, but if he had brought more defence to the e6 point with 19 ... ♗c8! White would have been at a loss to continue the attack.

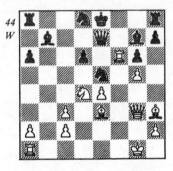

20   ♘e6!

In such positions there can be no half-measures; you must stop at nothing to boost your flagging initiative.

20   ...   ♗xf6
21   gf   ♕f7

The pawn on f6 is invulnerable because of 22 ♘c7+ followed by the win of the queen, but a line worth considering was 21 ... ♕xe6 22 ♗xe6 ♘xe6 23 ♗d4 ♔f7 24 ♗xe5 de 25 ♕xe5 ♖ac8 with unclear prospects.

22   ♘g7+   ♔f8
23   ♗h6   ♔g8
24   ♖d1   ♕c4?

In this involved position, Black makes a fatal error. His wish to untangle the cluster of pieces stuck in the corner is understandable, but this had to be done with greater care.

A tempting idea is 24 ... ♝c8?! 25 ♝xc8! (of course not 25 ♕xe5? ♕a7+) 25 ... ♖xc8, but here 26 ♘f5 (as in the game), or first 26 ♖xd6 and then 27 ♘xf5 would give Black a good deal of trouble.

The winning line was 24 ... ♕xf6! 25 ♖f1 ♕xg7 26 ♝xg7 ♔xg7 27 ♕f4 ♖e8 28 ♕f6+ ♔g8 29 ♕xd6 ♘df7 and Black's three pieces are stronger than White's queen and scattered pawns.

    25   ♘f5   ♕xe4 *(45)*

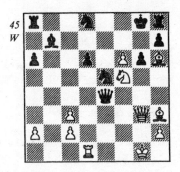

    26   f7+!

Very pretty! It emerges that Black can't play 26 ... ♔xf7 because of 27 ♘xd6+, or 26 ... ♘dxf7 because of 27 ♘e7 mate. Therefore the knight on e5, the chief support of Black's position, is deflected.

    26   ...   ♘exf7
    27   ♖e1   ♕xe1+

Or 27 ... ♕h1+ 28 ♔f2 ♕xe1+ 29 ♔xe1 which is even worse.

    28   ♕xe1   ♘e5
    29   ♕g3
                1-0

Shteinberg-Mukhin
World Junior Ch. Selection
Tournament, Moscow 1967
King's Indian

1	d4	♘f6
2	♘f3	g6
3	g3	♝g7
4	♝g2	0-0
5	0-0	d6
6	c4	c5
7	d5	♘a6
8	♘c3	♘c7
9	a4	♖b8
10	♖e1	a6
11	a5	b5
12	ab	♖xb6
13	♕c2!	

One of those unobtrusive moves which have a decisive bearing on the outcome of a game. White has been preparing e2-e4. Without renouncing this possibility he makes a useful waiting move, reserving the right to modify his plan on the analogy of the variation 13 ♖a2 e6 14 de ♘xe6 15 b3. As we shall see from what follows, the position of the queen on c2 considerably strengthens this variation, since the d1 square is freed for a rook which from there will be able to create immediate threats against the weak black d-pawn.

13	...	e5
14	de	♘xe6
15	♖d1	♗b7
16	♘a4	♗e4

The immediate 16 ... ♖b4 is worse; there could follow 17 ♗d2 ♗e4 18 ♕c1 ♖b3 19 ♗c3 ♗a8 (guarding against 20 ♘d2) 20 ♕c2 ♖b8 21 ♕d3 and Black cannot continue 21 ... ♘e4? because of 22 ♗xg7 ♔xg7 23 ♘e1 winning a pawn.

17	♕d2	♖b4
18	♘c3	

Of course not 18 ♕xd6? because of 18 ... ♗c2. Now, however, Black is faced with complex problems. With every move, the most vulnerable points in his position, the weak pawns on d6 and a6, stand out in sharper relief. 18 ... ♖xc4 19 ♕xd6 ♕xd6 20 ♖xd6 is unsatisfactory for Black, since in view of the threatened 21 ♘d2 he is unable to defend his a- pawn.

18	...	♗xf3

In the circumstances, comparatively best. Black temporarily gains control of the d4 point, thus shielding his pawn on d6.

19	♗xf3	♘d4
20	♖xa6	♖xc4
21	♗g2	d5

The only defence. The threat was 22 e3 ♘f5 23 ♗h3 when there is no saving the miserable pawn on d6, since 23 ... ♕c8? is met by 24

♖xd6, and 23 ... ♘g4? by 24 ♕e2.

22	♕d3!	

Threatening 23 ♘xd5.

22	...	♖b4
23	♗g5	♘e6 (46)

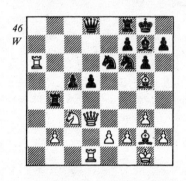

24	♘xd5	♖d4

A vital link in Black's defensive strategy. 24 ... ♖xb2? would lose to 25 ♗xf6 ♗xf6 26 ♖d6! The impression one has now, on the other hand, is that Black's threats on the d-file are highly unpleasant. Yet this too had been taken into account by White.

25	♗xf6!	♖xd3?

Over the course of the last ten moves, Black has conducted a difficult defence. Had he now played 25 ... ♗xf6 26 ♖a8 ♖xd3 27 ♖xd3 ♗xb2! his efforts would have been rewarded and the game would quickly have ended in a draw, White's insignificant advantage being inadequate to win. But under strong pressure from his opponent Black fails to hold out and commits a losing error.

26	♖xd3	♕e8

Curiously, there's no suitable place on the board for the black queen. For example: 26 ... ♕b8 27 ♖b6 ♕a7 28 ♖a3 ♕d7 29 ♖b7 etc.

27	♗e7	♕b5
28	♖b6	♕a5
29	♗xf8	♗xf8

It would have been better to check first with the queen, though the end result would still have been the same.

30	♗f3	♕e1+
31	♔g2	♘d4
32	♖b8	♔g7
33	♖b7!	

Now the white rooks commence the final, irresistible assault against the pawn cover round the enemy king.

33	...	♘xe2
34	♗xe2	♕xe2
35	♖f3	♗d6
36	♖bxf7+	♔h6
37	♘f6	g5
38	♖xh7+	♔g6

and Black **resigned** without waiting for the reply.

Miscalculating variations and combinations

In the course of a game, '*a chess-player's thought is concentrated chiefly on variations*' (Romanovsky).

Of the great multitude of variations considered, only an insignificant fraction will be carried out on the chessboard. These are the key lines which are unearthed by dint of intensive mental labour. We should add that a great deal of energy and time is often used unproductively in selecting the 'best' among several continuations of equal worth. In this 'best' continuation the opponent will have, perhaps, two or three replies at every turn. Working out these possibilities unavoidably leads to fatigue, which is just what gives rise to oversights and errors. The ability to discard what is superfluous and find your bearings quickly in any position is acquired through long, assiduous training.

From examining the nature of errors that players have made, one may conclude that they go wrong less often when working out lines which may be many moves deep but are forced. On the other hand, quiet and intermediate moves, as well as combinative strokes by the opponent, continue for a long time to be a blind spot even for very able chessplayers. The effort must be made to overcome this major failing, since very often the outcome is decisively influenced not so much by the strength of the unexpected move, as by the psychological effect of your own oversight, making it hard to regain your composure and find the strongest continuation.

Schüssler-Liu
World Junior Ch Groningen 1977
Sicilian Defence

1	e4	c5
2	♘f3	d6
3	♗b5+	♘c6
4	0-0	♗d7
5	♖e1	a6
6	♗f1	♗g4
7	h3	♗h5!?

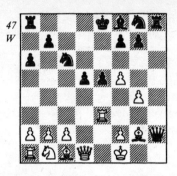

7 ... ♗xf3 was more circumspect, but the Singapore player aims to work up complications right away.

8	g4	♗g6
9	d4	cd
10	♘xd4	e5
11	♘f5	h5
12	♗g2	hg
13	hg	♗xf5
14	ef	♕h4

Both opponents have played the opening unconventionally and it is quite likely that both were satisfied with their positions. In return for White's central advantage Black has opened the h-file and is attempting to organise an attack on the white king.

15	♖e3	♕h2+
16	♔f1	d5! *(47)*

Black can't do without this move and takes the opportunity to play it.

17 ♘c3

Of course not 17 ♗xd5? 0-0-0 18 ♕f3 ♘d4 19 ♗xb7+ ♔b8 20 ♕e4 ♘f6, or 18 c4 ♗c5 19 ♘c3 (19

♖e2? ♕h1+) 19 ... ♘f6; in either variation Black achieves a quick win. However, a perfectly playable line is 17 ♕xd5 ♖d8 18 ♕f3 ♘d4 19 ♕e4 ♘f6 20 ♕xe5+ ♕xe5 21 ♖xe5+ ♗e7 22 ♘c3 ♘xg4 23 ♖e4 ♘f6 with a draw or 18 ... ♘f6 19 ♘c3 ♗c5 (19 ... ♘d4 is met by 20 ♕g3, when White already has the advantage) 20 ♘e4! ♗xe3 21 ♘f6+ gf 22 ♗xe3 and although White is the exchange down his chances are no worse.

17 ... 0-0-0

Not, of course, 17 ... d4 18 ♗xc6+ bc 19 ♕xd4 and White wins.

18 ♖d3

Again the pawn is immune: 18 ♘xd5? ♕h1+ or 18 ♗xd5 ♘f6 etc.

18 ... ♘f6
19 g5!?

A playable move which White was not to follow up properly. On the other hand, the excellence of White's 'central' strategy would have been underlined by the more logical 19 ♗g5! After 19 ... e4 20 ♖d2 there is no defending the pawn on d5, while after 19 ... d4 20 ♗xf6 gf 21 ♘e4 ♗e7 22 ♕f3 White's advantage is not to be doubted. What commences now, however, is tactical play to which both sides prove unequal.

19 ...   e4

20 ♖g3

A very attractive line was the exchange sacrifice 20 gf! ed 21 ♕xd3 gf 22 ♘xd5 ♗d6 23 ♕f3! ♔b8 24 ♗e3 ♘e5 25 ♕e4 with good prospects.

20 ...   ♗d6

21 gf   ♗xg3

22 fxg3?

This was evidently prompted by the false assumption that after 22 fxg7 ♖h5? Black holds the piece. But the answer 23 ♕g4! would then win for White.

Therefore Black would have to play the more modest 22 ... ♖hg8 23 fg ♕xg3 24 f6 ♕h4 25 ♘xd5 ♘b4 26 c4 ♘xd5 27 cd ♕xf6+ 28 ♔g1 ♕xg7 29 ♕c2+ ♔b8 30 ♗f4+ ♔a8 31 ♕xe4 ♕xb2 32 ♖e1 or 28 ... ♖xg7 29 ♗e3 ♕xb2 (29 ... ♖dg8? 30 ♖c1+ ♔b8 31 ♖c2) 30 ♖c1+ ♔b8 31 ♖c2 ♕e5 32 ♕d4. In either of these variations White would have a substantial plus, whereas after the move played it is Black who should win.

22 ...   ♕xg3

23 fg   ♖h2?

Missing the forced win that could have been achieved by 23 ... ♕xg7 24 ♗f4 (24 ♘xd5 ♖hg8) 24 ... ♖dg8 25 ♕d2 (25 ♕e2 ♖h1+) 25 ... e3 26 ♕xd5 (26 ♗xe3 ♖h2) 26 ... ♖h1+ 27 ♗xh1 ♕g1+ 28 ♔e2 ♕f2+ 29 ♔d3 ♘b4+ and White loses his queen.

24 ♕e2   ♕xg7

A bad line is 24 ... ♘d4? 25 ♕f2! ♕xf2+ 26 ♔xf2 ♘xf5 27 ♘xd5! ♘xg7 28 ♘b6+ and White wins.

25 ♗f4   ♘d4?

An oversight! After 25 ... ♖h4 a struggle with chances for both sides would lie ahead.

26 ♘xd5!   ♖xd5

There's nothing for it – the white can't be taken because of 27 ♘b6 mate.

27 ♕c4+   ♘c6

28 ♗xh2   ♖xf5+

29 ♔g1   ♕xb2

30 ♖f1?

White's extra piece should bring him a win and the quickest way to achieve this was 30 ♖e1! when, to avoid being mated, Black would have to exchange queens, making further resistance futile for him.

What is the explanation for such a large number of missed opportunities on both sides? We are hardly justified in criticising the players for poor combinative vision – after all, in the first part of the game many complex variations were calculated by them accurately. Most likely the explanation should be sought in inadequate physical stamina and the onset of fatigue, making it difficult not only to foresee the opponent's various intervening moves but to make any correct choice of the strongest among several continuations.

30	...	♖xf1+
31	♕xf1	♕xc2

Now White is left with only one pawn which gives Black some saving chances.

32	♕f5+	♔d8
33	♕d5+	♔e8
34	♗xe4?	

The win would definitely have been easier after the exchange of queens.

34	...	♕c1+
35	♔g2	♕b2+
36	♔h3	♕h8+
37	♔g2	♕b2+
38	♔h3	♕h8+
39	♔g3	♕g7+
40	♔f3	♕c3+
41	♔g4?	

The correct course was 41 ♕d3 ♘e5+ 42 ♗xe5 ♕xe5 43 ♗xb7 ♕f6+ 44 ♔g3 ♕g7+ 45 ♔f2 ♕f6+ 46 ♗f3 etc. Now, however, Black could have drawn by 41 ... ♘e7 42 ♕xb7 (42 ♕e5 ♕xe5 43 ♗xe5 f5+!) 42 ... f5+ 43 ♗xf5 ♘xf5 and Black will pick up White's bishop

or pawn.

41	...	♕g7+
42	♕g5	♕b2
43	♕g8+	♔e7
44	♕g5+	♔e8
45	♕e3	♔d8
46	♕d3+	♔e8
47	♕e3	♔d8
48	♗g3	♕xa2
49	♗h4+	f6

Fearing surprises in the variation 49 ... ♔c7 50 ♕f4+ ♔b6 51 ♗f2+.

50	♗xf6+	♔c7
51	♗g5	♕e6+

It might seem that Black has nothing more to fear now that he has centralised his queen.

52	♔g3	♔b8
53	♕f4+	♔a7
54	♕f2+	b6
55	♕f4	♕d7
56	♗f3	♘d4
57	♗g4	♘e6
58	♗xe6?	

He should have tried playing for the win in the endgame with two bishops against a knight. Unfortunately, in reference books this interesting ending receives no analysis or definite assessment. Yet practice shows how difficult it is to defend such a position. [This ending has now been proved a win by computer – Ed.]

By way of example we may quote Botvinnik-Tal 17th game, return World Ch. Match, Moscow 1961.

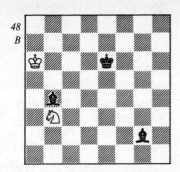

77 ... ♗f1+ 78 ♔b6 ♔d6 79 ♘a5 ♗c5+ 80 ♔b7 ♗e2 81 ♘b3 ♗e3 82 ♘a5 ♔c5 83 ♔c7 ♗f4+ 0-1 (On 84 ♔b7 ♔b5 85 ♘b3 ♗e3 Black wins the knight.)

In the present game, the same type of position could have arisen after 58 ♕e5 ♕c7 59 ♕xc7+ ♘xc7 *(49)*

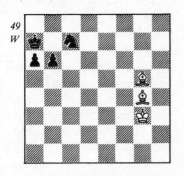

As you can verify without difficulty, no matter how Black arranges his pawns, he is unable to stop the white king from penetrating to c6, after which both pawns are lost.

58 ... ♕xe6 59 ♕c7+ ♔a8 60 ♗f4

♕e1+ 61 ♔g4 ♕d1+ 62 ♔g5 ♕d5+ 63 ♔f6 ♕b7 64 ♕d6 ♔a7 65 ♗e5 ♕c8 66 ♕e7+ ♕b7 67 ♕d6 ½-½

Miles-Bisguier
Birmingham 1973
Ruy Lopez

1	e4	e5
2	♘f3	♘c6
3	♗b5	♘f6
4	0-0	♘xe4
5	d4	♘d6
6	♗xc6	dc
7	de	♘f5
8	♕xd8+	♔xd8
9	♘c3	

An equally popular continuation is 9 b3 ♔e8 10 ♗b2 ♗e7 11 ♘bd2 maintaining a slight advantage.

9	...	♔e8
10	♘e2	♗e6
11	♘f4	♗d5
12	♘xd5	cd
13	♖e1!?	

Miles refrains from (or perhaps doesn't know about) the theoretical line 13 g4 ♘e7 14 ♗f4 ♘g6 15 ♗g3 c6 16 ♖fe1 ♗c5 17 c3 ♘f8 18 b4 with a slight plus for White, Fischer-Bisguier, USA 1963.

13	...	♗c5
14	♗f4	c6
15	♖ad1	h6
16	h3?	

White has developed his pieces unhindered and his position is preferable. He could have consolidated his advantage by 16 g4! ♘e7 17 ♘d4 so that after withdrawing his bishop to g3 he could prepare the advance of his f-pawn or play ♘d4-f5 if the occasion arose. Instead he hesitates and the advantage passes to Black.

16	...	g5
17	♗c1	♔e7
18	♘h2	

By now it's too late for 18 g4? ♘g7 19 ♘d4 ♗xd4! 20 ♖xd4 ♘e6 and 21 ... h5.

18	...	♖ag8
19	♘g4	h5
20	♘e3	♘h4?! *(50)*

After 20 ... ♗xe3 21 ♗xe3 g4 it isn't easy for White to find a satisfactory defence. But Black has no suspicion of his young opponent's interesting plan and plays for the attack straightforwardly. Now the threat is 21 ... g4 22 hg hg and 23 ... ♘f3+ with an immediate win.

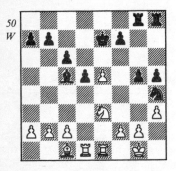

50 W

| 21 | ♘xd5+! |

This combination is based on Black's insecure king position and the lack of contact between his bishop and the rest of his pieces.

| 21 | ... | cd |
| 22 | ♖xd5 | b6? |

Unforeseen moves have an unpleasant psychological effect even on experienced grandmasters. True, finding the right rejoinder in the tense situation that has now arisen is not easy. 22 ... ♗b6?! might seem strong. Indeed, after 23 e6 f6?! (we shan't go into 23 ... fe 24 ♗xg5+ ♖xg5 25 ♖xg5 when White is better) 24 ♖d7+ ♔e8 25 b3? g4 26 ♖xb7 gh 27 ♖b8+ ♗d8 28 e7 ♘f3+ 29 ♔f1 hg+ 30 ♔e2 g1♘+! 31 ♔d1 ♔f7, Black wins. All very fine, but after 25 ♖e4! there is no defence against 26 ♖c4 and 27 ♖c8+. Therefore Black would have to play 23 ... f5! (depriving the white rook of the e4 square). The following variations show that after 24 ♖d7+ the chances are equal:

a) 24 ... ♔e8 25 ♗e3 (or 25 ♖xb7 g4, obliging White to force a draw with 26 ♖b8+) 25 ... g4 26 ♗xb6 gh (or 26 ... ab 27 ♗e3 ♖h6 28 ♖xb7 ♖gg6 29 ♖b8+ with a draw) 27 ♖d8+ ♔e7 28 ♖xg8 (28 ♖d7+ draws) 28 ... ♖xg8 29 ♗c5+ ♔e8 30 ♖e3 ♖xg2+ 31 ♔h1 ♖xf2 and after 32 ♖xh3 the game should very probably be drawn.

b) 24 ... ♔f6! is also possible: 25 b3 ♔g6 26 ♖xb7 ♖e8, aiming for ...

f5-f4 and ... ♘h4-f5 with complex play.

But perhaps the soundest continuation is 22 ... ♗b4! 23 ♖e4 ♔e6! 24 ♖b5 ♗e7 25 ♖xb7 ♗c5! (anything else would be worse: 25 ... ♖d8? 26 ♖xe7+ or 25 ... g4 26 ♖xa7 gh 27 ♖xe7+ ♔xe7 28 ♖xh4 ♖xg2+ 29 ♔f1! ♖hg8 30 ♔e2!) 26 ♖c4 ♖c8 27 b3 ♖hg8 and Black's chances are preferable.

23	e6	f5

Bisguier cannot be blamed for this move, for it might seem that after 23 ... f6 24 ♖d7+ ♔e8 25 ♗e3 the knot of black pieces on the kingside is incapable of stopping a mating attack by the white rooks. So Black keeps the f6 square free for his king to go to.

In fact, though, this plan is mistaken. In the variation just mentioned, Black could draw with 25 ... g4! 26 ♗xc5 gh 27 ♖e7+ ♔d8 28 ♖d1+ ♔c8 29 g3 ♘f3+ 30 ♔h1 bc 31 ♖dd7 etc.

24	♖d7+	♔f6?

It is only now, after this obvious-looking move, that Black is lost, whereas 24 ... ♔e8! would have drawn in the same way as in the last note.

25	♗d2	♔g6
26	b4	♗f8
27	e7	♗g7
28	♖e6+	♔h7
29	♗xg5	♘g6

The position of Black's pieces creates a tragicomic impression.

30	♖xa7	♖e8
31	♖d7	♘e5
32	♖d5	♖hg8
33	f4	♘c4
34	♖xf5	

By now White has five (!) pawns for his piece.

34	...	♗d4+
35	♔h1	♘e3
36	♖f7+	♖g7
37	♖h6+	
	1-0	

37 ... ♔g8 is answered by 38 ♖f8+ ♖xf8 39 ♖h8+.

Hönigl-Vladimirov
Junior International Tournament
Hallsberg 1976
French

1	e4	e6
2	d4	d5
3	♘d2	c5
4	ed	ed
5	♘gf3	♘c6
6	♗b5	♗d6
7	0-0	♘e7
8	dc	♗xc5
9	♘b3	♗d6
10	♘bd4	0-0
11	c3	♗g4
12	♕a4	♕d7
13	♗g5?!	

The well-tried ♗c1-e3 is preferable.

| 13 | ... | a6 |
| 14 | ♗e2?! | |

White's 13 ♗g5 would have

been perfectly logical if he could carry out the manoeuvre ♗g5-h4-g3, exchanging the black-squared bishops. But Black prevents this by exploiting the 'hanging' position of the bishop on e2. It follows that, in the struggle for the opening advantage, the bishop sortie to g5 was merely striking at thin air. Hence at this point White should have contented himself with an equal game: 14 ♗xc6 ♘xc6 15 ♘xc6 bc 16 ♘d4 c5 17 ♕xd7 ♗xd7 18 ♘e2 ♖fe8 19 ♗f4 ♗f8 20 ♖fe1, or even 15 ♗h4 ♘xd4 16 ♕xd4 ♗xf3 17 gf.

14	...	♖fe8
15	♖fe1	♘g6
16	h3?	

And this already is a tactical oversight. Instead, 16 ♘xc6 bc 17 ♘d4 c5! (17 ... ♗xe2?! 18 ♖xe2! could even lead to an inferior position for Black, since after the exchange of one of his rooks the other one would be tied to the defence of the weak a-pawn) 18 ♕xd7 ♗xd7 would have relieved White of all worries.

16	...	♘xd4
17	♕xd4 *(51)*	
17	...	♖xe2
18	♖xe2?	

Here is a striking example of psychological consternation following a miscalculation. 18 hg! ♖xb2 19 c4 ♖c2 20 ♕xd5 (20 ♖ec1!? is also possible, but not 20 cd? ♗c5)

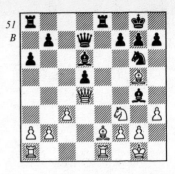

51
B

20 ... ♕c7 would have led to a position only slightly worse for White, whereas now he loses by force.

18	...	♗xf3
19	gf	♕xh3

White's shattered king position, added to the pawn he has lost, is too high a price for the exchange.

20	♕g4	♕h2+
21	♔f1	h6
22	♗e3	♘h4
23	♖ee1	

The only defence against the threatened 23 ... ♕h1+ 24 ♕g1 ♕h3+ and 25 ... ♘xf3+.

23	...	♖e8
24	♕d7	

The attempt to evacuate his king doesn't work: 24 ♔e2 d4! 25 cd (25 ♕xd4 ♘f5 and 26 ... ♖xe3+) 25 ... f5 26 ♕h5 ♖xe3+ 27 ♔xe3 ♘g2+, winning the queen.

24	...	♖e6
25	♔e2	♘g2
26	♖h1	♖xe3+
27	♔d2	♖e2+!

This sacrifice forces the win.

28	♔xe2	♘f4+
29	♔d2	♕xf2+
30	♔c1	♘d3+
31	♔d1	♕xf3+
32	♔d2	♗f4+
33	♔c2	♕e2+
34	♔b3	

0-1

Novikov-Kantsler
USSR Junior Ch., Daugavpils 1979
Caro-Kann

1	e4	g6
2	d4	♗g7
3	♘f3	c6
4	♘c3	d5
5	h3	♘f6
6	e5	♘e4
7	♘xe4	de
8	♘g5	c5
9	dc	♕a5+
10	♗d2	♕xc5
11	♗c3	♘d7

Of course not 11 ... ♗xe5? 12 ♗xe5 ♕xe5 13 ♕d8+! and White wins.

12 ♘xf7?

This should have led to loss. The correct line was played in a game Karasev-Nabolsin, Leningrad 1969: 12 ♗d4 ♕d5 13 e6! ♗xd4 14 ♕xd4! and White's position is better.

We can only conclude that the talented Harkov player, who recently achieved the master norm, possesses insufficient learning and

doesn't follow the periodicals. A still more disturbing fact is that in initiating complications with his last move, White had not foreseen his opponent's obvious retort and had confined himself to working out the crude 12 ... ♔xf7? 13 e6+ with a winning position.

12	...	0-0!
13	♕d2	♖xf7
14	e6	(52)

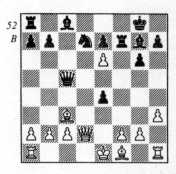

14	...	♖xf2!

As a result of this combination the white king comes under fire from all Black's pieces.

15	♕xf2	♗xc3+
16	bc	♕xc3+
17	♔e2	♕xc2+
18	♔e1	♕c3+
19	♔e2	♘e5
20	♕e1	♕b2+?

In a won position, Black kindly gives White a second chance. If some sort of explanation can be given for Novikov's oversight on move twelve (it is not impossible, for instance, that when playing 12

♘xf7 White forgot that castling was legal for Black), the reason for this mistake by the winner of the 1979 USSR Junior Championship is difficult to grasp. After 20 ... ♛d3+ 21 ♔f2 ♛d4+ 22 ♔g3 ♛d6! (22 ... ♝xe6 is also adequate) 23 ♛xe4 ♝xe6 Black's attack is irresistible.

21　♛d2　　♛b6

21 ... ♛xa1 22 ♛d8+ leads to a draw.

22	♛e3	♛xe6
23	♛b3	♔g7
24	♛xe6	♝xe6
25	♔e3	♜d8
26	♜c1!	

Thanks to a stroke of luck, White has managed to escape a quick defeat. However, even now his position does not inspire confidence – Black's material and positional ascendancy is beyond doubt. For many players, the heavy burden of a bad position is a weight too hard to carry and they prove incapable of offering protracted resistance. Much more rarely, you meet players on whom an inferior position acts as a stimulant. Their stubbornness increases; they ingeniously seek out all possible means of making the opponent's winning process difficult, they set him exacting problems over and over again. And it often happens that the opponent, weary of surmounting the many obstacles,

commits an error which reduces all his previous efforts to nothing.

White's last move reveals a determination to cause Black the maximum difficulty in the realisation of his advantage. The tempting 26 ♔xe4? would have led to an unpleasant position after 26 ... ♘c6 27 ♔e3 ♘b4 28 ♜c1 ♘xa2 29 ♜c7 ♜d7.

26	...	♝xa2
27	♜a1	♝c4
28	♔xe4	

Not 28 ♜xa7 ♜d1 winning material.

28	...	♝xf1
29	♜hxf1	♘c4?!

Black stumbles at the very first hurdle. 29 ...♘c6! was stronger.

30	♜fc1!	♘d2+
31	♔e3	♘b3
32	♜d1	♜xd1
33	♜xd1	♔f6
34	♜d5!	

Emphasising the awkward position of the black knight. The game should now be drawn.

34	...	a6
35	♜d7	♘a5
36	♜c7	♔e6
37	♔e4	♔d6
38	♜c8	♘c6
39	♜h8	a5
40	♜xh7	a4
41	♔d3	b5
42	♜g7?	

This should have lost. The simplest way of drawing was to

create a passed pawn on the kingside: 42 h4 and now:

a) **42 ... ♔c5** 43 g4 ♘e5+ 44 ♔c2 ♘xg4 45 ♖xe7 ♔d4 46 ♖d7+!

b) **42 ... ♔d5** 43 g4 e5 44 ♖d7+! ♔e6 45 ♖c7 ♔d6 46 ♖b7.

c) **42 ... a3** 43 ♔c3 ♘d4 44 ♖h8 e5 (44 ... ♔c5? 45 ♖c8+ ♘c6 46 g4 with 47 ♖xc6+ and 48 h5 to follow, could even lose for Black) 45 g4 b4+ 46 ♔xb4 a2 47 ♖a8 a1♕ 48 ♖xa1 ♘c2+ 49 ♔c3 ♘xa1, and in spite of his extra piece Black is unable to win! For example: 50 ♔b2 e4 (or 50 ... g5 51 hg ♔e6 52 ♔xa1 ♔f7 53 ♔b2 ♔xg6 54 ♔c3 ♔g6 55 ♔d3) 51 h5 ♔e5 52 hg, or 51 ... gh 52 gh ♔e5 53 h6 with an easy draw in all cases.

42	...	♔d5
43	♔c2	b4
44	♖xg6	♘d4+
45	♔b2	a3+
46	♔a2	e5
47	h4?!	

It's fairly easy to work out that pushing this pawn is now too late. But then, White also fails to save himself with 47 ♖g8 e4 48 ♖d8+ (48 ♖e8 ♘e6) 48 ... ♔c4 (48 ... ♔e5 is also possible) 49 h4 e3 50 h5 e2 51 ♖e8 ♘b5, after which further resistance is pointless.

| 47 | ... | e4 |
| 48 | ♖g3 | |

It's obvious by now that 48 ♖g8? is useless, since after 48 ... e3 the black king penetrates via e4.

| 48 | ... | ♘e2? |

Throws away the win. The path to victory was 48 ... ♘c2! 49 h5 (or 49 ♔b3 a2 50 ♔xa2 e3 51 ♖g8 e2 52 ♖d8+ ♔c6 53 ♖e8 e1♕ 54 ♖xe1 ♘xe1 55 h5 ♘xg2 56 h6 ♘f4 and 57 ... ♘g6) 49 ... e3 50 ♖g8 e2 51 ♖e8 (or 51 ♖d8+ ♔c4 52 ♖c8+ ♔d3 53 ♖d8+ ♘d4 54 ♖e8 b3+! 55 ♔xa3 ♘c2+ 56 ♔xb3 ♘e3) 51 ... b3+ 52 ♔xb3 ♘d4+ 53 ♔c3 a2, queening one of the pawns.

49	♖e3	♘c1+
50	♔b1	♔d4
51	h5!	

This is what Black had missed.

| 51 | ... | ♔xe3 |
| 52 | h6 | |

½-½

The draw was agreed in view of 52 ... ♔d2 53 h7 a2+ 54 ♔b2 a1♕+ 55 ♔xa1 ♔c2 56 h8♕ ♘b3+ 57 ♔a2 ♘c1+ with perpetual check.

Inadequate knowledge of basic endgames

A player is rarely able to finish off a chess game by a mating attack or combination. More often, the advantage he has acquired needs to be converted in the endgame. For this reason every strong player needs to be able to play endgames well. He has to know about a large number of theoretical endings so as to have the possibility of reducing to one of the familiar advantageous positions. There is, moreover, one other important circumstance which should not be forgotten, namely:

The role of the endgame is by no means restricted to the final phase of the play. The entire course of a game is to a significant extent determined by considerations of what the possible chances are if the main pieces should be exchanged and an endgame reached.

B. Blumenfeld

There are difficulties that arise from the very moment when a number of pieces including the queens have been exchanged. Can such a position be considered an endgame?

The answer is supplied only by a concrete examination of the particular case. From relying on outward signs (the exchange of queens), you can come to false conclusions and expose your king – in what you suppose to be an endgame – to lethal danger of the kind associated with a complex middlegame.

An understanding of all we have just said is gained through long, persistent work. Unfortunately, not many are capable of doing it. The consequence is a one-sided development in chessplayers – openings in good order, tactics nearly always up to standard, and ... scanty endgame knowledge.

**Dolmatov-Yermolinsky
National Youth Games
Moscow 1977**
Sicilian Defence

1	e4	c5
2	♘f3	d6
3	d4	cd
4	♕xd4	a6
5	♗e3	♘c6
6	♕d2	♘f6
7	♘c3	e6
8	0-0-0	

So far, play has followed Schweber-Quinteros, Argentina 1969. *ECO* recommends 8 ... ♗e7 with a minimal plus for White.

8 ... b5? (53)

This gives White the possibility of reducing to the better endgame by force.

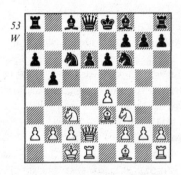

53
W

9	e5!	de
10	♕xd8+	♘xd8
11	♘xb5!	ab
12	♗xb5+	♗d7
13	♖xd7!	♘xd7
14	♖d1!	

14 ♘xe5? is inferior: 14 ... ♗d6
15 ♗xd7+ ♔e7 or 15 ♘xd7 ♖xa2.

14	...	♖a5
15	♗xd7+	♔e7
16	♗b6	♖d5
17	♖xd5	ed
18	♘xe5	♔d6!
19	♗xd8	♔xe5
20	♗b6 (54)	

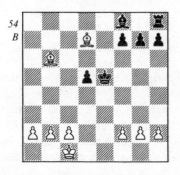

54
B

The endgame that has been reached is clearly in White's favour. But he has to surmount quite a few obstacles to achieve the win. The greatest difficulties arise if the black-squared bishops are exchanged. For this reason 20 ... d4!? looks plausible, so as to answer 21 a4?! with 21 ... ♔d5 followed by 22 ... ♗c5. For example: 22 ♗e8 ♗c5! 23 ♗xf7+ ♔c6 24 ♗xc5 ♔xc5 25 ♗b3 ♖f8 26 f3 ♖f6 and Black holds the draw. However, with 21 ♗c6! White thwarts his opponent's plan, since on 21 ... ♗d6? he continues, not with 22 a4? ♖c8 23 ♗f3 ♗c5 24 a5

♔d6 25 ♔d2 ♖b8 26 ♗xc5 ♔xc5 27 a6 ♔b6 28 ♗e2 ♔a7 29 b3 f6 30 ♗c4 ♖d8 which draws, but with 22 f4+! winning easily.

Nor does Black achieve his aim with an immediate 20 ... ♗b4 21 c3 ♔d6 22 cb ♔xd7 23 a4! It isn't hard to see that White wins with the help of his pawn on b2.

Later it was established that the strongest continuation in the diagrammed position is 20 ... ♗e7! (see the game on page 182 below). And yet Yermolinsky, who a few months later was to achieve a master norm, not only failed to find this move but proved incapable of offering his opponent any resistance. All his subsequent play simply arouses astonishment; his aimless pawn moves waste time and deserve the severest censure.

20	...	♔d6
21	♗b5	g5
22	a4	♗g7
23	c3	f5
24	♔c2	h5
25	a5	♖b8?

This move too is bad, since it gives White the chance of pushing his a-pawn with tempo.

26	b3	♗e5
27	a6!	♗xh2
28	a7	♖a8
29	c4	dc
30	bc	h4
31	♔d3	♗g1

32	c5+	♔d5
33	♗d7	♗xf2
34	♗xf5	
	1-0	

Azmaiparashvili-Yurtayev
World Junior Ch. Selection
Tournament, Sochi 1978
Indian Defence

1	♘f3	g6
2	c4	c5
3	♘c3	♗g7
4	e3	♘f6
5	d4	0-0
6	♗e2	cd
7	ed	d5
8	0-0	♘c6
9	♗g5	♘e4
10	cd?!	

By transposition of moves and with colours reversed, a variation of the Tarrasch Defence has been reached. White's last move is dubious and hands over the initiative to Black. 10 ♘xd5?? loses a piece to 10 ... ♘xg5 11 ♘xg5 e6, but after the correct 10 ♗e3 the game is level.

10	...	♘xg5
11	dc?!	

A second inaccuracy, landing White in an inferior position. The cause of it is a faulty approach to the study of openings. While examining in minute detail the formations that belong to their own repertoire, the majority of young players, up to the time they

gain the master title, don't, as a rule, bother even to look through games that fall outside their chosen sphere. We shall return to this question later. For the present, we would point out that this position has long been known, and that after the better 11 ♘xg5 ♘xd4 Black has no more than a slight edge.

11	...	♘xf3+
12	♗xf3	bc
13	♗xc6	♖b8
14	♕d2?!	

White would have fewer troubles after 14 ♖b1 ♗xd4 15 ♗e4.

14	...	♕xd4
15	♕xd4?	

And this further mistake already puts White in a critical situation. We can surmise that the reasons for it were most probably psychological. Finding himself unexpectedly in the worse position, White became flustered and played a move that led to the loss of a pawn. After the correct 15 ♖ad1 his position would still have been tenable, for example:

a) 15 ... ♕b6 16 ♘d5 ♕c5 17 b4.
b) 15 ... ♕b4 16 ♘d5 ♕d6 17 ♕e3.
c) 15 ... ♕xd2 16 ♖xd2 ♗a6 17 ♖c1.

15	...	♗xd4
16	♖fd1	e5
17	♖d2	*(55)*

It's easy to convince youself that White is unable to save his

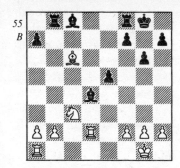

pawn, after which his position is lost. However, as we shall see again (in Izhnin-Yurtayev on page 85), endgame technique is not a strong point with the highly talented Yurtayev. The remainder of the game is a vivid illustration of this.

17	...	♖xb2
18	♖xb2	♗xc3
19	♖ab1	♗xb2
20	♖xb2	♗e6
21	f3	♖c8
22	♗a4	♖c5?

A serious lapse. Black has to avoid exchanging the queenside pawns, since the attempt to exploit his material advantage in a rook or bishop ending with pawns on only one wing would be doomed to failure against correct defence. His purpose could have been served by the modest 22 ... ♖c7! After 23 ♔f2 (not 23 h4? ♖c4 24 ♗b3 ♖b4) 23 ... ♔g7 24 ♔g3 g5! he could have improved his

position with the pawn advance ... h7-h5-h4.

23	♖b7	a6
24	♖a7	a5
25	♗b3	♗xb3
26	ab	♖b5

Black has managed to obtain a position in which the exchange of pawns is prevented. If his rook and pawns were on the sixth rank, winning the game would be an entirely realistic proposition. As it is, the sixth rank will be controlled by the white rook which radically alters the verdict.

27	h4	♔g7
28	♔h2	h5
29	♖a6!	♔f8
30	♖a7	♔g7
31	♖a6	♖xb3

Leading to a theoretically drawn position. He could have tested White in the variation 31 ... ♔f8 32 ♖a7 f5 33 ♖a8+ ♔f7 34 ♖a7+ ♔e6 35 ♖a6+ ♔d5 36 ♖xg6 ♖xb3 37 ♖g5 f4 38 ♖xh5 but this position too is a draw, since 38 ... ♖b8 is met by 39 g3 and 38 ... a4 by 39. ♖h8.

| 32 | ♖xa5 | ♔f6 |
| 33 | ♖a4 | g5? |

This loses a pawn, though without affecting the outcome of the game.

| 34 | ♖a6+ | ♔f5 |
| 35 | ♖h6 | |

and the players agreed a **draw** a few moves later.

Sochagin-Petrushin
1st Category Tournament
Leningrad 1968
King's Gambit

1	e4	e5
2	f4	ef
3	♘f3	♗e7
4	♘c3!	

This is stronger than the usual 4 ♗c4 ♘f6! 5 e5 ♘g4 6 0-0 ♘c6 7 d4 d5 with equality, or 5 ♘c3 ♘xe4! 6 ♘e5 ♘g5.

4	...	♗h4+
5	♔e2	d6
6	d4	♗g4
7	♗xf4	♘c6
8	♕d3	♕d7
9	♔d2	

Despite White's loss of the right to castle, his position is preferable in view of the strong placing of his pawns and pieces in the centre.

9	...	♗xf3
10	gf	♘ge7
11	♗g3	♗xg3
12	hg	d5
13	ed	

If 13 ♗h3 then 13 ... f5.

13	...	♘b4
14	♕e4	♘bxd5
15	♘xd5	♕xd5
16	♕xd5	♘xd5
17	♖e1+	♔d7

Black evidently supposes that the endgame stage has been reached and boldly moves his king towards the centre. But now White

subjects it to an attack thoroughly characterised by middlegame features – a pawn storm and sacrifices. 17 ... ♔f8 was more prudent.

18	c4	♘f6
19	♗h3+	♔c6

And here 19 ... ♔d8 was better.

20	♔c3	

A simpler way was 20 ♖e7 ♖hf8 21 ♖he1 when 21 ... ♖ae8? fails against 22 ♗d7+!

20	...	♖he8
21	b4	♖xe1

Or 21 ... b6 22 b5+ ♔b7 23 ♖e5 (23 f4 is also good), with a big advantage.

22	♖xe1	♖e8
23	b5+	♔d6

Losing at once. However, 23 ... ♔b6 would not have saved him either: 24 c5+! ♔a5 25 ♖xe8 ♘xe8 26 ♔c4 b6 27 ♗d7 ♘f6 28 c6 a6 29 a4 with an easy win thanks to the unanswerable threat of d4-d5-d6.

24	c5+!	♔d5 (56)

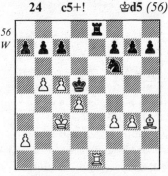

25	♗f1!	

1-0

Showing that it won't come to an

endgame. Black resigned as there is no defence against 26 ♗c4 mate.

Izhnin-Yurtayev
USSR Junior Team Ch., Lvov 1976
Sicilian

1	e4	c5
2	♘f3	d6
3	d4	cd
4	♘xd4	♘f6
5	♘c3	g6
6	♗e3	♗g7
7	f3	0-0
8	♕d2	♘c6
9	♗c4	♗d7
10	h4	♘e5
11	♗b3	♖c8
12	0-0-0	♘c4
13	♗xc4	♖xc4
14	h5	♘xh5
15	g4	♘f6 (57)

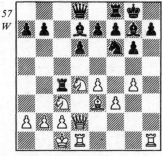

16   ♘de2

The up-to-the-minute fashion in this variation that has been analysed inside out. The main line is 16 ♗h6 ♘xe4! 17 ♕e3 (the variation 17 ♘xe4? ♖xd4 18 ♕h2 ♗e5 19 f4 ♖xd1+ 20 ♖xd1 ♗h8!

21 ♗xf8 ♕b6, or 19 ♕h4 ♖xe4! 20 fe ♕b6 21 c3 ♖c8 is still less favourable for White) 17 ... ♖xc3 18 bc ♘f6 19 ♗xg7 ♔xg7 20 ♘e2 ♕b6 with an unclear position, Zuckerman-Velimirović, Vrsac 1973. While analysing this game the young candidate masters I. Vilner and V. Temkin unearthed an interesting possibility: 20 ♕h6+ ♔g8? 21 g5 ♘h5 22 ♖xh5! gh 23 ♖h1 ♕c8 24 ♖xh5 ♗f5 25 ♘xf5 ♕xf5 26 g6 ♕xg6 27 ♖g5 and White wins. However, after the correct 20 ... ♔h8! (aiming to meet 21 g5 with 21 ... ♘h5 22 ♖xh5?! gh 23 ♖h1 ♖g8 24 ♖xh5 ♖g7), the position remains unclear.

White can also play 16 e5 when a game Adorjan-Ostojić, Olot 1974, continued 16 ... ♘xg4 17 fg ♗xe5 18 ♕g2 and White won quickly with a rook sacrifice on h7.

In his annotations to this game, Grandmaster Matanović stated that 17 ... ♗xg4 was unplayable because of 18 ♗h6 with a won position. Indeed, after the inviting 18 ... ♖xd4? 19 ♕xd4 ♗xh6+ 20 ♖xh6 ♗xd1 21 ♕xd1 de 22 ♕h1 it's hard for Black to defend. However, 18 ... ♗e5!? 19 ♗xf8 ♕xf8! 20 ♘de2 ♕g7 gives a position that can only be evaluated after substantial practical testing.

It may possibly have been with this last variation in mind that (after 16 e5 ♘xg4 17 fg) Black 'risked' 17 ... ♗xg4!? in a game Y.Yakimavichius (Lithuania)-A. Sokolov (Moscow), in this same Junior Team Tournament. Unfortunately the principal continuation remained 'behind the scenes', since instead of 18 ♗h6 White played 18 ♖dg1. There followed: 18 ... de 19 ♕h2 h5 20 ♖xg4 ed 21 ♗f2, and now 21 ... ♕c8! (indicated by R.Kimelfeld and M.Yudovich jun.) would have been very strong.

A year later, at the National Youth Games in Moscow, the variation was played again, in the game Dvoiris-Asanov. After 16 e5 ♘xg4 17 fg ♗xg4, White again refrained from 18 ♗h6 in favour of 18 ♖dg1. After 18 ... de, taking into account the recommendation just mentioned, he played 19 ♖xg4 (instead of 19 ♕h2). There followed: 19 ... h5 (19 ... ed, which would transpose into the game Yakimavichius-Sokolov, was worth considering) 20 ♖xh5 ed? (going in for the theoretical duel, Black ought to have carefully analysed this position and been ready, above all, to meet White's obvious reply. It is therefore hard to understand this mistake which leads to a quick defeat. Of course he couldn't play 20 ... gh? 21 ♗h6 hg 22 ♕g5, when mate is unavoidable. But 20 ... ♖xd4! 21

♗xd4 ed 22 ♘e4 gh 23 ♖xg7+ ♔xg7 24 ♕g5+ would have drawn) 21 ♖h1 ♖c6 (21 ... de is answered, not by 22 ♕h2? ♕d2+! which wins for Black, but by 22 ♕xd8 ♖xd8 23 ♖xc4, and White should win) 22 ♕h2 f5 23 ♖xd4! ♕c7 24 ♗f4 ♕a5 25 ♖d5 ♖c5 26 ♕h7+ ♔f7 27 ♖g1 1-0.

| 16 | ... | ♖e8!? |

At present, 16 ... ♕a5 enjoys no great popularity.

| 17 | ♗h6! |

A line worth considering is 17 ♗d4!? ♕a5 18 g5 ♘h5 19 ♗xg7 ♔xg7 20 ♘f4 ♘xf4 21 ♕xf4 ♗e6. In the 1978 USSR Junior Team Championships in Tashkent, Shulman (Latvia) against Zlochevsky (Moscow) played 22 ♘d5? here, and there followed: 22 ... ♗xd5 23 ♖xh7+ ♔xh7 24 ♕h4+ ♔g8 25 ♖h1 ♖xc2+! 26 ♔xc2 ♖c8+ 27 ♔d1 ♗b3+ 28 ab ♕a1+ 29 ♔d2 ♕xg2+ 30 ♔e3 ♖c3+ 31 ♔f4 ♖xb3, and Black won.

In place of the losing move 22 ♘d5? White could have obtained the better ending by 22 ♖xh7+! ♔xh7 23 ♕h4+ ♔g8 24 ♖h1 ♕a5 25 ♕h7+ ♔f8 26 ♕h8+ ♕xh8 27 ♖xh8+ ♔g7 28 ♖xe8 (indicated by A.Geller).

17	...	♗h8
18	e5	♘xg4
19	fg	♗xg4
20	ed	♕xd6
21	♕e1?	*(58)*

This whole variation – but without the moves 17 ♗h6 ♝h8 – had been seen in the game Martin-Tarjan (Torremolinos 1974). In that game, the move 20 ♕e1 was perfectly logical, since after 20 ♕xd6 ed White's bishop is *en prise*. The analogous continuation in the present game can most likely be explained by a wrong method of studying opening variations. Recollecting that 20 ♕e1 had occurred in Martin-Tarjan, Izhin played this move automatically, without considering that White's bishop is on h6 not e3, and that after 21 ♕xd6! ed 22 ♖xd6 ♝g7 (the white bishop is too strong, and has to be exchanged) 23 ♗xg7 ♔xg7 24 ♔d2! Black has a tough struggle for the draw ahead of him.

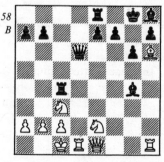

58
B

21 ...   ♝xc3!

A very powerful move that had gone unnoticed in Martin-Tarjan, where White gained a win after Black's queen had retreated to a6. Also 21 ... ♕c6!? is not bad: 22 ♝d2 (the threat was 22 ... ♝xe2) 22 ... b5, with initiative for Black.

22	♕xc3	♕xd1+
23	♔xd1	♖xc3
24	bc	♖c8
25	♖h2	♖xc3?!

Let us try to sum up the course of the struggle so far. Both opponents have played a complex opening line according to the most up-to-date precepts. But whereas Black's play reveals an understanding of the ideas of the variation, and his opening has been inseparably linked to the middlegame (21 ... ♝xc3!), White's play creates the impression of disjointed thrusts based on recollections of a game seen previously. Thus, the strong move 17 ♗h6! was made fortuitously and was not followed up (White didn't play 21 ♕xd6!); Black's combination (21 ... ♝xc3) took his opponent unawares.

The fact remains that up to here the level of play has been fairly high. Yet now the endgame commences, and . . . it looks as though substitute players take over. Technical faults follow one after another, and, at the finish of the game, serious deficiencies emerge in the conduct of simple theoretical endings. Black's last move complicates the winning of his well played game; the correct line was 25 ... f6! 26 ♗e3 e5, and the black pawns are set in motion.

| 26 | ♔d2 | ♖h3? |

He shouldn't exchange his rook. It was still not too late for 26 ... ♖a3 27 ♘c1 f6 etc.

| 27 | ♖xh3 | ♗xh3 |
| 28 | ♘f4! | |

Now after 29 ♘d5 Black has to give up a pawn.

28	...	♗d7
29	♘d5	f6
30	♘xe7+	♔f7
31	♘d5	g5
32	♔e3	♗e6
33	♔d4	♔g6
34	♗f8	♗xd5
35	♔xd5	h5
36	♔e4	f5+
37	♔e5	

This is quite adequate to draw. But if we try to explain the following blunder by time-trouble (this is only a supposition), a candidate master might nonetheless have been expected to know about the familiar theoretically drawn ending that arises after 37 ♔f3 (Black cannot exploit the presence of pawns on the queenside). For example: 37 ... b6 38 c4 f4 39 c5 bc 40 ♗xc5 a6 41 ♔e4 h4 42 ♗d4 h3 43 ♗g1 ♔h5 44 ♔f3, or 38 ... h4 39 c5 bc 40 ♗xc5 a6 41 ♗b6 g4+ 42 ♔f4 h3 43 ♗g1 etc.

| 37 | ... | b6 |
| 38 | ♗b4? | |

It is only after this move that White is lost. A simple draw would have resulted from 38 c4! h4 39 c5 bc 40 ♗xc5 h3 (40 ... f4 leads to identical variations) 41 ♗g1 f4 42 ♔e4 ♔h5 43 ♔f3.

38	...	h4
39	♗e1	h3
40	♗g3	f4
41	♗h2	f3

0-1

Implementing a wrong strategic plan

Evaluation of a position is performed on the basis of objective factors (assets or defects) characteristic of it, such as the pawn skeleton, the stationing of the pieces (especially the kings), the control of open files and the centre etc. As his skill develops, a player comes to assess positions with sufficient precision. And yet at moments when an exertion is needed to overcome wishful thinking and decide on the correct plan for his subsequent operations, he doesn't always prove equal to it.

Costigan-Rohde
USA 1978-9
Sicilian Defence

1	e4	c5
2	♘f3	e6
3	b3	

Not the best policy against such an independent-minded player as Rohde. From analysing his games you can tell that he endeavours to avoid convention himself, and steers the game away from long theoretical variations as soon as he can.

3	...	♗e7
4	♗b2	♘f6
5	e5	♘d5
6	c4	♘f4!?

The familiar continuation is 6 ... ♘b6!? (or 6 ... ♘c7) 7 ♘c3 f6 8 ♘e4 fe 9 ♘xe5 0-0 10 d4 cd 11 ♕xd4 ♗b4+ 12 ♘c3! ♘c6. Black has clearly the worse position in the centre (Keres, Nei).

| 7 | h4!? | d6 |
| 8 | g3! | |

A mistake would be 8 h5? de 9 d4!? e4! saving the piece.

8	...	♘g6
9	ed	♗f6
10	♘c3?!	

A beginner doesn't miss the chance of setting his opponent a trap, even at the cost of worsening his own position. He has no great pretensions. But in master practice, such play cannot be justified under any circumstances. White is now preventing 10 ... ♕xd6? on account of 11 ♘e4. For the sake of this meagre achievement he has rejected the interesting continuation 10 ♗xf6!? ♕xf6 11 d4 cd 12 ♘xd4 ♘c6 13 ♘xc6! ♕xa1 14 ♗g2 followed by 15 h5.

| 10 | ... | ♘c6 |
| 11 | ♘g5?! | |

Wasting time. White's persistent attempt to post a knight on e4 is easily thwarted by Black.

| 11 | ... | ♗d4! |
| 12 | ♕h5? | |

White doesn't want to acknowledge his own errors and merely increases their ill effects. This kind of thing is typical of many young players. They are ashamed to admit their miscalculations and endeavour to cover them up by conceiving a strategic plan in which the inferior moves can be utilised. But such a policy cannot bring success and in the present game White is very quickly routed. It remains to be added that after 12 ♘f3! the game is level.

12	...	♕xd6
13	♗g2	♕e5+
14	♔f1	

14 ♕e2 ♘b4 15 ♗e4 f5 16 ♗b1 was preferable.

| 14 | ... | h6 |
| 15 | ♗xc6+ | |

Obviously the only way to save his piece.

15	...	bc
16	♕f3	0-0
17	♖e1?!	

The correct line was 17 ♘h3 followed by 18 h5 and 19 ♘f4 (R. Byrne, E. Mednis). After the move played White can no longer carry out this manoeuvre and the knight is unable to take part in the game.

17	...	♛c7
18	♘h3	e5
19	g4? *(59)*	

Making defeat inevitable. With 19 h5 ♘e7 20 g4 it was possible to organize resistance, since 20 ... e4 is unplayable owing to the undefended position of Black's knight, while 20 ... f5 is met by 21 g5 and White holds on.

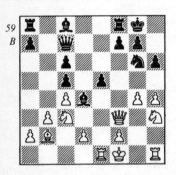

19	...	e4!

Now Black opens up the f-file and concludes the game with a direct attack.

20	♛xe4	f5
21	♛c2	fg
22	♛xg6	gh
23	♘d1	♗f5
24	♛h5	♗d3+
25	♔g1	♛g3 mate

Makarichev-Vladimirov
Lvov 1976
Ruy Lopez

1	e4	e5
2	♘f3	♘c6
3	♗b5	♘f6
4	0-0	♘xe4
5	d4	♗e7
6	de	

Another familiar continuation, 6 ♛e2 ♘d6 7 ♗xc6 bc 8 de ♘b7 or 8 ... ♘f5, leads to the freer game for White.

6	...	0-0
7	♛d5	

7 ♖e1 can be met by 7 ... d5 8 ed ♗xd6! 9 ♗xc6 bc, and for his broken pawn position Black has enough compensation in the form of actively placed minor pieces.

7	...	♘c5
8	♗e3	a6

A new move. The line known to theory is 8 ... ♘e6 9 ♘c3 a6 10 ♗c4 d6 11 ed ♛xd6 12 ♖ad1 with slightly the better position for White.

9	♗xc5	

Now 9 ♗c4 d6 10 ed ♛xd6 11 ♘c3 ♘b4 12 ♛xd6 ♗xd6 13 ♘d4 ♗d7 leads to complete equality.

9	...	ab
10	♘bd2?! *(60)*	

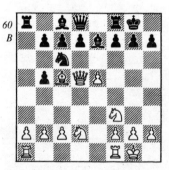

A more interesting line was seen in Lanka-Asanov, Kapsukas 1978: 10 ♗xe7 ♕xe7 11 ♘c3! (11 ♕xb5 ♖a5) 11 ... b4 12 ♘b5 ♖a5 13 a4 and now it was essential for Black to play 13 ... ba 14 ♖xa3 ♖xa3 15 ♘xa3 ♕e6 with an equal game (Moiseyev).

At a stage of the game when there is an absence of forced variations, envisaging the general course of play, even if only for the next five or ten moves, often presents the players with a serious problem. For, on conceiving a plan, it is impossible *'to carry out your designs in their entirety, with total precision. That would be practicable only in cases where the opponent didn't offer any resistance to your intentions.'* (Romanovsky)

The ability to tell just when a specific plan needs to be worked out, in accordance with the demands of the position, depends on a player's experience and level of skill.

10 ...   b4!

A strong move, blocking the opponent's queen's wing. It emerges that in spite of White's better development and spatial advantage, Black's position is no worse. The backward pawn on a2 and the advanced one on e5 require defending and curb the mobility of White's pieces. In determining his plan for the next phase of the game, Makarichev should have taken into account the defects of his position and simplified with 11 ♗xe7 ♕xe7 12 ♘c4 b6 13 ♘d4 ♗b7 14 ♘xc6 ♗xc6 15 ♕d4. Instead he played carelessly:

11 ♘b3?

. . . and soon found himself in difficulties:

11	...	♗xc5
12	♕xc5	♖e8
13	♖fe1	b6
14	♕c4	♗b7
15	♕f4	h6

Unlike his opponent, Black is playing very constructively. He now wishes to increase the pressure against the pawn on e5 by transferring his knight to g6, and to this end he protects the f7 point against raids by the white knight.

16 h4?

This serious weakening of the kingside, resulting from the wish to forestall Black's manoeuvre, further increases the difficulties of defence which were considerable in any case. Evidently White had to decide on 16 a3!?, since 16 ♘bd4 ♘xd4 17 ♘xd4 ♕g5 18 ♕xg5 hg 19 ♘b5 ♖a5 is thoroughly bad.

16 ...   ♘e7!
17 h5

17 ♕xb4 ♗xf3 18 gf ♘g6 is even worse. But now Black is able to eliminate the main defender of the

e-pawn.

17	...	♗xf3!
18	♕xf3	♘c6
19	♕f5	♕g5
20	♕xd7	♘xe5
21	♕h3	

On 21 ♕d5, Black would have the pleasant choice between transition to much the better endgame with 21 ... ♘g4 and the win of a pawn with 21 ... ♕xh5 when White would have to continue 22 ♘d4, since 22 f4? fails against 22 ... ♖ad8 23 ♕b5 c6 with an immediate win.

21	...	♖xa2
22	♖ad1	

Taking the rook would lead to loss: 22 ♖xa2 ♘f3+ 23 ♕xf3 ♖xe1+ 24 ♔h2 ♕h4+ 25 ♕h3 ♕xf2 26 ♖a8+ ♔h7 27 ♕d3+ f5 28 ♕d4 ♕e2 29 ♕d3 ♕e5+.

22	...	♖xb2
23	♖e2	c5
24	♖de1	(61)

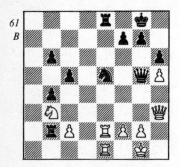

| 24 | ... | ♖xc2 |

The same themes in a new setting. After this sacrifice the co-operation of White's pieces is destroyed and his king ends up in a mating net.

25	♖xc2	♘f3+
26	♕xf3	♖xe1+
27	♔h2	♕h4+
28	♕h3	♕e4
29	♖d2	♕e5+!

An essential finesse.

30 g3 c4 31 ♘d4 ♕d5 32 f3 c3 33 ♖e2 ♖d1 34 ♖e4 f5 35 ♖e8+ ♔h7 36 ♘e6 ♕a2+ 37 ♕g2 ♖d2 38 ♘f8+ ♔g8 39 ♘g6+ ♔f7 40 ♖f8+ ♔e6 41 ♘f4+ ♔d7 0-1

Huzman-Nenashev
National Youth Games,
Leningrad 1982
Queen's Indian

1	d4	♘f6
2	c4	e6
3	♘f3	b6
4	a3	♗a6
5	♕c2	♗b7
6	♘c3	c5
7	d5	ed
8	cd	♘xd5
9	♗g5	f6
10	♘xd5	♗xd5
11	0-0-0	♗e6
12	♗f4	♘c6
13	e3	c4?

Black's effort to create complications, which in the end lead to his own destruction, results from a superficial appraisal of the final position in the forced variation 13 ... ♗e7 14 ♗a6 0-0 15 ♗b7 ♘a5! 16 ♗xa8 ♕xa8. For a chess master there is no difficulty in ascertaining that White's minimal material plus cannot compensate for Black's many threats. But to be aware of this, you have to look deeply into the position, which Black did not do.

14	♗xc4	♘b4
15	ab	♗xc4
16	♕e4+	♗e7 (62)

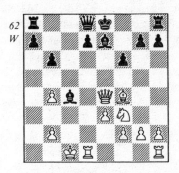

17   ♖xd7!!

Retribution for Black's rash play. He can't play 17 ... ♔xd7 18 ♖d1+ ♔e8 19 ♕c6+, when White picks up a bishop in addition to the queen. It's interesting that not long before this game, a similar catastrophe on d7 had occurred in the same opening variation in Lputian-Farago, Erevan 1982: 11 ♗f4 ♕e7 12 0-0-0 ♕e4 13 ♖xd5! ♕xd5 14 e3 ♕e6 15 ♗d3 ♘c6 16 ♖d1 ♖d8 17 ♗f5 ♕f7 18 ♗c7 g6 19 ♕e4+ ♕e7 (63)

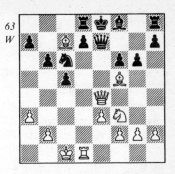

20 ♗xd7+!! There followed 20 ♖xd7 21 ♕xc6 ♖g8 22 ♖d6 and Farago resigned three moves later.

17	...	♕xd7
18	♕xa8+	♔f7

18 ... ♕d8 is unplayable because of 19 ♕c6+; so is 18 ... ♗d8 on account of 19 ♖d1 ♕e7 20 ♖xd8+!

19   ♕xh8   ♗f8!

Finding himself in a lost position, Nenashev searches about for counterchances. The straightforward 19 ... ♗d3 would be parried by 20 ♕a8!

20	♕xh7	♗d3
21	♕h5+	♗g6
22	♘e5+!	fe
23	♕xe5	♕d3
24	♕c3	♕e4!

Threatening 25 ... ♗xb4. But even this is no help.

25	f3	♕b1+
26	♔d2	♕xh1

Now Black actually has a piece more but the bad placing of all his pieces leads to his defeat.

27 ♕c4+   ♔f6

27 ... ♔e7 28 ♕c7+ ♔e8 29 ♕c6+ would not alter matters.

28 ♕c6+ ♔f7 29 ♕d5+ ♔e8 30 ♕e6+ ♔d8 31 ♕xg6 ♗xb4+ 32 ♔c2 ♕e1 33 ♕d3+ ♔c8 34 ♗g3 ♕a1 35 ♕f5+ ♔d8 36 ♕d5+ ♔c8 37 ♕c6+ ♔d8 38 ♗h4+ 1-0

The problem of the clock in practical play

Often, in the course of a game, while considering his moves, a player is faced with a problem which is usually solved intuitively – he has to *examine a small number of variations as many moves deep as he can, or else a large number to a depth of just two or three moves* (Kotov).

Making, in addition, an assessment of the end position after each concrete calculation, the brain performs a large task on which time is spent up. The most usual time-control for chess competitions is forty moves in two or two-and-a half hours. Most players find this thinking time sufficient. Nonetheless, games in which hectic time-scrambles do occur are not infrequent. One view is that time-trouble is peculiar to the 'human computer' type of player, who tries to perform a comprehensive calculation and assessment of all variations that arise during the game. But this

view of the matter hardly explains it in full. After all, among time-trouble addicts there are both strong players and weak ones, some who calculate quickly and accurately and others whose analysis is full of mistakes. To gain proper insight into this question we have to consider what most time is spent on. If we exclude the rare cases when complex combinations, containing quiet unobtrusive moves, have to be worked out, most time is used in forming strategic plans. A grandmaster in time-trouble, for example, will not as a rule overlook a forced sacrificial combination, but will feel uncomfortable in a positional dilemma.

The closer to time-trouble, the less strategy and the more tactics, Grandmaster Bronstein confirms. However, blindly copying the precepts of grandmasters for playing in time-trouble leads to no good. Even grandmasters make errors when short of time, and young players often become so flustered that a large advantage they have acquired loses all significance and the result becomes a matter of chance.

An addiction to time scrambles usually originates early in life. The most frequent causes for it are not weak analytical abilities but a lack of self-confidence, the re-checking of variations examined already and hesitation between several continuations of roughly equal merit. The addiction grows stronger with the years and it then often becomes impossible to cure it. For this reason, it is imperative to combat it at the earliest possible stage.

The following interesting thoughts by outstanding chess specialists may offer good advice to time-trouble addicts on how to eliminate this dire ailment:

Many players make the following serious mistake: in an involved position they strive above all to find a combinative solution to the problems facing them, and only after failing to find anything do they 'content' themselves with a positional cotinuation. This is the wrong approach; in situations that offer a mass of combinative lines of roughly equal value, we must straightaway switch over to a positional continuation, for choosing between lots of complicated variations is not worth the effort and we therefore boldly and proudly decline to do it. It's a different matter if the number of variations is restricted, or if their value is unequal; then we must go to work on them.

Nimzowitsch

One must play training games in which the time situation is taken into account above all else ... and continue these exercises until the habit of making suitable use of one's time has been acquired.

Botvinnik

Very often, players try to explain their defeats by time shortage. 'I lost in time trouble' they will say, in an attempt to make excuses for themselves and detract from the opponent's achievement. This pernicious, un-self-critical attitude is pure delusion.

A loss is a loss and there can be no excusing it. The real causes underlying it ought, however, to be brought to light, so that they can be successfully extirpated by suitable methods of training.

In the Nottingham tournament of 1936, Alekhine was two pawns up in an endgame against Tylor, but made a gross blunder which threw away his easy win. In his notes to the game, he writes:

In my view, to say that White was in severe time trouble is no more of an excuse than (for instance) it would be for a criminal to say that he was drunk when he committed his crime. An experienced master's failure to cope with the clock should be considered just as great a fault as the oversight itself.

The following instructive episode helped me to understand this matter properly.

In the post-war years I frequently faced Soviet Master N. Kopilov in tournaments. My score from these encounters did me little credit, and the more games I lost to him, the more eager I was to get even. I would use large amounts of thinking time and obtain the advantage, but eventually in time trouble I would commit crude errors and lose yet again. In one of the games, with an extra pawn and the better position, I threw away my queen two moves before the time control. This happened notwithstanding the scrupulously correct behaviour of my opponent, who didn't rush things in my time trouble but would write his move down and only then press the clock, slowly and as if reluctantly.

To my shame I have to confess that it was more than my nerves could stand. I swept the chessmen across the board and started signing the scoresheet. Picking the pieces up, Kopilov reacted to my outburst very calmly.

'It's no good getting worked up' he said. 'I don't get worse positions by playing worse than you. We just have different approaches to the game. You use up lots of time and energy to get the advantage, you get tired and finish up in time trouble. *I* play quickly, I stay fresh and I can keep thinking clearly. Your mistakes don't happen by accident, there are reasons for them. They come from not using your resources in the proper way.'

Words of wisdom!

Now and then a player actually uses his own time trouble as a psychological weapon. In a bad position which is impossible to save by normal methods, he will deliberately leave himself with just a few minutes for the remaining ten to fifteen moves, in an attempt *'to use this seemingly unfavourable situation to draw the opponent out of his natural rate of moving and dislodge the normal state of his emotions'* (V. Malkin).

There are cases when such tactics bring success. Losing his self-control, and not wanting to give the player in time trouble the chance of thinking when it is not his move, an inexperienced opponent will start playing fast himself. The mutual errors which ensue may disrupt the rightful course of the game and produce unexpected results. To avoid such accidents, you have to develop the ability to carry on playing without paying attention to your opponent's time trouble, or at any rate to make no more than two moves at a time in rapid succession. The technique of this last method is very simple. You select some continuation and play your move; the opponent makes the expected reply and you quickly move again, after which it is essential for you to have a careful think about the new position. Playing by 'short bursts' is highly unpleasant for the opponent in time trouble, who has difficulty finding the right answer to the second move of each pair.

Kasparov-Lanka
USSR Junior Ch Tbilisi 1976
Sicilian Defence

1	e4	c5
2	♘f3	♘c6
3	d4	cd
4	♘xd4	g6
5	c4	♗g7
6	♗e3	♘f6
7	♘c3	♘g4
8	♕xg4	♘xd4
9	♕d1	♘e6
10	♕d2	♕a5
11	♖c1	b6
12	♗e2?!	♗b7
13	f3	f5
14	ef	gf
15	0-0	♖g8
16	♖fd1	d6
17	a3	f4
18	♗xf4	♕f5! *(64)*

So far both sides had been playing quickly, especially Kasparov who evidently supposed that after his game with Yurtayev in 1975 (see page 61) he was familiar with all the subtelties of the position. But this naive assumption was

naturally to prove false. Latvian players have always devoted much time to the analysis of fashionable variations. In this case, uncovering a defect in a line recommended by Kapengut, they had managed to find a new continuation that causes White trouble. Once again, then, Kasparov found himself on unfamiliar ground and had difficult problems to solve over the board. None of this would have happened, of course, if he had taken sufficient pains in analysing his game against Yurtayev.

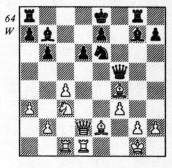

64
W

19 ♗e3

More than half an hour of precious time was used on this move. An equal game would have resulted from 19 ♗g3 ♗d4+ 20 ♗f2 (20 ♔f1?! is dangerous: 20 ... ♖xg3! 21 hg ♕h5 22 ♔e1 ♕h2 23 ♗d3 ♗xf3! with a sharp attack, or 23 ♕d3 ♕xg3+ 24 ♔d2 ♘c5 25 ♕xh7 ♘b3+, regaining the sacrificed exchange with the better position), and now:

a) **20 ... ♕h3** 21 ♗f1 ♗xf3 22 ♗xd4 ♘xd4 (22 ... ♘f4? loses to 23 ♖c2 ♘e2+ 24 ♔f2, or 23 ... ♗xg2 24 ♗xg2 ♖xg2+ 25 ♕xg2 with a big material advantage to White) 23 g3! (the obvious-looking 23 ♔h1? loses to 23 ... ♘e2! 24 ♕xe2 ♗xe2 25 gh ♗f3+ 26 ♗g2 ♗xg2+ 27 ♔g1 ♗f3+) 23 ... ♖xg3+ (he can't play for a win with 23 ... ♗xd1? 24 ♕xd4, or 23 ... ♕h4? 24 ♗g2! ♗xd1 25 ♖xd1) 24 hg ♕xg3+ 25 ♗g2 ♗xg2 26 ♕xg2 ♘f3+ 27 ♔f1 ♘h2+ with a draw.

b) Black appears to have no serious attack in the line **20 ... ♘f4** 21 ♕xd4 ♖xg2+ 22 ♔f1 ♘xe2 (22 ... ♕h3 23 ♔e1) 23 ♘xe2 ♕xf3 24 ♖c3 etc. (L. Yudasin).

19	...	♗e5
20	♘d5	

There's nothing for it. 20 ♔h1? leads to a bad position after 20 ... ♕h5 21 h3 ♕g6 22 ♗f1 ♕g3 23 ♔g1 ♕xh3, while 20 ♘e4? loses outright: 20 ... ♗xe4 21 fe ♕h3 22 ♗f1 ♗xh2+ 23 ♔f2 ♕g4! 24 ♔e1 ♗g3+ 25 ♗f2 ♖f8.

20	...	♕h3
21	♗f1	♕xh2+
22	♔f2	♕h4+?

Driving the king out to e2 in front of the bishop is obviously a tempting idea, and yet there was much more to worry White in an advance of the h-pawn. This had to be prepared by 22 ... ♖c8!, so as to induce 23 b3, closing the d1-a4 diagonal to the white queen; for 23 ♕c2? is unsatisfactory after 23 ... ♕h4+ 24 ♔e2 ♘d4+ 25 ♗xd4 ♗xd4 26 ♘e3 ♖g5 with an overwhelming position for Black.

23	♔e2	♖c8
24	b3	♘c5
25	♗f2	♕h2
26	♕c2	♖g6
27	♖e1	♕h6
28	♔d1	♖e6
29	♗e3	♕h5

An original position has arisen with both kings uncastled. All the same, the initiative lies with Black, as his king is better sheltered than his opponent's. White is therefore obliged to play accurately.

For example, 30 ♘f4? is unplayable: 30 ... ♗xf4 31 ♗xf4 ♖xe1+ 32 ♔xe1 ♕h4+ 33 g3 ♕h1, and Black wins a pawn.

A stronger line is 30 b4!? ♘d7! with complex play, since again White can't continue 31 ♘f4 on account of 31 ... ♗xf4 32 ♗xf4 ♖xe1+ 33 ♔xe1 ♕h4+ 34 g3 ♕h1, winning a pawn on f3. If Black tries for more, he is unsuccessful. For example, 30 ... ♗g3 31 ♖e2 (31 ♗f2? leads to the worse position for White: 31 ... ♖xe1+ 32 ♗xe1 ♗xe1 33 ♔xe1 ♘e6; alternatively 32 ♔xe1 ♕e5+ 33 ♔d1 ♗xf2 34 ♕xf2 ♗xd5 35 cd ♕xd5+ 36 ♔e2 ♕a2+, or 33 ♔e2 ♗xd5 34 cd ♘d3+) 31 ... ♘d7

(31 ... ♛h1?! looks suspect: 32 bc
♜xc5? 33 ♔d2! ♝xd5 34 ♝xc5,
and White wins. An unclear
position arises after 32 ... ♝xd5 33
♔d2! On the other hand, 33 cd?!
♜xe3 34 ♜xe3 ♛xf1+ 35 ♔d2
♛xg2+ 36 ♔d3 ♛xc2+ 37 ♜xc2
♜xc5 gives Black the better
ending) 32 ♘f4 ♝xf4 33 ♝xf4
♜xe2 34 ♔xe2! and White can
continue the defence successfully.
In many of the variations just
mentioned, the decisive blow is
delivered by the black knight, so
Kasparov takes the crucial decision
to exchange it.

30	♝xc5!?	♜xc5
31	b4	♜c8
32	♛e4	

Threatening 33 ♘f6+.

32	...	♔f7
33	♝d3	♜h6
34	g4	♛g5
35	f4!	♛xg4+
36	♝e2	♛h4
37	♝f3	e6
38	♜h1?	*(65)*

The game was played in the last
round. Kasparov was a point
ahead of Lanka and level with the
Kazan representative R. Gabdrakh-
manov, whose opponent, Z.Sturua
of Tbilisi, had half a point less.
Therefore a single wrong move by
any of these contenders for first
place could have a decisive
bearing on the result of the
tournament.

This circumstance undoubtedly
left its mark on the tense struggle
in the present game, in which
Kasparov was left with scarcely a
minute, and Lanka not much
more that two minutes, for the last
seven moves before the time
control. This accounts for the
errors by both sides which were to
mar the finish of an interesting
game.

Here White could have forced a
draw with 38 fe ♛xe4 39 ♝xe4 ed
40 ♝xd5+ ♝xd5 41 cd ♜xc1+ 42
♔xc1 de 43 ♜xe5 ♜h2.

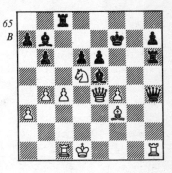

65
B

38	...	♛xf4!
39	♜xh6?	

This should have lost at once.
But then, 39 ♘xf4 ♝xe4 40 ♝xe4
♜xh1+ 41 ♝xh1 ♝xf4 would have
led slowly but surely to the same
result.

39	...	♛xh6
40	♝g4	ed?

In the heat of the time-scramble
Black misses the simple 40 ...
♝xd5! – putting an end to the

fight.

| 41 | ♕f5+ | ♕f6 |

And a better line here was 41 ...
♔g8 42 ♕e6+ ♕xe6 43 ♗xe6+
♔g7 44 ♗xc8 ♗xc8 45 cd ♗g4+ etc.

| 42 | ♕xh7+ | ♕g7 |
| 43 | ♕f5+ | ♗f6? |

After 43 ... ♔g8! 44 ♕e6+ ♔h8,
the checks, and with them
the game, would come to a
stop.

44	♕d7+	♔g8
45	♗e6+	♔h8
46	♕xg7+	♗xg7
47	♗xc8	♗xc8
48	cd	♗g4+
49	♔e1	♗b2?

The three extra moves that
Black made after the time control
didn't alter the verdict on the
position, but this last move –
which he sealed – definitely spoils
the win which he could have tried
to achieve by 49 ... ♗f3.

| 50 | ♖c2 | ♗xa3 |

Black can achieve nothing
tangible after 50 ... ♗e5 51 ♖c7.

51	♖h2+	♔g7
52	♖g2	♗xb4+
53	♔f1	♔f6
54	♖xg4	♗c3
55	♖e4	♔f5
56	♖e7	♗e5
57	♖xa7	♔e4
58	♖b7	♗d4
59	♔e2	♔xd5
60	♔d3	

½-½

*What's the explanation for so many
mistakes by both sides? Time
trouble, of course.*

Bronstein

Korzubov-Kasparov
National Youth Games
Moscow 1977
Sicilian Defence

1	e4	c5
2	♘f3	e6
3	d4	cd
4	♘xd4	♘f6
5	♘c3	d6
6	♗e3	a6
7	f4	b5
8	a3	♗b7
9	♕f3	♘bd7
10	♗d3	♖c8
11	0-0	♗e7

The exchange sacrifice played
in Kovacs-Szabo (Budapest 1972)
did not prove justified: 11 ...
♖xc3? 12 bc ♘c5 13 ♕h3 ♘fxe4
14 c4, with the better chances for
White.

| 12 | ♖ae1 | 0-0 |
| 13 | ♕g3?! | |

A new move, the chief idea
of which remained undisclosed in
this game. Usually White plays the
queen to h3, in order after 13 ...
♘c5 to withdraw the bishop to f2
adn to be able, if occasion arises,
to transfer this piece to h4 or start
an attack by pushing the g-pawn.
Possibly Korzubov was intending
to answer 13 ... ♘c5 by plunging

into obscure play with 14 f5?! e5 15 ♘de2 ♗xe4? 16 ♗h6 ♘h5 17 ♕g4 ♗xd3 18 cd ♘xd3 19 ♕xh5 gh 20 ♘d5, and White has a very powerful attack.

Things also turn out quite well for him after 15 ... ♘fxe4? 16 ♗xe4 ♘xe4 (16 ... ♗xe4? loses a piece to 17 ♗xh6 ♗f6 18 b4) 17 ♘xe4 ♗xe4 18 ♗h6 ♗f6 19 ♘c3 ♗xc2 20 ♘d5 ♔h8 21 ♘xf6 gh 22 ♕h4 and Black can hardly repulse the attack without heavy losses. However, after the cool 15 ... ♔h8! it's hard to see how White can strengthen his position, whereas Black's threats are becoming serious.

The other possible continuation looks even less attractive: 14 e5 ♘h5 15 ♕g4 ♘xd3 16 cd g6. We therefore have to conclude that Korbuzov's last move was made on the assumption that Kasparov, who always strives for the initiative, would be enticed into sacrificing the exchange and would fall into a cunning, masked trap.

13   ...   ♖xc3?!

At first sight this looks very strong. But in chess you cannot always evaluate a position by outward appearances. Concrete, precise calculation is always required.

14   bc   ♘xe4
15   ♗xe4!   ♗xe4 *(66)*

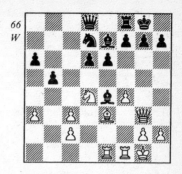

66
W

16   f5!

This splendid move creates numerous threats in the centre and on the kingside. To start with, Black has to save himself from 17 ♗h6.

16   ...   ♗h4!?

Perhaps he should have opted for 16 ... ♗xf5 17 ♘xf5 ef 18 ♗h6 ♗f6 19 ♖xf5 ♘e5 (but not 19 ... ♔h8? 20 ♕xd6! gh 21 ♖d1) 20 ♖ef1 ♘g6 21 ♗g5 ♗xg5 22 ♖xg5 ♕c7, when in view of White's many pawn weaknesses, Black can count on drawing.

17   ♕xd6   ef?!

In this sharp position Kasparov makes the kind of oversight that is rare in his play. Capturing the rook would have maintained the balance: 17 ... ♗xe1! 18 fe ♘f6! (the only move, which Black had evidently missed. Indeed, a bad position results from 18 ... ♗xh4 19 ef+ ♖xf7 20 ♖xf7 ♔xf7 21 ♕e6+ ♔f8 22 ♕xe4, or 19 ... ♔h8

20 ♘e6 ♛e7 21 ♛xd7! ♛xd7 22 ♘xf8 and 23 ♘g6+; or 18 ... fe 19 ♖xe1 ♘f6 20 ♛xe6+ ♔h8 21 ♗g5 ♗b7 22 ♗xf6) 19 ef+ ♔xf7 20 ♛e6+ ♔g6 21 ♖xe1 ♛d5 with a level game.

| 18 | ♖d1 | ♛e8 |

Indirectly defending the pawn on f5.

19	♗f4	♗e7
20	♛xa6	♘c5
21	♛xb5	♛a8
22	♖d2	♛xa3
23	♘b3	♘e6
24	♗e3!	g6

It was better to refrain from this move and bring the queen back into play with 24 ... ♛a8.

| 25 | ♛e5 | ♖c8 |
| 26 | ♖d7 | ♗d8 |

He has to control the f6 square.

| 27 | ♘c5! | |

In spite of time shortage, Korzubov finds a very powerful continuation, proceeding to attack his opponent's weakened kingside.

| 27 | ... | ♗g5!? |

An ingenious retort, which unexpectedly plays a decisive part in determining the result of the game. At this point Korzubov had considerably more time left than Kasparov, but he spent almost all of it – eight precious minutes – looking for a decisive continuation in answer to his opponent's unexpected move.

28	♘xe6	♗xe3+
29	♔h1	♗h6
30	♛f6	♖f8

In normal circumstances Black would of course have resigned. But the players' clocks presented a familiar spectacle – Kasparov had one minute left, Korzubov had two.

| 31 | ♘xf8 | ♛a2 |
| 32 | ♛e7? | |

After 32 ♘xh7! or 32 ♖d8 a few seconds would be enough to win with.

| 32 | ... | ♛c4 |
| 33 | ♖fd1 | ♗e3 |

Now mate with 34 ... ♗xg2+ is threatened. The only way to defend against it is to give back some of the extra material with 34 ♛xf7+! But that always goes so much against the grain.

| 34 | ♛h4?? | ♗g2+ |
| 35 | ♔xg2 | ♛xh4 |

and, succeeding in making his last five moves before the time control, **Black won**.

3 Chessplayers of Positional and Combinative Styles

Every chess master evolves a style corresponding to his individual character.

Réti

Some lengthy debates are conducted about who should be classed as a player of the positional type and whose style is basically combinative.

It should be observed that there is not, and cannot be, any wholly unequivocal opinion on this question.

The one thing that can be said for certain is that there are weak players and strong ones. The former as well as the latter may incline either to combinative play or to positional play. But whereas the weak player often regards a combination as an end in itself and feels moral satisfaction from the mere fact of having combined, the strong player uses a combination exclusively as a means to gaining an advantage.

In some positions that arise in play, there will be two paths leading to the decisive advantage – either a mating attack resulting from a complex combination many moves deep, or else forced exchanges which lead to a prolonged but technically won endgame. In this case players can be divided up according to which path they would choose, in keeping with their temperament and the views they have formed on chess. Among many others, Alekhine and Tal would give preference to a combination. Capablanca and Petrosian would favour the positional solution. Does this mean that the former can be called combinative and the latter positional players?

An answer to this question is given by P. Romanovsky, chess master and trainer, in his book *The Middlegame*:
"Chessplayers can play cautiously, riskily, sharply, boldly, experimentally, cunningly, circumspectly, subtly, ingeniously, etc, but they cannot play positionally or combinatively, inasmuch as both of these elements, known to us from chess practice, are united in a

single creative process. Taking away either element means truncating this process in its most important, its most fundamental aspect."

And the final word on this issue is spoken by World Champion Anatoly Karpov in his article *After the Match that Never Was*: "Whereas all Tal needed to do to become World Champion was to nonplus and stun his rivals with sacrifice after sacrifice (Petrosian was just as good at combining, but he kept his talent in check, playing purely positionally) – at present, this is not enough to achieve major successes. You have to do *everything* sufficiently well (with no discernible defects), as well as as being able to do *something* excellently."

These thoughts are borne out by the tenor of the following two games by distinguished players of our time.

English Opening

	1	c4	g6
	2	♘c3	♗g7
	3	g3	c5
	4	♗g2	♘c6
	5	b3	

With the struggle for the centre in view, 5 e3! or even 5 e4!? seems more logical. The slow move White plays enables Black to develop his pieces quickly and harmoniously.

	5	...	e6!
	6	♗b2	♘ge7
	7	♘a4?!	

White conducts the opening irresolutely. The bishop exchange involves loss of time. He should have carried on developing with 7 ♘f3 d5 8 cd ♘xd5 9 ♖c1, so as to prepare the exchange of black-squared bishops after 10 ♕c2.

	7	...	♗xb2
	8	♘xb2	0-0
	9	e3	d5
	10	♘f3	♘f5!

Preventing the advance d4, Black gradually acquires a spatial advantage.

	11	0-0	b6
	12	♘a4	

Now 12 d4? is dangerous because of a possible exchange sacrifice: 12 ... cd 13 ♘xd4 ♘cxd4 14 ed ♗a6 15 ♖e1 dc! 16 ♗xa8 ♕xa8 17 bc ♖d8, with serious threats on the long diagonal.

	12	...	♗b7
	13	cd	ed
	14	d3	

As before, 14 d4 cd 15 ♘xd4 ♘cxd4 16 ed ♕f6 17 ♘c3 ♖fd8! is unfavourable for White.

	14	...	♕f6
	15	♕d2	♖ad8
	16	♖fd1	♖fe8!

Putting a stop for good to the possibility of 17 d4? because of 17 ... cd 18 ♘xd4 ♘cxd4 19 ed

♘xd4! 20 ♕xd4 ♖e1+ and Black wins.

17	♖ab1

17 ♖ac1! was more accurate.

17	...	♘d6
18	♘e1	d4
19	e4	♕e7
20	♘c2?!	

The other possible continuation looks unattractive: 20 f4 f5 21 e5 ♘b5, and after the exchange of white-squared bishops both black knights obtain comfortable posts on d5 and e6.

20	...	f5
21	ef	♘e5!
22	f4	

After 22 ♗xb7 ♕xb7 23 ♘e1 ♘xf5, White has no counterplay at all. Black would gain an overwhelming advantage by doubling rooks on the e-file.

22	...	♘f3+
23	♗xf3	♗xf3
24	♖e1	*(67)*

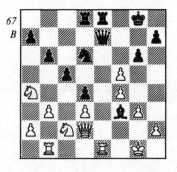

67
B

24	...	♕e2!

Reducing to a distinctly advantageous endgame.

25	♖xe2	♖xe2
26	♕xe2	

Annotators of this game unanimously note that on 26 ♕c1!? Black was intending 26 ... ♖g2+ 27 ♔f1 ♖xh2 28 ♘e1 ♗d5, when in spite of his large material plus it's hard for White to activate his pieces. For example: 29 ♖b2 ♖h1+ 30 ♔f2 ♘xf5, and 31 ♖e2 fails against 31 ... ♖h2+; or 29 ♘b2 ♘xf5 30 ♔g1 ♖h1+ 31 ♔f2 ♖e8 32 ♘c4 ♖h2+ 33 ♔g1 ♖ee2, with unavoidable mate.

26	...	♗xe2
27	♘b2	

White hastens to bring this knight into play. The attempt to keep his extra pawn would have led to a miserable position: 27 fg ♗xd3 28 gh+ ♔xh7 29 ♖c1 ♖e8 30 ♘e1 ♗b5 31 ♘b2 ♖e2 etc.

27	...	gf
28	♖e1	♗h5
29	♘c4	♘xc4
30	bc	♖e8
31	♔f2	♖xe1
32	♔xe1	♔f8
33	♔d2	♔e7
34	♘e1	a6
35	a4	

The threat was 35 ... b5, but now another White weakness becomes fixed, which together with the poor mobility of his knight deprives him of any saving chances.

35	...	a5
36	♔c2	♗e8
37	♔b3	♗c6

The bishop is doing a tremendous job – on the one hand it has tied White's king to the defence of a pawn, on the other hand it stops the knight from freeing itself.

38	♔a3	♔f6
39	♔b3	♔g6
40	♔a3	♔h5
41	h3	♔g6

The king has carried out its 'dark mission' of inducing another pawn to occupy a white square, where the bishop will go after it.

42	♔b3	♔g7!

An important gain of tempo, as the following will show.

43	♔a3	♔f6
44	♔b3	♗e8
45	♘g2	

Centralising the knight would not have brought relief: 45 ♘f3 ♗h5 46 ♘e5 ♗d1+ (the possibility of this check is the result of Black's 42nd move) 47 ♔a3 ♔e6 48 ♘c6 ♗c2 49 ♘e5 h6 50 g4 fg 51 hg ♗d1, and White is in *zugzwang*.

45	...	♗h5
46	♔c2	♗e2
47	♘e1	♗f1
48	♘f3	♗xh3
49	♘g5	♗g2
50	♘xh7+	♔g7
51	♘g5	♔g6
52	♔d2	

White's position is hopeless; other continuations also failed to save him, for example: 52 ♘e6 ♔h5 53 ♘c7 ♔g4 54 ♘d5 ♔xg3 55 ♘xb6 ♔xf4 56 ♔d2 ♗c6 57 ♔e2 ♔g3.

52	...	♗c6?!
53	♔c1	♗g2!

Black makes the correct decision – before picking up the pawn he must activate his king to the full, so that White's knight can't plug the gap on g4 by the manoeuvre ♘h3-f2.

54	♔d2	♔h5
55	♘e6	♗c6
56	♘c7	♔g4
57	♘d5	♔xg3
58	♘e7	♗d7
59	♘d5	♗xa4
60	♘xb6	♗e8?!

60 ... ♗c6 was more precise, but such minor details can no longer affect the result.

61	♘d5	♔f3
62	♘c7	♗c6
63	♘e6	a4
64	♘xc5	a3
65	♘b3	a2
66	♔c1	

White can't afford to take the pawn: 66 ♘xd4+ ♔xf4 67 ♘b3 ♗a4 68 ♘a1 ♔g3.

66	...	♔xf4
67	♔b2	♔e3
68	♘a5	♗e8
69	c5	f4
70	c6	♗xc6

71	♘xc6	f3
72	♘e5	f2
	0-1	

King's Indian Defence

1	♘f3	♘f6
2	g3	g6
3	c4	♗g7
4	♗g2	0-0
5	0-0	♘c6
6	♘c3	d6
7	d4	a6
8	d5	♘a5
9	♘d2	c5
10	♕c2	e5

The opening stage of the game is concluded. White has acquired some space advantage, thanks to advancing his d-pawn to the fifth rank. Black, on the other hand, having blocked the centre, can start preparing a breakthrough on either of the wings.

11	b3	♘g4
12	e4	

12 h3 would be answered by 12 ... ♘h6. The defence of the h-pawn might then cause White unnecessary bother.

12	...	f5
13	ef	

The necessary continuation; otherwise, after 13 ... f4, Black would obtain a spatial plus on the kingside and chances of an attack.

13	...	gf
14	♘d1!	

Aimed against 14 ... f4, which

White would answer with 15 ♗e4! After that, 15 ... fg is not dangerous because of 16 fg! when the second rank is easily defended by the queen, while the square e3 is secure against forays by the enemy knight. The intermediate move 16 ♗xh7+? would lose: 16 ... ♔h8 17 fg e4! and White loses a piece.

14	...	b5
15	f3	e4!
16	♗b2	ef
17	♗xf3	♗xb2

The bishop exchange weakens Black's king position. A stronger move was 17 ... ♘e5.

18	♕xb2	♘e5
19	♗e2	f4
20	gf	♗h3? *(68)*

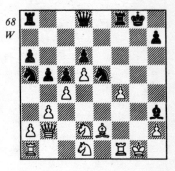

20 ... ♖xf4 was preferable, when Black's position is no worse. For example, 21 ♖xf4 ♕g5+ 22 ♔h1 ♕xf4, or 21 ♘e3 ♕g5+ 22 ♔h1 ♖xf1+ and 23 ... ♖a7. Now White plays an unexpected combination.

| 21 | ♘e3! | ♗xf1 |

It's too late for 21 ... ♖xf4 22
♖xf4 ♕g5+, upon which Tal gives
23 ♖g4! ♗xg4 24 ♘xg4 ♘xg4 25
♗xg4 ♕xg4+ 26 ♔h1, and 'all
Black's pieces disappear from the
board, leaving him with only the
wretched knight on a5 and the
rook on a8 – and thus settling the
outcome.'

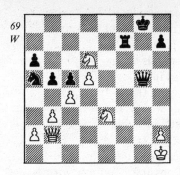

| 22 | ♖xf1 | ♘g6 |
| 23 | ♗g4 | ♘xf4 |

Leads to loss, but Black's
position is bad anyway. 23 ... ♕f6
would be met by 24 ♗e6+ ♔h8 25
♕xf6+ ♖xf6 26 f5 ♘e5 27 ♘e4,
with a won endgame.

24 ♖xf4!

The rare case of a second
exchange sacrifice. White's attack
becomes irresistible.

24	...	♖xf4
25	♗e6+	♖f7
26	♘e4	♕h4

Or 26 ... ♖a7 27 ♘f5! winning
at once.

| 27 | ♘xd6 | ♕g5+ |
| 28 | ♔h1 | ♖a7 |

On 28 ... ♕xe3, the continuation
would be 29 ♗xf7+ ♔f8 30 ♕h8+
♔e7 31 ♘f5+ ♔d7 32 ♗e6+!
winning the queen.

| 29 | ♗xf7+ | ♖xf7 (69) |
| 30 | ♕h8+! | |

1-0

If you try to draw conclusions
about these two games from the
standpoint of 'who's who', it
seems clear that the first one was
played by an adherent of the
positional style, while in the
second the pieces were managed
by a chessplayer whose credo is
tactics. But don't jump to conclusions, reader; turn to the end of
the chapter, where the names of
the players are disclosed.

A few years ago, one distinguished
grandmaster, in conversation with
me, was sharply criticising the
play of another equally distinguished grandmaster, on the
grounds that the latter, in a level
position, would stir up mind-
bending complications even if (let
us say) the analysis of ten
variations showed that seven were
in his favour while two led to
equality and one gave him the
worse game. In such a labyrinth of
possibilities, most of his opponents
would fail to find the right
continuation, and would lose.

"I'm different", concluded the
grandmaster I was talking to.
"After I've done such a colossal

amount of work and used up loads of time, I end up rejecting this sort of possibility, even though I know it stands a very good chance of working. I'm just not capable of playing that way."

It would be foolish to seek the truth in either of these opposite attitudes to chess. In the last resort everyone aims to play as strongly as possible, and everyone has to achieve this purpose by the means most suited to himself. Most likely, both grandmasters are right – as is borne out by their remarkable results.

In 1959 at the USSR Championship in Tbilisi, I watched Tigran Petrosian – World Champion in the making – whose propensity is for quiet play, analysing some adjourned games, surrounded by chess trainers and a few participants in the tournament (some of whom were acknowledged tacticians). In the course of this analysis he was so quick at finding the most complex tactical strokes with their many ramifications, which most of those present had missed, that you began to have the impression of looking not at a chessboard but into a kaleidoscope.

It is just this quickness in unearthing the concealed resources of chess positions that is one of the most important indications of a top-class player (or one *destined*

for the top class).

Dvoiris-Kasparov
USSR Junior Ch Vilnius 1975
Sicilian Defence

1	e4	c5
2	♘f3	♘c6
3	d4	cd
4	♘xd4	♘f6
5	♘c3	d6
6	♗c4	e6
7	♗e3	♗e7
8	♕e2	a6
9	0-0-0	♕c7
10	♗b3	0-0
11	g4	♘xd4
12	♖xd4	b5

This is considered more reliable than 12 ... e5 13 ♖c4 ♕d8 14 g5 ♘e8 (on 14 ... ♘d7, *ECO* recommends 15 ♘d5, but White can go straight for the attack with 15 h4!? b5 16 ♖xc8! ♖xc8 17 ♘d5, when Black is in a very dangerous position despite his extra exchange) 15 ♖g1 ♗d7 16 ♘d5 ♗b5 17 ♗b6, and it isn't easy for Black to equalise (*ECO*).

13	g5	♘d7
14	♕h5	♖d8 (70)
15	♘d5?	

This continuation has long since been discarded. But the alternatives also fail to give White a decisive plus. Black's position is not at all bad. He has no weaknesses, and when required his pieces can be brought across to

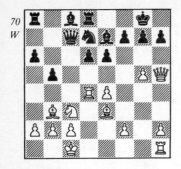

the defence of his king. For example, Velimirović in *ECO* gives 15 e5? de! (15 ... d5? 16 ♗xd5) 16 ♖h4 ♘f8 17 ♘e4 ♗b7 18 ♘f6+ ♗xf6 19 gf ♗xh1 20 fg ♔xg7 21 ♗h6+ ♔g8 22 ♕g5+ ♘g6 23 ♕f6 ♖d1+! followed by 24 ... ♕d8+. To supplement this analysis, Nikitin gives 16 ♘d5? ed 17 ♗xd5 ed 18 ♕xf7+ ♔h8 19 ♗xd4 ♗xg5+ 20 ♔b1 ♕e5! 21 ♗xe5 ♘xe5, and Black has more than enough for the queen.

After 15 e5? Black may also play 15 ... ♘xe5!? This is given a question mark by Velimirović, on the assumption that White wins with 16 ♖h4. However, 16 ... h6 17 gh g6! leads to an obscure position, where White's advantage, if any, is not easy to demonstrate.

15 ... ed
16 ♗xd5 ♘e5!

The whims of fashion? We come upon them at every turn – in the arts, at work, in everyday life. Chess too has been unable to insulate itself from them.

Games by young players register the opening fashions like a barometer. No sooner have their elders employed some new continuation with success in a tournament, than thousands of younger players incorporate it into their repertoire. The vast majority of them, however, while conscientiously learning up the first ten or fifteen moves, don't know what to do afterwards.

The twelve-year-old Kasparov was a pleasant exception. Even at such an early age he succeeded in avoiding the problems of his repertoire by thorough analysis of characteristic middlegames. Only a few individuals are capable of this, and as a rule they are the very ones who will attain a high level of success.

Many readers may react to this with an ironic smile. It's all very well to make predictions (they will say), when probability has become fact. Isn't Kasparov firmly installed on the Olympus already?

Well, permit me to ask a question in return, reader. Are there many players who at the age of nine or ten make use of the full amount of thinking time that they are given? From a small number, there are two I can recall: Boris Spassky and Gary Kasparov.

It's 'trivial' things like this which make able players stand

out, and which can form a basis
for predictions . . .

According to Nikitin's analysis,
Black's last move refutes the
sacrifice.

17 f4!?

An unforeseen reply. The
analysis examines 17 ♗xa8 ♗g4
18 ♕h4 ♗f3, with the better game
for Black.

17 ... g6?!

Black could have turned his
assets to account by 17 ... ♗g4 18
♕h4 (a possibility is 18 ♗xf7+!?
♘xf7 19 ♕xg4, with an obscure
position which nonetheless favours
Black) 18 ... ♖ac8 19 c3 h5! (this is
the only move to secure Black's
advantage, whereas 19 ... ♗e2? 20
fe de 21 ♗xf7+ would give White
the better position, and 19 ... ♗f3
20 fe ♗xh1 21 e6 leads to
unnecessary complications) 20 fe
(after 20 h3, the tempting 20 ...
♘f3?! 21 ♕f2 ♘xd4 22 hg leads to
a position where Black's material
edge is of little importance;
however, 20 ... ♘g6! assures him
of a decisive plus, for example
21 ♕f2 ♗e6 22 f5 ♗xd5 and 23 ...
♘e5; alternatively 22 ♗xe6 fe 23
f5 ef 24 ef ♘e5, or 23 ♕f3 e5) 20 ...
de 21 ♖d2 (21 ♖d3 loses to 21 ...
♖xd5 22 ♖xd5 ♕c4 23 ♖xe5 ♗a3)
21 ... b4 22 c4 ♖xd5 23 ed ♕xc4+
24 ♔b1 ♗f5+, with a pleasant
choice of winning continuations.

18 ♕h4 ♘f3

19	♗xf7+	♔g7
20	♕h6+	♔xf7
21	♕xh7+	♔e8
22	♕xg6+	♔d7
23	♕f5+	♔e8
24	♕g6+	♔d7
25	♖d3	

White declines the draw, and
though two pieces down tries to
find a way to win. But there
is insufficient justification for
this.

25	...	♕c4
26	♖hd1	♗b7
27	♕h7	♗xe4
28	♖xd6+	♔e8

Of course not 28 ... ♔c8? 29
♖xd8+ and 30 ♕d7+.

| 29 | ♕h8+ | ♗f8 |

After 29 ... ♔f7 a draw could be
agreed at once, but by now it is
Black who is trying to evade the
perpetual check.

30	♖xd8+	♖xd8
31	♖xd8+	♔xd8
32	♕xf8+	♔d7
33	♕g7+	♔e8
34	♕h8+	♔f7
35	♕f6+	♔g8
36	♕d8+	♔h7
37	♕d7+	♔g6
38	♕e8+	♔f5
39	♕d7+	♕e6
40	♕xe6+	♔xe6
41	b3	♘xh2
42	c4	bc
43	bc	♘g4
44	♔d2	♔f5

| 45 | a3 | ♗b1 |

½-½

**Kasparov-Roizman
Minsk 1978**
Ruy Lopez

1	e4	e5
2	♘f3	♘c6
3	♗b5	♘d4
4	♘xd4	ed
5	0-0	♗c5

Playable, though a more popular line, is 5 ... c6 6 ♗c4 ♘f6 7 ♖e1 d6 8 c3 ♘g4! 9 h3 ♘e5, or 6 ♗a4 ♘f6 7 d3 d5 8 ed ♘xd5 9 ♖e1+ ♗e7, with a minimal plus for White in either case.

| 6 | d3 | c6 |
| 7 | ♗c4 | |

More usually the bishop is withdrawn to a4, but Kasparov likes clear-cut variations; the threat now is 8 ♗xf7+.

| 7 | ... | d6 |
| 8 | f4 | ♘f6 |

After 8 ... ♘e7 Black has to reckon with the continuation 9 f5 d5 10 ♗b3.

| 9 | e5?! | |

Prompted by a wish to complicate the game as quickly as possible.

| 9 | ... | de? |

A strange oversight for such a strong master. After 10 fe? Black wants to station his knight on d5 in complete comfort; but this is not to be.

He should have played at once

9 ... ♘d5 10 ed 0-0 11 ♗xd5 cd 12 f5 ♗xd6, when Black's position is no worse.

10	♗xf7+	♔xf7
11	fe	♕d5
12	ef	gf
13	♘d2	♖g8

On 13 ... ♗f5, White plays 14 ♘e4! all the same.

14	♘e4	♗e7
15	♗f4	♖g6
16	♕e2	♗g4
17	♕f2	♖ag8
18	♖ae1	h5 *(71)*

Black is in a difficult situation. His kingside weaknesses and insecure king position are making themselves felt. His last move has the purpose of strengthening the pressure of his rooks along the file, for now White will be unable to post a minor piece on g3.

However, White's unexpected retort steers the game on a completely different course.

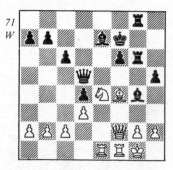

71
W

| 19 | ♗g5! | ♕d8 |

Black can't play 19 ... ♖xg5, on

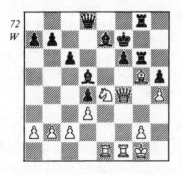

account of 20 ♘xf6 with an immediate win; for example, 20 ... ♕f5 21 ♘xg4 ♕xf2+ 22 ♖xf2+ etc.

In addition, Kasparov indicates that "the counterattacking move 19 ... ♗h3 is refuted by 20 ♘xf6 ♗xf6 21 ♕xf6+! with a quick mate, or 20 ... ♕xg2+ 21 ♕xg2 ♗xg2 22 ♖xe7+!"

20   ♕f4   ♗e6
21   h4

Obviously the only move, after which White's bishop no longer has any retreat. On the other hand, a new threat arises: 22 ♗xf6! ♗xf6 23 ♘g5+, or 22 ... ♖xf6 23 ♕e5! etc.

21   ...   ♗d5 (72)

A striking denouement would occur after 21 ... ♗g4 22 ♗h6 ♖h8 23 ♘g5+ ♔g8 24 ♖xe7! ♕xe7 25 ♕b8+; if 24 ... ♖gxh6 (or 24 ... ♖hxh6), then 25 ♕e4. On 23 ... ♔e8, White wins with 24 ♖xe7+ ♔xe7 25 ♖e1+ ♔d7 26 ♘f7, or 24 ... ♕xe7 25 ♕b8+ ♕d8 26 ♖e1+ etc.

22   g4!!

An astonishing move! The black rook defends the critical point f6, and in order to drive it away White decides on a continuation that looks so risky – his own king too is now left without pawn cover. Yet Kasparov has calculated accurately, as the further course of the game shows.

22   ...   ♔g7?!

Loses immediately. Resistance could have been prolonged (but that is all) by 22 ... ♗xe4 23 ♕xe4! (after 23 gh? ♖xg5+ 24 hg ♗d5, Black can defend) 23 ... hg 24 ♕e6+ ♔f8 25 ♗f4! By thwarting Black's attempt to exchange queens and threatening to advance the h-pawn, White would still win. Kasparov also gives the following beautiful variations: "22 ... ♖h8 23 ♗xf6! ♖xg4+ 24 ♕xg4 hg 25 ♗xe7+ ♔xe7 26 ♘c5+, or 23 ... ♗xf6 24 g5 ♗xe4 25 ♖xe4 ♔g7 26 ♖e6 ♖f8 27 ♔h2, and Black's position is very bad, although he can still prolong the fight."

The remaining moves were:

23   gh   fg
24   ♕e5+   ♔h6

Or 24 ... ♗f6 25 ♘xf6 ♖xf6 26 hg, winning for White.

25   hg   gh
26   ♖f5   ♔xg6
27   ♔h2

1-0

Talent is not easily weighed!

Already at the age of ten, the young Baku player became known at national level. From then onwards his successes increased from one tournament to the next, and in 1978, at the age of fifteen, he gained first place in the Sokolsky Memorial Tournament at Minsk, exceeding the master norm by 3½ points.

All these years Kasparov has been accumulating experience and perfecting his skill, but the hallmark of his play – a love for sharp positions – has remained unchanged.

Alexander Kochiev became a master at seventeen – two years later in life than Kasparov. His play makes a less striking impression. Nonetheless, he became a grandmaster by the age of twenty (a feat attained by few), and there are many things in chess which he knows how to do excellently.

Kochiev is not considered a combinative player. His style is universal. He is equally good at defending and attacking, but is perhaps most successful of all in the exploitation of accumulated small advantages. No doubt such qualities are enough in themselves to make a strong player, but an account of Kochiev's chess personality would be incomplete if it failed to bring out one other distinctive feature of his play.

Since his youth he has been able to sense the approach of danger in good time, to diagnose the mounting crisis in a game. In such moments his play becomes transformed, and he strives to utilise all possibilities for confusing his opponent and making the win difficult for him.

Kochiev-Sochagin
Leningrad 1969
King's Indian Defence

1	c4	♘f6
2	♘c3	g6
3	e4	d6
4	d4	♗g7
5	f3	0-0
6	♗g5	♘bd7
7	♕d2	c5
8	d5	a6
9	h4	

9 ♗h6! – and only afterwards 10 h4 – was more precise. In that case Black wouldn't have been able to carry out the plan of development which later on was to cause White difficulties.

9	...	h5!
10	♘h3	♘e5! *(73)*

Going over games from national and international tournaments together with young players, you often hear the perplexed question: "What use is this to us? We don't play such openings! Wouldn't it be better to look at something from our own repertoire?"

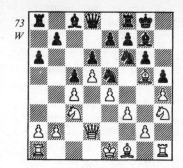

73
W

We shan't go into arguments about what would be better or worse, yet some answer to this question has to be offered.

The point is that combinative motifs and strategic ideas, upon which a plan in a game of chess is built up, may be identical in different openings.

Let us try putting a somewhat free interpretation on the pronouncement by the World Champion which we have already quoted. Let us say: you have to have good knowledge of the chess heritage, as well as excellent knowledge of your own repertoire.

Only when this is the case can a player be said to possess a wide outlook – to possess the ability to utilise, in his games, everything which he has so far justified himself in practice.

An example will make this clear.

In the Ruy Lopez, after the well-known moves 1 e4 e5 2 ♘f3 ♘c6 3 ♗b5 a6 4 ♗a4 d6 5 ♗xc6+ bc 6 d4 f6 7 ♗e3 ♘e7 8 ♘c3 ♘g6 9 ♕d3 ♗e7 10 h4, we reach a position that holds interest for us.

In reply to White's attack against the central pawn on e5, Black has been carefully fortifying it (4 ... d6; 6 ... f6; 8 ... ♘g6). However, White's last move (10 h4) justifies what looks like an inconsistency on Black's part – the surrender of the centre with 10 ... ed!? 11 ♘xd4 ♘e5 12 ♕e2 c5 13 ♘b3 0-0 14 0-0-0 ♕e8 (74).

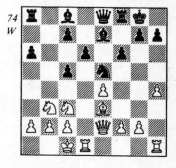

74
W

Let us look for something in common between the last two diagrammed positions, for all their fundamental differences. The common factor is not hard to spot – it is the unassailable black knight in the centre. The knight can be driven away only by f4, and in that case it would transfer itself to the g4 square weakened by the advance of the h-pawn, and would put a brake on White's attempts to work up a kingside initiative.

11	♗e2	♗d7
12	♘f2	♕a5
13	f4	

White is obliged to start active operations; otherwise Black will seize the initiative with 13 ... b5.

13	...	♘eg4
14	♘xg4	hg
15	e5	

White would have liked to prepare this break with 15 0-0-0. But there is no time for that, in view of 15 ... b5 16 e5 b4.

15	...	de
16	fe	♘h5
17	♕e3	

Some interesting lines arise after 17 e6?! fe 18 ♗xg4 ♘g3 19 ♖g1 ♖ad8 20 ♗xe7! ed! (20 ... ♖de8?! looks tempting: 21 ♗xf8? ♗xc3 22 ♕xc3 ed+, with an immediate win. However, 21 d6! would secure White the advantage) 21 ♗xd8 ♗xc3 22 ♗xa5 ♖e8+ 23 ♔f2 ♘e4+ 24 ♔e3 ♘xd2+ 25 ♔d3 ♗xa5 26 ♗xd7 ♖e7 27 ♗g4 ♘xc4, or 23 ♔d1 ♗xg4+ 24 ♔c2 ♗xd2 25 ♗xd2 ♗f5+ 26 ♔b3 ♖e2 with plenty of initiative for the sacrificed exchange.

17	...	f5

Looks very energetic, but more difficult problems would have faced White after 17 ... ♕c7 18 ♗xe7 ♗xe5! 19 ♗xf8 ♖xf8. The active placing of Black's pieces, with the white king stuck in the centre, would more than compen-

sate for the lost exchange.

18	0-0	

White has a bad position after 18 ♗xe7 f4 19 ♕d2 ♗xe5.

18	...	♕c7
19	♗xe7	♗xe5
20	d6!	

The only move.

20	...	♗xd6
21	♗xd6	♕xd6
22	♖ad1	♕c6

22 ... ♕e6 was more precise: 23 ♕xc5 ♖ac8 24 ♕d6 ♕e3+ 25 ♔h2 ♖c6 26 ♕xd7 ♕g3+ 27 ♔g1 ♕e3+ 28 ♔h1 ♘g3+ 29 ♔h2 ♘xe2 30 ♘xe2 ♕xe2 with equal chances. Now, however, Black has some difficulties to overcome.

23 ♘d5 ♔g7 24 ♕e5+ ♔h6 25 ♕e3+ ♔g7 26 ♕e7+ ♖f7 27 ♕e5+ ♔h7 28 ♗xg4 ♖e8 29 ♕c3 ♖e4 30 ♗xh5 gh 31 ♘f6+ ♕xf6 32 ♖xd7 ♔g6 33 ♕xf6+ ♖xf6 34 b3 b5 35 cb ab 36 ♖c7 c4 37 bc bc 38 ♖c1 ♖xh4 39 ♖1xc4 ♖xc4 40 ♖xc4 ♖a6 41 a4 ♔g5 42 ♔f2 f4 43 ♔f3 ♖b6 44 ♖c5+ ♔g6 45 ♖b5 ♖c6 46 a5 ♖c4 47 ♖b8 ♖a4 48 ♖a8 ♔h6 49 a6 ♔g5 50 a7 ♔h4 51 ♔f2 ♖a3 ½-½.

As a rule it is very difficult to perform an exact analysis of a sacrifice taking into account all the sub-variations, even just a few moves deep; more often, such an aimless expenditure of energy leads to nervous strain, time-trouble and undeserved defeat.

Spielmann

Kochiev-Fyodorov
Leningrad 1971
King's Indian Defence

1	c4	♘f6
2	♘f3	g6
3	g3	♗g7
4	♗g2	0-0
5	0-0	d6
6	d4	♘bd7
7	♘c3	e5
8	b3	♖e8
9	e3	c6
10	♗b2?!	

Until this game, no doubt had been cast on White's last move. But the events which now follow expose its drawbacks. It seems that the few adherents of this variation will have to opt for a different continuation here, for example 10 ♕c2, when 10 ... e4? is unplayable because of 11 ♘d2 d5 12 cd, and White takes over the c-file.

10	...	e4
11	♘d2	d5
12	f3	

This would seem entirely logical; White opens up the f-file, and, with his lead in development and his strong centre, seizes the initiative ... But then, these are all merely general considerations. The concrete events point to a different conclusion.

12	...	ef

After 12 ... ♗h6 13 fe ♗xe3+ 14 ♔h1 ♗xd2 15 ♕xd2 de 16 d5, White obtained a big advantage in Kochiev-Panchenko, Riga 1971. An even worse choice is 14 ... ♗xd4 15 ed cd 16 ♘f3, when White has a formidable attack, Zatsepin-Vasyukov, Moscow 1950.

13	♕xf3	dc
14	bc?	

The start of an unfortunate plan which lands White in a bad position. But good advice is already hard to give. The apparently more promising 14 ♘xc4?! causes Black no difficulties. A game Zak-Simagin, Sochi 1951, continued 14 ... ♘b6 15 ♘e5 ♗e6 16 ♖ad1 ♕e7 17 e4 ♖ad8 18 ♘e2 ♘fd7 19 ♘d3 f5, with the better position for Black.

14	...	♘c5
15	♘d5	(75)

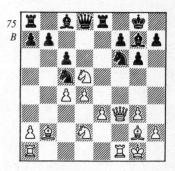

15	...	♘g4!!

A paradoxical move. Black allows a pawn to be taken – with

check, too – reckoning that White will afterwards have difficulty re-establishing the co-ordination of his pieces. In the game Cherepkov-Shianovsky, Leningrad 1950, Black played weakly: 15 ... ♘a4?! 16 ♘xf6+ ♗xf6 17 ♕xf6 ♕xf6 18 ♖xf6 ♘xb2 19 e4, with an obvious advantage to White.

16 ♕xf7+

It's hard to resist this continuation, especially since clear methods of holding the balance are not to be found. For example, 16 h3 ♘h6 17 ♘f4? ♘a4 18 ♗c1 ♖xe3! Alternatively, 17 ♗a3 ♘a4! 18 ♘f6+ ♗xf6 19 ♕xf6 ♕xf6 20 ♖xf6 ♘f5 21 ♘f1 ♗d7! (preventing 22 ♖xc6) 22 g4 ♔g7 23 g5 h6, or 21 g4 ♖xe3 22 gf ♖xa3 23 ♖f1 ♗xf5 24 ♘e4 ♔g7 25 d5 ♘c3. In all these cases Black has a won position.

16 ... ♔h8

17 ♘f4?

This should have led to loss. But as analysis shows, White's position is bad already, and finding the right continuation in the bewildering maze of possibilities is extremely difficult:

a) **17 ♘c7?** ♖e7 18 ♕xg7+ ♔xg7 19 dc ♗f5 20 ♖xf5 ♕xd2! and Black wins.

b) **17 dc?** ♗xb2 18 ♘c7 ♖e7 19 ♕f8+ ♕xf8 20 ♖xf8+ ♔g7 21 ♘xa8 ♔xf8. Black's advantage is indisputable.

c) **17 ♗a3** cd 18 ♗xc5 ♘xe3 19 ♗xd5 ♘xd5? 20 cd b6 21 ♖ae1 ♗h3 22 ♗e7 ♗xf1 23 ♗xd8 ♖xe1 24 ♘f3! ♗xd4+ 25 ♔h1 ♖xd8 26 ♘xe1 ♗c4 27 ♘g2 ♗xd5 28 ♕e7 ♖c8 29 h4, and although Black's bishops are bearing down on the white king, an immediate win is not to be found. However, in this variation Black can play more strongly: 19 ... ♘xf1! 20 ♖xf1 b6! 21 ♗xa8 bc, and despite material equality White's position is hopeless. After 19 ♖fe1 ♗e6?! 20 ♕xe8 ♕xe8 21 ♖xe3 ♗h6 22 ♖e2 ♗xd2 23 ♖xd2 the position looks unclear, but 19 ... ♗f5! puts White once again in a critical situation.

d) **17 h3**. After this, a position arises in which one false step by either side can be immediately fatal. The correct move for Black is 17 ... ♗e6! With this he gains an important tempo, after which White once again stands on the brink of disaster. For example, 18 ♕c7? cd 19 ♕xd8 ♖axd8 20 hg dc 21 ♗a3 ♘d3 22 ♗xb7 c3 23 ♗a6 cd 24 ♗xd3 ♗xg4, or 22 g5 b5 23 ♖ab1 c3 24 ♘e4 b4, and in both cases Black easily wins.

It isn't as simple for Black to realise his advantage in the variation 18 ♕xg7+?! ♔xg7 19 dc+ ♔g8 20 hg cd 21 ♖ad1 ♕g5 22 ♖f4, although his large material plus should enable him to win in the end.

One last possibility remains to

be examined: **18 ♕f3!?** cd 19 hg dc 20 ♗a3 ♘d3 21 ♖ab1 ♕a5 22 ♖xb7. Now 22 ... ♕xa3? leads to a curious draw: 23 ♖xg7! ♔xg7 24 ♕f6+ ♔g8 25 ♗xa8 ♘c5 26 dc ♕xe3+ 27 ♕f2, with an approximately equal endgame.

Yet after 22 ... ♕xd2! Black attains an overwhelming position, since 23 ♖xg7 no longer works: 23 ... ♔xg7 24 ♕f6+ ♔g8 25 ♗xa8 ♕xe3+ and 26 ... ♖xa8. In addition, Black can improve on his play with 18 ... ♗xd5!? (instead of 18 ... cd) 19 ♕xg4 ♗xg2 20 ♔xg2 ♖xe3! (20 ... ♘a4? is wrong because of 21 ♗a3 ♖xe3 22 ♘b3). Now White cannot save himself with the combination 21 ♖f7 ♘a4 22 ♖xg7!? ♔xg7 23 d5+ ♘xb2 24 ♕d4+ ♕f6 25 ♕xe3 ♘xc4 26 ♘xc4 ♕xa1 27 ♕e7+ ♔g8 (27 ... ♔h8? leads to a draw: 28 ♘e5 ♕xa2+ 29 ♔g1 ♕xd5 30 ♘f7+ ♔g7 31 ♘g5+ ♔h6 32 ♘f7+ etc.) 28 ♕e6+ ♔h8 29 ♘e5 ♕xa2+ 30 ♔g1 ♕xd5 31 ♕f6+ ♔g8 32 ♘g4 ♕d1+ 33 ♔g2 ♕d2+ 34 ♔g1 ♖e8, putting an end to the struggle.

We may conclude, then, that the entire opening variation is unfavourable for White.

17 ...   ♗f5?!

Not the best continuation. The immediate 17 ... ♘h6?! is dubious, not because of 18 ♕xg7+? ♔xg7 19 dc+ ♔g8, when either 20 ♘e4

♖xe4! or 20 ♖ad1 ♗g4 leads to a win for Black, but because of 18 ♘xg6+ hg 19 ♕xg6, and counter-threats arise for White. The correct method was to insert a preliminary 17 ... ♘a4! driving the white bishop off the long diagonal, and only then to play 18 ... ♗f5.

18 e4   ♘h6?

A second careless move, finally letting slip the win which could have been achieved fairly simply by 18 ... ♗xd4+ 19 ♗xd4+ ♕xd4+ 20 ♔h1 ♘xe4 21 ♘xe4 ♗xe4.

19 ♕xg7+!   ♔xg7
20 dc+   ♔g8
21 ef   ♕xd2
22 ♖f2   ♕e3? *(76)*

A stronger line was 22 ... ♖e1+ 23 ♗f1! ♕b4 24 ♖xe1 ♕xe1 25 fg, with chances for both sides.

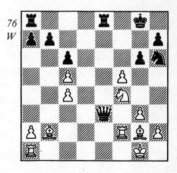

23 ♘d5!

After this move White is left with only one minor piece for the queen, yet the exposed position of Black's king outweighs this large material plus.

23	...	cd
24	♗xd5+	♔f8
25	♗c1!	♛xc5

Counter-sacrificing the queen would not have saved the game: 25 ... ♛xf2+ 26 ♔xf2 ♘xf5 27 ♗xb7, and White should win.
26 ♗xh6+ ♔e7 27 f6+ ♔d7 28 ♖d1 ♖ad8 29 f7 ♖f8 30 ♗f3+ ♔c8 31 ♖xd8+ ♖xd8 32 ♗d5 b5 33 f8♛ ♖xf8 34 ♗xf8 ♛b6 35 c5 ♛a5 36 ♗d6 1-0.

The following game was played when Kochiev had already gained the grandmaster title.

Balashov-Kochiev
Lvov 1978
King's Indian Defence

1	♘f3	♘f6
2	c4	g6

In spite of the difficulties that Black has to contend with in the King's Indian Defence, Kochiev plays the black side of this opening with surprising consistency, especially when he has managed to avoid the Sämisch Variation.

He has thoroughly studied the structures typical of this defence, and acutely discerns the moment when the slightest inaccuracies on his opponent's part permit him to seize the initiative.

| 3 | b3 | |

You might say that Black has scored a psychological success

already. An excellent connoisseur of the openings, Balashov this time prefers to deviate from theoretical continuations. Yet in top-class play there is little to be achieved by such means.

3	...	♗g7
4	♗b2	0-0
5	g3?!	

The initial cause of his subsequent difficulties. In such positions it's better to develop the white-squared bishop with 5 e3. The point of this is to restrict the dangerous advance of the black e-pawn and to secure the important d4 square for a knight.

5	...	d6
6	d4	♘bd7
7	♗g2	e5
8	de	de

Undoubtedly stronger than 8 ... ♘g4 (aiming to take on e5 with the knight), for now Black constantly threatens to advance his central pawn as far as e3.

| 9 | 0-0 | |

Of course not 9 ♘xe5? ♘g4 10 ♘d3 ♗xb2 11 ♘xb2 ♛f6 and Black wins.

9	...	e4
10	♘e1	♛e7
11	♘c2	♖d8
12	♘c3	♘c5
13	♛c1	c6
14	♘e3	a5
15	♖d1	♖xd1+
16	♛xd1	♘g4

17 ♕d2

By exchanges, White attempts to neutralise the mounting pressure from Black's pieces. But as a result of the unfortunate 5 g3? his position is a constricted one, and he has to tread carefully. Thus, the exchange of a further piece with 17 ♘xg4? would lead to a lost position: 17 ... ♗xg4 18 ♕d2 (the threat was 18 ... ♘d3) 18 ... ♖d8 19 ♕e3 ♕d6! (after the tempting 19 ... ♗d4? 20 ♘d5! ♗xe3 21 ♘xe7+ ♔f8 22 ♘xc6 White has a won endgame) with the fearsome threat of 20 ... ♕d2.

17	...	a4
18	b4	♘xe3!

An essential finesse! The immediate 18 ... a3? is refuted by 19 ♘cd5! cd 20 ♗xg7 (but not 20 ♘xd5? ♕f8?) 20 ... ♘xe3 21 ♗c3 ♘xc4 22 ♕d4, and Black's position is worse.

19	♕xe3	a3
20	♘d5	cd
21	♗xg7	♔xg7
22	bc	dc
23	♖c1	♗f5
24	♖xc4!	

24 g4? might appear to draw, but in fact this is not the case: 24 ... ♗xg4 25 ♕xe4 ♕xe4 26 ♗xe4 ♗xe2 27 ♗xb7 ♖a5 28 c6 ♖c5 29 ♖c3 ♗f3! 30 ♔f1 ♗xc6 31 ♗xc6 ♖xc6 32 ♔e2 ♔f6 33 ♖xa3 ♔e5 34 ♔d2 ♔d4 35 ♖a7 ♖f6, or 25 ♗xe4 ♗xe2! 26 ♗xb7 ♕xe3 27 fe ♖a5,

with analogous variations.

24 ... ♕e5

There is no other way for Black to strengthen his position. All his hopes are pinned on the a-pawn.

25 ♖c3? (77)

It was hard to decide on a queen endgame in which the opponent would have a passed pawn on the sixth, yet it was precisely here that White had appreciable drawing chances. For example: 25 ♗xe4 ♗xe4 26 ♕xe4 ♕a1+ 27 ♔g2 ♕xa2 28 ♕xb7 ♕xc4 29 ♕xa8 ♕xc5 30 e4! ♕c3 31 e5, with the threat of 32 ♕a6.

Now Black wins quickly.

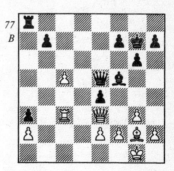

25	...	♕d5
26	g4	

Defending the point h3, but overlooking something else in the process.

26	...	♗xg4
27	♖xa3	♕d1+
28	♗f1	♗xe2!

0-1

A pretty finish.

Whoever wishes to develop a capacity for independent chess thought must avoid anything in chess which lacks life: artificial theories that rest on very few examples and an immense amount of contrivance; the habit of shying away from danger; the habit of needlessly taking over variations and principles employed by others, and repeating them unreflectingly; self-satisfaction and conceit; reluctance to admit one's errors . . . in short, anything conducive to routine, or to anarchy.

Emanuel Lasker

Rohde-Seirawan
USA 1976
Scandinavian Defence

1	e4	d5
2	ed	♕xd5
3	♘c3	♕a5
4	♘f3	♘f6
5	♗c4	

This game, packed with the gripping drama of a struggle with no quarter, is of interest for another reason too: the two opponents, still very young at that time, are the most talented representatives of the large group of American chess masters who made a name for themselves in the second half of the 1970s.

Seirawan, who was to become World Junior Champion, favours a quiet manoeuvring game. His opponent Rohde, winner of the international junior tournament at Schilde (1976), is clearly marked out as a tactician. Knowing that in reply to 1 e4 Seirawan adopts all kinds of variations in virtually all of the half-open defences, and not wishing to come up against something unexpected in the opening, Rohde is the first to turn away from well-trodden paths. The books consider that a line suggested long ago by Lasker gives White the advantage: 5 d4 ♗g4 6 h3 ♗h5 7 g4 ♗g6 8 ♘e5 c6 9 h4 ♘bd7 10 ♘c4 ♕c7 11 h5 ♗e4 12 ♘xe4 ♘xe4 13 ♕f3.

5	...	♗g4
6	h3	♗h5
7	♕e2	♘bd7
8	g4	♗g6
9	b4!?	

The quiet 9 d3 is not in Rohde's style. As the game develops, we shall constantly observe White playing his moves on alternate flanks, and aiming a variety of tactical stabs at his opponent.

At the moment, this pawn is invulnerable: 9 ... ♕xb4?! 10 ♖b1, and it is not clear where Black is going to castle.

9	...	♕b6
10	h4	h6

10 ... h5? is inferior: 11 g5 ♘g4 12 ♘d5 ♕d6 13 d4. So is 10 ... ♘xg4? 11 h5 ♗f5 12 ♘d5 ♕d6 13 ♘d4 and 14 ♘b5. In both variations, White has a big

advantage.

| 11 | h5 | ♗h7 |
| 12 | a4 | c6 |

After 12 ... ♘xg4? 13 ♘d5 ♕d6 14 b5 0-0-0 15 ♗a3, Black's queen has no satisfactory retreat.

| 13 | g5 | hg |
| 14 | ♘xg5 | ♗g8 |

14 ... e6 loses to 15 ♘xf7!

| 15 | a5 | ♕c7?! |

The pawn could have been taken: 15 ... ♕xb4 16 ♖a4 ♕d6 17 ♘ce4 ♘xe4 18 ♘xe4 ♕c7. But Black doesn't want to comply with his opponent's plan of complicating the game as much as possible.

16	b5	cb
17	♘xb5	♕c6
18	♖h3 *(78)*	

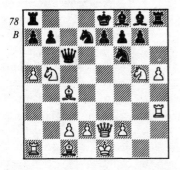

78
B

It's not often you see such a position arising from the opening of a game between players in the master class!

| 18 | ... | a6 |
| 19 | ♘c3 | e6 |

19 ... ♕g2?! could be met by

20 d4 ♕g1+ 21 ♕f1 ♕xf1+ 22 ♔xf1 ♖xh5 23 ♖xh5 ♘xh5 24 ♖b1, and in spite of his extra pawn it isn't easy for Black to find a defence against White's increasing initiative.

| 20 | ♗b2 | ♕g2!? |

At last Seirawan proves that he too is no coward. A quieter game would have resulted from 20 ... ♖c8 21 d3 ♗e7.

21	♕e3	♗c5
22	d4	♗xd4
23	♕xd4	♕xg5
24	♘e4	♘xe4
25	♕xe4	♗h7
26	♕d4	♖g8

26 ... ♗f5? 27 ♕xg7 ♖xh5 28 ♕xg5 ♖xg5 29 ♖h8+ ♘f8 30 0-0-0 is scarcely attractive; it's difficult for Black to parry his opponent's many threats.

| 27 | ♖e3! | ♕xh5?! |

27 ... ♕f6 was more cautious.

28	♗a3!?	♕xa5+
29	♔f1	♗f5
30	♖d1	0-0-0

Black is hard pressed. He would lose with 30 ... e5? 31 ♕d6 0-0-0 32 ♗b4 ♕c7 33 ♗xf7 followed by ♖c3, or 30 ... ♕c7? 31 ♖c3 ♕d8 32 ♗d3 ♘f6 33 ♗xf5 ♕xd4 34 ♖xd4 ef 35 ♖e3+ ♘e4 36 f3.

| 31 | ♗d6 | ♕b6 |
| 32 | ♕c3? | |

The first serious oversight in this game.

With the sacrifice of both his

rook's pawns White has compelled the black king to castle, but even so it has not found a peaceful haven. There was an immediate win here with 32 ♖c3!! To save himself from the threatened mate, Black would have to shed a piece.

32	...	♕c6
33	♗xa6	♘c5!
34	♗xb7+!	

Both sides are playing resourcefully.

| 34 | ... | ♔xb7 |
| 35 | ♖b1+ | ♔a8? |

The losing move; Black was counting on 36 ♗xc5?

35 ... ♔c8 would have forced a draw: 36 ♗xc5 ♕h1+ 37 ♔e2 ♗g4+ 38 f3 ♕g2+ (indicated by R.Byrne and E.Mednis). But now White springs an unpleasant surprise on his opponent.

36	♕xc5!	♕h1+
37	♔e2	♗g4+
38	♔d2	♖xd6+
39	♕xd6	♕xb1
40	♖a3+	♔b7
41	♖b3+	♕xb3
42	cb	

The uncomplicated technical part of the game which now remains is carried out faultlessly by Rohde.

42	...	♗f5
43	♕d7+	♔b6
44	♔c3	♖h8
45	♕xf7	♖h3+
46	♔b4	♖h4+

47	♔a3	g6
48	♕f6	♖h3
49	♕d8+	♔b5
50	♕b8+	♔a5
51	♕a7+	♔b5
52	♕b7+	♔c5

He can't repeat with 52 ... ♔a5? because of 53 f3 with the unanswerable threat of 54 b4 mate (Byrne, Mednis).

53	♔a4	♖d3
54	♕c7+	♔d5
55	b4	♖d4
56	♔a5	♗d3
57	♕c5+	♔e4
58	f3+	

1-0

Rohde-de Firmian
US Junior Championship 1976
Sicilian Defence

1	e4	c5
2	♘f3	d6
3	d4	cd
4	♘xd4	♘f6
5	♘c3	a6
6	♗e2	e5
7	♘b3	♗e6
8	♗g5	♗e7
9	f4	ef
10	♘d4!	

Rohde is a very interesting player. As with some of the best representatives of the young generation in the USSR, his play is characterised by creative breadth and a total absence of conventionality. In every game, he strives to find new paths from the very beginning – to set demanding problems for his opponent to solve on his own. In this case, by an original manoeuvre in a variation that has been played inside out, he has succeeded in molesting the white-squared bishop which might have seemed completely invulnerable; he confronts his opponent with the unpleasant choice of assenting to an exchange or losing time parrying this threat.

10 ...   ♕a5

It isn't easy for Black to find a plan of counterplay. 10 ... 0-0 11 0-0 would not alter the situation, while 10 ... ♘xe4?! would clearly be disadvantageous because of 11 ♘xe4 ♗xg5 12 ♘xe6 fe 13 ♘xg5 ♕xg5 14 ♕xd6 (Byrne, Mednis), or 11 ♗xe7 ♘xc3 12 ♗xd8 ♘xd1 13 ♘xe6 fe 14 ♖xd1 ♔xd8 15 ♖xd6+ with the better game for White.

11 ♗xf4   ♘xe4
12 ♘xe6   fe *(79)*

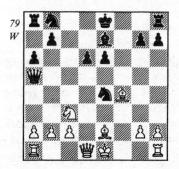

An unexpected check, adding to the weaknesses in Black's camp – which were numerous in any case.

13 ...   g6
14 ♕d4   ♘f6
15 ♗f3   e5

It looks as if White's expedition has resulted in material losses. But this has all been foreseen by Rohde.

16 ♕c4!   ♘bd7

Of course not 16 ... ef? 17 ♕c8+ ♕d8 18 ♕xb7 (Byrne, Mednis).

17 ♗h6!?   ♕c5
18 ♕e6   ♕b4?!

He should have tried to co-ordinate his pieces with 18 ... ♕c7 19 0-0-0 ♘c5 20 ♕h3 ♕d7 21 ♕xd7+ ♔xd7 (it's hard for Black to hold the balance in the line 21 ... ♘fxd7 22 b4 ♘e6 23 ♗xb7 ♖b8 24 ♗d5) 22 ♗g7 ♖he8 23 ♗xf6 ♗xf6, when White's initiative compensates for the pawn minus.

19 0-0-0   ♘c5
20 ♕h3   ♔f7

Black can't manage to regroup properly. 20 ... ♕c4?! (intending 21 ... ♕e6) is met by 21 ♗d5 as in the game, while the attempt to deprive White of the d5 square with 20 ... e4 would be decisively refuted as follows: 21 a3! ♕b6 (otherwise 22 ♗g7, 23 ♗xf6 and 24 ♘xe4) 22 ♖he1! ef 23 ♗g7 (now we see the point of White's 21st move: Black hasn't a queen

13 ♗h5+!

check on f4 available) 23 ... f2 24
♗xf6! (after 24 ♖xe7+?! ♔xe7 25
♗xf6+ ♔f7 26 ♗xh8 ♖xh8 27
♘d5 ♕d8 28 ♖f1 ♕g5+ 29 ♘e3
♔g7 30 ♖xf2 ♖e8, the position is
none too clear; in this line, it isn't
too late for White to lose with 27
♕f3+ ♔g7 28 ♕xf2?? ♘b3+) 24 ...
fe♕ 25 ♖xe1, with a mating attack.

| 21 | ♗d5+ | ♘xd5 |
| 22 | ♘xd5 | ♕a5 |

After 22 ... ♕h4 23 ♖hf1+ ♔g8
24 ♘xe7+ ♕xe7 25 ♕f3, White
has a won game.

23	♖hf1+	♔e8
24	♘xe7	♔xe7
25	♗g5+	♔e8
26	♖xd6	♕xa2

The sole defence against the
threatened 27 ♖e6+; but of course
Black is not able to save the game.

| 27 | ♕e3! | ♕a1+ |

Or 27 ... ♘d7 28 ♕a3 ♕c4 29
♕d3 ♕xd3 30 ♖e6 mate (Byrne,
Mednis).

28 ♔d2 ♕xf1 29 ♕xe5+ ♔f7 30
♖f6+ ♕xf6 31 ♕xf6+ ♔g8 32 ♕e7
h6 33 ♗f6 ♖h7 34 ♕xc5 ♖d7+ 35
♗d4 ♖ad8 36 c3 ♖d5 37 ♕c7
♖5d7 38 ♕e5 ♔h7 39 g4 ♖f8 40 h4
♖fd8 41 h5 gh 42 ♕f5+ 1-0.

Chiburdanidze-Zaichik
Baku 1979
Sicilian Defence

1	e4	c5
2	♘f3	♘c6
3	d4	cd
4	♘xd4	♘f6
5	♘c3	e6
6	♘db5	d6
7	♗f4	e5
8	♗g5	a6
9	♘a3	b5
10	♘d5	

Although the Women's World
Champion nearly always strives
for the initiative, for attack and
combinations, in this case she tries
to steer the game into purely
positional paths, thereby demon-
strating that her opponent's strong
points – ingenuity and excellent
tactical vision – are very well
known to her.

| 10 | ... | ♗e7 |
| 11 | ♘xe7!? | ♘xe7 |

The reason for capturing this
way is that after 11 ... ♕xe7 12 c3
0-0 13 ♘c2 it isn't easy for Black
to free himself with a central
break.

| 12 | ♗d3?! | |

White obtains a slight advantage
after 12 ♗xf6 gf 13 ♕d2 ♗b7
14 0-0-0 d5 15 ed ♗xd5 16 c4!

| 12 | ... | ♗b7 |

Not liking the look of 12 ... d5
13 ♗xf6 gf 14 ed ♕xd5 15 ♕e2
♗b7 16 f3, with the better position
for White.

| 13 | ♕e2 | ♘d7 *(80)* |
| 14 | b4! | |

Chiburdanidze demonstrates the
many-sidedness of her talent. This
difficult positional move discloses

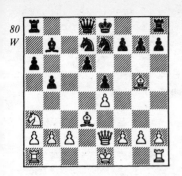

the dark side of Black's set-up – the weakness of his queenside pawns.

| 14 | ... | f6 |
| 15 | ♗d2 | f5! |

Stronger than 15 ... d5!? 16 ed ♗xd5 17 0-0 0-0 18 c4 bc 19 ♘xc4, with a slight advantage for White.

16	c4	♘f6
17	f3	fe
18	fe	♘c6
19	cb	♘d4
20	♕e3	ab
21	♘xb5	0-0
22	0-0!	

Seeking material gains could have had awkward consequences after 22 ♘c3?! (on 22 ♘xd4? ed 23 ♕xd4 ♘xe4! Black obtains a very strong attack) 22 ... ♘g4 23 ♕g5 ♘f2 24 ♗c4+ ♔h8 25 ♕xd8 ♖axd8 26 0-0 ♘xe4 27 ♘xe4 ♗xe4 and Black is very actively placed in the centre.

22	...	♘xb5
23	♗xb5	♗xe4
24	a4!	

Of course not 24 ♖xf6? ♕xf6 25 ♕xe4 ♕f2+ and 26 ... ♕xd2.

| 24 | ... | d5 |
| 25 | ♗c6 | ♖c8? |

It was essential to play 25 ... d4! *(81)* at once, giving rise to a highly interesting endgame which should, it seems, have ended in a draw.

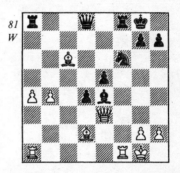

The tempting queen sacrifice 26 ♕xe4? doesn't work: 26 ... ♘xe4 27 ♗xe4 (27 ♖xf8+ ♔xf8!) 27 ... d3! 28 ♗xa8 ♕d4+! and Black's pawns become mobile. So White should play 26 ♕b3+ ♔d5 27 ♗xd5+ ♕xd5 28 ♕xd5+ ♘xd5 29 ♖fc1 ♖fc8 30 b5 e4 (not 30 ... ♖xc1 31 ♗xc1 e4 32 a5 e3 33 a6 d3 34 ♗xe3! and White wins; in this line, if 31 ... ♘c3, then 32 b6!) 31 ♖xc8+ ♖xc8 32 ♖c1 ♖xc1+ 33 ♗xc1 e3 34 ♗xe3! (34 ♔f1? d3 35 ♗b2 ♘f4, and Black wins) 34 ... de 35 a5 ♘c7 36 b6 ♘a6 – draw.

| 26 | b5 | d4 |
| 27 | ♕b3+ | ♔h8 |

It's too late now for 27 ... ♗d5?

because of 28 &xd5+ &xd5 29
&xd5+ ♘xd5 30 ♖xf8+ &xf8 31
a5 e4 32 b6 etc.

| 28 | &b4 | &xc6 |

28 ... ♖g8? loses to 29 ♖xf6! So
Black has to part with the
exchange.

| 29 | &xf8 | &b7 |

29 ... &d5? loses to 30 &xg7+
&xg7 31 &g3+ &f7 32 &xe5 &c4
33 ♖f4 etc.

| 30 | &f7! |

Putting paid to all Black's
hopes based on an advance of his
pawns and an attack against g2.

| 30 | ... | &xf8 |
| 31 | &xb7 | d3 |

31 ... e4 could be met by 32
♖xf6!

| 32 | a5 | e4 |
| 33 | a6 | |

Here too 33 ♖xf6 would have
been very strong, but White had
precisely calculated the winning
continuation which now follows.

33	...	e3
34	&xc8!	&xc8
35	a7	&a8
36	b6	e2
37	b7	ef&+
38	&xf1	&xb7
39	a8&+	&xa8
40	♖xa8+	♘g8

It may look as if White has
considerable technical difficulties
to surmount before achieving the
win. In fact, though, the path to
victory is not complicated. Any
movement of Black's kingside
pawns will create a weakness,
where the white king will eventually
penetrate.

41	♖d8	h6
42	♖xd3	♘f6
43	&f2	&h7
44	&f3	&g6
45	&f4	♘h5+
46	&e5	&g5
47	♖d4	♘f6
48	h4+	&h5?

Hastens defeat. Still, after 48 ...
&g6 49 g4, the end result would be
unalterable.

| 49 | &f5 | ♘g8 |
| 50 | ♖d7 | |

1-0

The game on pages 104-107 was
played in the USSR Team Cham-
pionship, Moscow 1964, between
Smyslov (White) and Tal (Black).
The beautiful combinative attack
(pages 107-108) was carried out by
Tigran Petrosian in his World
Championship match with Spassky,
Moscow 1966.

What is necessary for success?
*Innate chess talent, a stable
character, special preparation, and
a resilient nervous system that can
stand hard work.*

Botvinnik

4 Developing a Repertoire

Well, what *is* needed to make a good player?

Three requirements as a minimum – ability, knowledge and understanding.

The most complex thing, perhaps, is what is associated with chess understanding. There is a wide gulf between the ability to calculate a combination a few moves deep and a refined positional assessment. A very important means towards bridging this gulf is supplied by a knowledge of archetypal middle-game positions, which comes from analysis of opening structures in your repertoire, and from playing through games in national and international tournaments – which have to be studied, not just looked over.

Every chessplayer forms his own approach to the assessment of positions. One player has a penchant for playing with an isolated pawn in the centre; another finds this unacceptable. One player loves complex combinative play, another prefers simple positions. The aim should be to eliminate one-sidedness in the development of your skills, and to make your style of play universal – to enjoy attacking and defending in equal measure, and to master endgame technique.

'Know yourself.'

"One of the surest ways to improve is to annotate games for the press", wrote Botvinnik as long ago as the beginning of the fifties. This thought still crops up today in his public lectures and pronouncements.

Of course, conducting an objective analysis of one of your games without sufficient experience is not so simple. And yet even a player of little experience should, in the course of his analysis, be capable of unearthing the chief mistakes and submitting some correct recommendations. What is essential is to ascertain the prospects that open up for both sides, while giving as much as possible in the way of relevant supporting variations. It is very important to disclose in what circumstances the losing errors were made, and what was the reason for them. If the causes of error recur (time trouble – playing on your *opponent's* time trouble – inability to conduct a lengthy calculation of forced variations – underestimates of weaknesses in your camp – bad endgame technique, etc.), the right conclusions must be drawn, and ways must be found for eliminating the defects.

Annotating a game takes 12-16 hours on average. For convenience, the whole task may be divided into five steps:

a) Play through the game quickly, taking 15-20 minutes, so as to call to mind again what you had thought and felt.

b) Go over the game in the course of an hour, and make a synopsis of its characteristic critical stages.

c) In the course of 3-4 hours, analyse the critical stages in detail.

d) Analyse the opening phase, taking care to fill any gaps in your knowledge of this or that variation – gaps which may have had a direct or indirect bearing on an unsuccessful choice of opening in the game. For this, 3-4 hours are needed.

e) Go through the game and put together the commentary as a whole (4-5 hours).

Often, in the process of an-notating, you will convince your-self that an overall plan which did bring you a win in the game was nonetheless faulty. This fact should be self-critically disclosed, and not concealed in the undergrowth of an inevitably specious analysis; theory and practice are united. The work finds its culmination in the conclusions about your typical, repeated errors – inadequacy of opening preparation, weak technique in endings, etc.

Zak-Sorokin
Leningrad 1946
Slav Defence

1	d4	d5
2	c4	e6
3	♘c3	c6
4	♘f3	

I was insufficiently prepared for 4 e4!? which was fashionable at that time and leads to sharp play with varied possibilities for both sides: 4 ... de 5 ♘xe4 ♗b4+ 6 ♗d2 (6 ♘c3 c5 gives equality) 6 ... ♕xd4 7 ♗xb4 ♕xe4+.

In this position **8 ♘e2** has been played without much success for White: 8 ... ♘a6 9 ♗f8 ♘e7! 10 ♗xg7 ♘b4 11 ♕d6! (but not 11 ♗xh8? because of 11 ... e5 with a winning attack) 11 ... ♘d3+ 12 ♔d2 ♘f5 13 ♕xd3 ♕xd3+ 14 ♔xd3 ♘xg7, with a level game (Holmov-Novotelnov, Sochi 1951); or 8 ... ♘d7 9 ♕d6 c5! 10 ♗xc5

♘xc5 11 ♕xc5 ♗d7, again with equality.

8 ♗e2 has caused Black more worries, but here again players have gained equality with careful defence:

a) **8 ...** ♘a6 9 ♗c3 ♘e7 10 ♗xg7 ♖g8 11 ♗c3 ♘d5! (after 11 ... ♕xg2? 12 ♕d2 ♕xh1 13 0-0-0 White obtained a winning attack in Bronstein-Kotov, Budapest 1950) 12 cd ♕xg2 13 de! (13 ♗f3? ♕xh1!) 13 ... ♗xe6 14 ♗f6 ♖g6 15 ♗h4 ♕xh1 16 ♕d6 ♕xg1+ 17 ♔d2 ♕g5+ 18 ♗xg5 ♖xg5 19 ♔e1 ♖d8, and Black has enough for the queen (Romanovsky).

b) A quieter game results from **8 ...** c5 9 ♗xc5 ♕xg2 10 ♕d4 ♘d7 11 ♗f3 ♕g5 12 ♗b4 ♕e5+ 13 ♘e2 ♕xd4 14 ♘xd4 ♘e5 15 0-0-0 ♗d7 (unnecessary complications arise if the pawn is taken: 15 ... ♘xc4? 16 ♘f5! ef 17 ♖he1+ ♗e6 18 ♗xb7, and White has a won position) 16 ♗xb7 ♖b8 17 ♗d6 ♖xb7 18 ♗xe5 f6 with equality – Sapundzhiev-Popov, Bulgaria 1961.

4	...	♘f6
5	♗g5	

I played this move unhesitatingly, since 5 e3 ♘bd7 6 ♗d3 dc 7 ♗xc4 b5 8 ♗d3 a6 9 e4 c5 gives a position from the Meran Variation, one of the branches of which had been analysed in detail by Georgian players including my opponent:

10 e5 ♘g4 11 ♘g5 (I didn't know of the game Botvinnik-I.Rabinovich, Leningrad 1926, where White played much more strongly: 11 ♗g5! ♕b6 12 ♗e4 ♗b7 13 ♗xb7 ♕xb7 14 0-0) 11 ... cd 12 ♘xf7 ♕h4 13 g3 ♕h5! (on 13 ... ♕h3? 14 ♘e4 ♕g2 15 ♕xg4 ♕xh1+ 16 ♔e2, White has a won position) 14 ♘xh8 dc 15 ♗e4 ♗b4 16 ♔f1 ♖a7 17 ♗f4 g5 18 h3 gf 19 ♕xg4 ♕xg4 20 hg ♘xe5 21 bc ♗xc3 22 ♖c1 b4 23 gf ♘xg4 24 ♖xh7 ♖xh7 25 ♗xh7 ♗b7 26 ♗d3 ♗xh8 27 ♖c7 ♘h2+ 28 ♔g1 ♘f3+ – draw.

All this could be avoided by means of 10 d5 c4 11 de, and now:

a) **11 ... cd** 12 ed+ ♕xd7 13 ♘e5 ♕e7! (the obvious-looking 13 ... ♕e6? is worse: 14 ♘xd3 b4 15 ♘xb4!) 14 ♘xd3 (Black has more difficult problems after 14 ♗f4!) 14 ... b4 15 ♘e2 ♕xe4 16 0-0 ♗e7 17 ♖e1 ♕b7, with equality (Portisch-Trifunović, Sarajevo 1962).

b) **11 ... fe!?** 12 ♗c2 ♗b7 13 0-0 ♕c7 14 ♕e2 ♗d6 15 ♘g5 ♘c5 16 f4 e5 17 a4 h6 18 ♘f3 ♘d3 19 ♗xd3 cd 20 ♕xd3 ♖d8 21 ♕e2 ♕c4` with somewhat the better game for White (Uhlmann-Fuchs, East Germany 1963). If instead 14 ♘g5?! then 14 ... ♘c5 15 f4 h6! 16 e5? (stronger 16 ♘f3, after which Black has a choice of continuations leading to unclear play: 16 ... ♘cxe4 17 ♕e2, or 16 ...

☖d8) 16 ... hg 17 ♗g6+ ♔e7 18 ♕e2 ♘fd7 19 f5 ♔d8 20 fe ♘xe6 21 ♗f5 ♔c8 22 ☖d1 ♗c5+ 23 ♔h1 ♘d4 24 ♕g4 ♘xf5 25 ♕xf5 ♕xe5, with a won position for Black (Ftacnik-Panchenko, Sochi 1977).

But at the time these variations were not yet known.

5 ... dc
6 e4

6 a4 ♗b4 7 e4 has also been seen: 7 ... ♗xc3+! 8 bc ♕a5 9 e5 ♘e4 10 ☖c1 (Black has the better prospects after 10 ♗d2 ♕d5 11 ♕c2 c5, as in Donner-Kotov, Venice 1950) 10 ... ♘d7 11 ♗e3 ♘b6 with equal chances (Donner-Pomar, Lugano 1959.

6 ... b5
7 e5

Possible replies to 7 a4 are 7 ... ♕b6, 7 ... ♗b4 and 7 ... b4.

7 ... h6
8 ♗h4

Grandmaster Geller has tried 8 ♗xf6!? a few times. In Geller-Bronstein (Moscow 1949), there followed 8 ... gf 9 a4 ♘d7 10 ab cb 11 ♘xb5 fe 12 ♘xe5 ♗b4+ 13 ♘c3 ♗xc3+ 14 bc ♘xe5 15 de ♕xd1+ 16 ☖xd1 ♗a6 17 ♗e2, with a slight advantage to White. Geller-Simagin (Szczawno Zdroj, 1950) varied with 9 ... ♗b7 10 ef a6 11 ♗e2 ♘d7 12 ♘e5 ♘xf6 13 0-0 ♗g7 14 ♗f3 ♕b6, with a slight plus on Black's side. Geller-Foltys (Szczawno Zdroj, 1950) saw 9 ... ♗b4 10 ef ♕xf6 11

♘e5? (stronger 11 ♗e2) 11 ... c5! 12 ♗e2 ♘d7 13 0-0 cd 14 ♘g4 ♕g7 15 ♘xb5 h5, with a won position for Black.

8 ... g5
9 ef

This continuation was first played in a game Ragozin-Böök (Helsinki 1946).

White seems to be able to achieve more in the main line: 9 ♘xg5 hg 10 ♗xg5 ♘bd7 11 g3 ♕a5 (L.Radchenko recommends the interesting sacrifice 11 ... b4?! 12 ♘e4 ♘xe4 13 ♗xd8 ♔xd8 14 ♕c2!? f5 15 ♗xc4, with a sharp position. In place of 14 ♕c2, possible moves are 14 ♗xc4, 14 ♕f3 and 14 ♗g2) 12 ef b4 13 ♘e4 ♗a6 14 ♕f3 (but not 14 ♗g2 c3 15 bc bc 16 ♕c2 ☖b8 17 a3 ☖b2 18 ♕xc3 ♗b4 and Black wins, Kramer-Berliner, USA 1945) 14 ... 0-0-0 15 ♗g2 c3! 16 b3! with 17 ♗f1 to follow. It would be a mistake to play 16 bc? ♗c4 17 ♘c5 ♘e5! or 16 ♘xc3 ♘b8! 17 ♘e4 ☖xd4 18 ♗e3 b3+ 19 ♘c3 ♗a3! 20 ab ♗xb2, with a won game for Black in both cases.

All this I knew in its essentials, but I nonetheless refrained from 9 ♘xg5, since I didn't want to allow the complications – which at that time were unclear to me – arising after 9 ... ♘d5! 10 ♘xf7 ♕xh4 11 ♘xh8 ♗b4 12 ♕d2! (White has no advantage after

12 ♖c1 ♛e4+ 13 ♗e2 ♘f4 14 ♛d2
♘d3+ 15 ♔f1 ♘xc1 16 ♘xe4
♗xd2 17 ♘xd2 ♘xa2 – Smyslov)
12 ... c5 13 0-0-0 cd 14 ♛xd4 ♛g5+
15 f4 (15 ♔b1? ♘c6) 15 ... ♘xf4 16
♔b1 ♗xc3 17 ♛xc3 ♗b7 with
chances for both sides (Korelov-
Sveshnikov, 1972); or 13 ... ♘c6
14 ♘g6 ♗xc3 15 bc ♛g5 16 ♛xg5
hg 17 h4 ♔f7 18 h5 ♘xc3 19 ♖d2
cd 20 h6 ♔xg6 21 h7 ♗a6! (21 ...
♗b7? 22 h8♛ ♖xh8 23 ♖xh8 d3
24 ♖xd3! and White wins) 22
h8♛ ♖xh8 23 ♖xh8 d3, and
Black's minor pieces are no worse
than White's rooks.

9 ... gh
10 ♘e5 ♛xf6

Forced, in view of the threatened
11 ♘xf7 ♔xf7 12 ♛h5+.

11 a4!?

During analysis of the Ragozin-
Böök game, which continued
11 ♗e2 ♘d7, it was established
that after 11 ... ♗b4? 12 ♗f3 ♗b7
13 a4 a6 14 ab ab 15 ♖xa8 ♗xa8 16
♛a1 and 17 ♛a7, White wins a
piece. With the move played, I was
naively hoping to disguise this
trap and use it to catch out my
experienced opponent. In fairness,
one should note that this move is
no worse than any others in the
position. One may also mention
11 g3 ♘d7 12 ♛e2 (12 f4 is weaker
– 12 ... ♘xe5 13 de ♛d8 14 ♗g2
♛xd1+ 15 ♖xd1 ♗d7 16 ♘xb5
♖b8 17 ♘xa7 ♖xb2, with the

better ending for Black) 12 ...
♘xe5 13 de ♛e7, with a level game
(Bronstein-Botvinnik, Moscow 1951)
or 12 ... c5!? 13 ♗g2 cd 14 ♘xd7
♗xd7 15 ♘d5 ♛g7 16 ♘c7+ ♔d8
17 ♘xa8 ♗b4+ 18 ♔f1 d3, when
instead of the correct 19 ♛d1!
White mistakenly played 19 ♛e4?
in Mocete-Class (1955), and lost
quickly after 19 ... ♛xb2 20 ♖d1
♗c5 21 ♛xh4+ ♔e8. In the
present game, confronted with
something unexpected, my opponent
thought for 40 minutes and
played:

11 ... ♗b7!

As already mentioned, my
'preparation' for this game had
merely amounted to an attempt to
catch Black in a trap. With my
illusions gone, I now had to do
some calculation, and concluded
that the key diagonal a8-h1 must
not be given up without a fight.
For example: 12 ab? c5! 13 ♛a4 cd
14 b6+ ♔d8 15 ♛a5 ♗d6! 16 ba+
♔e7 17 ab♛ ♖hxb8, and Black
wins.

12 ♗e2 c5!
13 ♘xb5 ♘a6
14 ♗h5 ♖h7
15 0-0 ♖g7
16 g3?

Inconsistent! After the correct
16 ♗f3 ♗xf3 17 ♛xf3 ♛xf3 18
♘xf3 h3 19 g3, White's position
may well be preferable even,
despite the pawn minus.

| 16 | ... | cd |
| 17 | ♕xd4 | ♖d8? |

Returning the compliment, after which the chances are equal again. 17 ... ♗d5 18 ♖ae1 ♗c5 would have forced White to sacrifice the exchange with 19 ♕xd5 ed 20 ♘g4+ ♕e7 21 ♘f6+ ♔f8 22 ♖xe7 ♗xe7 23 ♘xd5 ♗c5, when Black has all the winning chances.

| 18 | ♕xa7 | ♕xe5 |
| 19 | ♕xb7 | hg (82) |

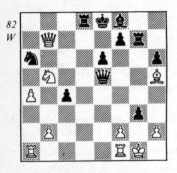

20 ♗f3?

It was essential to make do with perpetual check by 20 ♕c6+ ♖d7 21 ♕c8+ ♖d8. Serious mistakes of this kind used to occur very often in my games just at the crucial moment. There are many examples I could give, and all of them have the same cause – an inability to keep carrying out analyses of long variations throughout the whole course of a game. This was evidently connected with the long gaps between my appearances in competitions – one or two tourna-

ments a year – and with the peculiarities of my constitution.

I did have an understanding of all this even at that time, but I didn't draw the appropriate conclusions – which can only be regretted.

| 20 | ... | gf+ |
| 21 | ♔h1 | ♗c5! |

Now Black completely exposes the white king, and resistance becomes hopeless.

22	♕xa6	♖g1+
23	♖xg1	fg♕+
24	♖xg1	♗xg1
25	♕c6+	♔f8
26	♔xg1	♕e1+
27	♔g2	♖d2+
28	♔h3	♕e5!

0-1

So White lost the game through weak technique in calculation.

It is generally thought that the solving of combinations and studies (sometimes from diagrams, without using a board) improves your calculation technique. Without disputing the definite value of that method, I would call attention to the opinion of Romanovsky, Levenfish, Kotov and many other authorities, who have held that the most effective way is to analyse games –ones that are full of tactical complications.

Such games, with annotations supplied, abound in anthologies of the chess careers of Chigorin,

Alekhine, Tal and other grand-masters.

You should pick out games in accordance with your chosen opening repertoire, copy them into a notebook – without the annotations, of course – leave it on one side for about a month, so that any glimpse of the commentary in the source book will have been forgotten, and then proceed to the analysis.

Doing it this way, you can assess the quality of your work by comparing the two commentaries. To begin with, of course, the results will be disheartening. With time, though, your accumulated experience will tell, and in the end the results you achieve will not suffer from the comparison.

A method for working on the openings has to be very seriously thought out and laid down. Chess players possessing outstanding memory powers can allow them-selves the luxury of employing an immense variety of openings. For the majority, this is scarcely feasible.

You can well restrict yourself to studying a narrow opening reper-toire in depth – which, as we have stated, facilitates the transition to a favourable middlegame on the basis of a sound strategic plan. In any event, the collecting of essential material must be carried on from day to day. Pick out and copy the relevant game from tournaments and matches of recent years, as well as any interesting ideas from older tourna-ments books; add to these any commentaries appearing in the press, then undertake an analytical examination of the material you have collected. Working on these lines, you easily perceive that no handbook, not even the most up-to-date, can give such detailed insight into all the refinements of the variation you are studying. It can be stated in all likelihood that enriching yourself with the ideas characteristic of a specific opening equips you adequately to perform a critical study of published analyses. As a result your an-notations will gain in precision, and the new ideas you find will sometimes radically alter the assessment of a variation. This is how theoretical novelties are born.

Chiburdanidze-Dvoiris
USSR Ch ½-final Tallinn 1980
Sicilian Defence

1	e4	c5
2	♘f3	d6
3	d4	cd
4	♘xd4	♘f6
5	♘c3	a6
6	♗g5	e6
7	f4	♘bd7

8	♕f3	♕c7
9	0-0-0	b5?

Previously 9 ... ♗e7 had been played. Despite individual failures, that move does seem sounder than the game continuation. The premature attempt by Black to develop a queenside initiative is very attractively refuted by the Women's World Champion. But an interesting point is that shortly before, Black had suffered a crushing defeat in this variation in the game Chudinovskikh-Kuporosov (Arkhangelsk 1980). After 10 e5! ♗b7 11 ♕h3 de 12 ♘xe6 fe 13 ♕xe6+ ♗e7 14 ♘xb5 ab 15 ♗xb5, a position arose which was known to theory and was assessed by the books as favouring Black, in view of 15 ... ♗e4 – on which Chudinovskikh was intending 16 ♖d2! 0-0-0 17 ♕xe7 h6 18 ♗xf6 gf, and then either 19 ♗a6+ or 19 ♖hd1. The game actually went 15 ... ♗d5 16 ♖xd5! ♘xd5, and now not 17 ♕xd5 ♖c8! with advantage to Black, but 17 ♖d1! after which "Black has a huge material plus – an extra rook and minor piece – but the threats to his king are unanswerable" (Chidinovskikh). We must suppose that Maia Chiburdanidze was not yet acquainted with that game; in her home analysis, she found a different solution to the problem

confronting her.

10	♗d3	♗b7
11	♖he1	♕b6 (83)

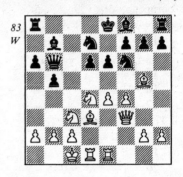

83
W

| 12 | ♘d5! |

Considerably stronger than the familiar 12 ♘b3.

| 12 | ... | ed?! |

After this, events proceed on forced lines. Black had to risk taking the knight on d4, although Dvoiris very obviously had cause to assume that precisely this continuation had undergone the most thorough analysis. After 12 ... ♕xd4 13 ♗xf6 gf 14 ♗xb5 ♕xd1+ 15 ♕xd1 ab 16 ♘c7+ ♔e7 17 ♘xa8 ♗xa8 18 ♕d3, "Black has three pieces for the queen, but White is winning a second pawn; in addition, Black has an unsafe king position" (V.Chekhov). The attempt to hold on to the queen is no better: 14 ... ♕c5 15 b4! ♕a7 16 ♘xf6+ ♔e7 17 ♗xd7 ♔xf6 18 ♕c3+ ♔e7 19 ♕xh8 ♔xd7 20 ♕xh7, and White has a won position.

13 ♘c6!

This striking move wrecks the Black position. The sacrifice has to be accepted; if 13 ... d4, then 14 e5! is immediately decisive.

13	...	♗xc6
14	ed+	♗e7
15	dc	♘c5
16	♗xf6	gf
17	♗f5	♛c7

If 17 ... ♖d8, then 18 ♛e3 wins.

18	b4!	♘e6
19	♛h5	♘g7
20	♗d7+	♔f8
21	♛h6	d5
22	♖xe7!	

Impressive conduct of the attack by Chiburdanidze.

| 22 | ... | ♔xe7 |
| 23 | ♖e1+ | ♔f8 |

Of course not 23 ... ♘e6 24 ♗xe6 fe 25 ♛g7+ ♔d6 26 ♖xe6+.

24	♛xf6	♔g8
25	♖e7	♖f8
26	♗e6	♛xe7
27	♛xe7	fe

Or 27 ... ♘xe6 28 f5 etc.

28	c7	h5
29	♛xf8+	
	1-0	

Chiburdanidze-Tukmakov
USSR Ch 1st League 1980
Sicilian Defence

1	e4	c5
2	♘f3	d6
3	d4	cd
4	♘xd4	♘f6
5	♘c3	a6
6	♗g5	e6
7	f4	♛c7?!!

Grandmaster Tukmakov has been playing the Najdorf Variation for many years. Having studied in detail the refinements of this opening scheme and the middle-game characteristic of it, he is reluctant to give it up; and in spite of the setbacks for Black in recent competitions, he attempts to rehabilitate the system. Clearly, by choosing the dubious continuation 7 ... ♛c7!? – in which White even has additional attacking possibilities after the doubling of Black's pawns on the kingside – Tukmakov is taking a serious risk. Nonetheless, despite his failure in the present game, this kind of decision deserves to be emulated. For it is only by going the whole way in the practical application of your theoretical views that you can attain thorough clarity about positions which, even after pains-taking home analysis, will have remained obscure.

8	♛f3	b5
9	0-0-0	b4
10	e5	♗b7
11	♛h3	de

Up to here, play has followed Psakhis-Tukmakov (Frunze 1979), which continued 12 ♘cb5 ab 13 ♗xb5+ ♗c6! 14 fe ♗xb5 15 ef ♗d7! and Black defended successfully. However, in analysing that theoretically important game, the Women's World Champion has unearthed an interesting possibility which had gone unnoticed by both players.

12	fe!	♕xe5
13	♗xf6	♕xf6?

In a game against L.Yudasin (Minsk 1981), after a thorough study of this position, Tukmakov came back with an improvement for Black: 13 ... gf! 14 ♗b5+ ab 15 ♖he1 ♕f4+! (15 ... bc is inferior; Yudasin gives 16 ♖xe5 fe 17 ♘xe6 ♖xa2 18 ♘c7+ ♔e7 19 ♕h4+ f6 20 ♕b4+ ♔f7 21 ♕b3+. Alternatively, 17 ... fe 18 ♕h5+ ♔e7 19 ♕xe5 ♖xa2 20 ♕c7+ ♔f6 21 ♖f1+ etc.) 16 ♔b1 ♖a6 17 ♕h5 bc 18 ♘xe6 ♖xe6 19 ♖xe6+ ♗e7 20 ♕xb5+ ♗c6 21 ♖xc6 ♘xc6 22 ♕xc6+ ♔f8 23 ♕xc3 ♗d6 and White has a difficult game.

14	♘cb5!	♗c5 (84)

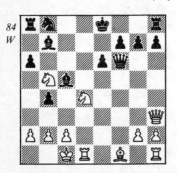

This position, which is critical for the whole variation, was evaluated differently by the two players.

15 ♘xe6!

In analysing the position, Tukmakov, had probably devoted most of his attention to the complications arising after 15 ♘c7+, leaving out of account the move played, which brings White a quick win.

15	...	ab

15 ... fe is met by 16 ♕h5+.

16	♗xb5+	♘c6
17	♗xc6+	♗xc6
18	♘c7+	♔f8
19	♘xa8	♕f4+
20	♔b1	♕b8
21	♖hf1	♗e7
22	♕e6	

1-0

Whereas in ordinary opening systems the basis of a correct approach is not the learning up of variations but an understanding of the opening ideas, in gambit systems a precise knowledge of variations is quite indispensable, since the dynamic equilibrium resulting from a sacrifice can often be sustained only by finding the sole correct move time and again – which isn't so easy when playing over-the-board with limited thinking time.

This is illustrated when we consider how to build up a repertoire in answer to 1 e4. There are two ways of solving this problem. One is to select some half-open system and study its hidden possibilities thoroughly enough to remove any fear of surprises that your opponent might have prepared against you.

Granted a certain rationale in this method, which does enable a player to achieve perfectly adequate competitive results, a more purposeful approach (from the point of view of improving your play most rapidly) is to opt for 1 ... e5! In this case, it often happens that from the very first moves the game enters the realm of tactical complexities, the analysis of which will quickly contribute to raising your class of play. Admittedly, this entails much more work.

Thus, after 1 e4 e5, you have to be prepared for the following possibilities on White's part (most of the recommendations have been made on the basis of material supplied in *ECO*).

King's Gambit

In this opening, attention must be give to the game Hartston-Spassky (Hastings 1965-66):

1	e4	e5
2	f4	ef
3	♘f3	d5
4	ed	♘f6
5	♗b5+	

Other continuations cause Black no difficulties. For example, 5 ♘c3

♘xd5 6 ♘xd5 ♛xd5 7 d4 ♗e7! or 5 c4 c6 6 d4 ♗b4+ 7 ♘c3 cd 8 ♗xf4 0-0 9 ♗e2 dc 10 ♗xc4 ♘d5! In both variations White is forced to work for equality.

5	...	c6
6	dc	♘xc6!

This move is condemned in old opening manuals on account of 7 d4 ♛a5+? 8 ♘c3 ♗b4 9 0-0! ♗xc3 10 ♛e2+ with advantage to White. However, in answer to

| 7 | d4 | |

Spassky played:

| 7 | ... | ♗d6 |

And there followed:

8	♛e2+	♗e6
9	♘e5	0-0
10	♗xc6	bc
11	♗xf4	♘d5
12	♗g3	f6
13	♘f3	

A bad line is 13 ♘xc6 ♗xg3+ 14 hg ♛d6, with a difficult position for White.

13	...	♗xg3+
14	hg	♜e8

And Black obtained the advantage. It remains to be added that after the possible 9 ♘g5 0-0 10 ♘xe6 fe 11 ♛xe6+ ♚h8 12 ♗xc6 bc 13 0-0 ♛c7 14 ♛h3 ♜ae8 *(85)*

Black has sufficient compensation for the sacrificed pawn.

Apart from this variation, it is necessary from the outset to have some idea – even if only in general terms – of the Bishop's Gambit

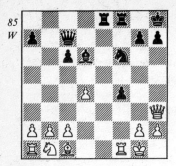

and the Steinitz Gambit.

Vienna Game

Given your aim to play sharp positions, one variation where the material balance is disrupted must be included in your repertoire without fail:

1	e4	e5
2	♘c3	♘f6
3	♗c4	♘xe4!
4	♕h5	♘d6
5	♗b3	♘c6
6	♘b5	g6
7	♕f3	f5
8	♕d5	♕e7
9	♘xc7+	♔d8
10	♘xa8	b6 (86)

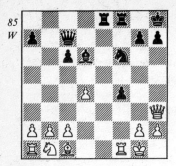

Practice has shown that the very strong initiative Black enjoys gives full compensation for his material losses. For example:

a) **11 ♘xb6** ab 12 ♕f3 ♗b7 13 ♕d1 ♘d4 14 ♔f1 ♕g5 15 f3 f4 16 c3 ♘f5 17 ♘h3 ♕h5 18 ♕e2 ♘h4 19 ♘f2 ♘xf3 (Chistiakov-Estrin, Moscow 1957).

b) **11 ♘f3** ♗b7 12 d4 ♘xd4 13 ♗g5 ♘xf3+ 14 ♕xf3 ♕xg5 15 ♗d5 e4 16 ♕b3 (16 ♕c3? ♗xd5 17 ♕xh8 ♕e7 gives Black the better position) 16 ... ♗a6 17 ♕a4 (here too 17 ♕c3 is bad: 17 ... ♘e8! 18 ♕xh8 ♗h6, winning at once) 17 ... ♗h6, and White's position is becoming difficult to defend.

c) In the last few years, the continuation **11 d3 ♗b7 12 h4!?** f4 13 ♕f3 ♘d4 14 ♕g4 has become popular. In this position *ECO* recommends 14 ... ♗h6, to stop White exchanging queens with 15 ♕g5. But this doesn't seem to be essential, since after 14 ... ♗xa8! 15 ♕g5?! ♕xg5 16 hg ♗e7 Black's position is clearly preferable.

A game between two young schoolboys (2nd category tournament, Leningrad 1979) saw **8 ... ♕f6?** 9 ♘xc7+ ♔d8 10 ♘xa8 b6 11 d3? ♗b7 12 h4? After the unexpected 12 ... ♘e7! 13 ♗g5 ♘xd5 14 ♗xf6+ ♘f6, Black obtained a won position.

Yet 8 ... ♕f6? has been known to be bad for a long time, since instead of 11 d3? White can gain the advantage by 11 ♘xb6 ab 12 d4! ♘xd4 13 ♘f3 ♗b7 14 ♕xd4!

A more popular continuation (after 1 e4 e5 2 ♘c3 ♘f6) is: **3 f4 d5 4 fe ♘xe4 5 ♘f3** (Black obtains good play after 5 ♕f3 ♘c6 6 ♗b5 ♘xc3 7 bc ♕h4+ 8 g3 ♕e4+ 9 ♕xe4 de 10 ♗xc6+ bc 11 ♘e2 ♗e7 12 ♖f1 0-0) **5 ... ♗e7 6 d4 0-0 7 ♗d3 f5 8 ef ♗xf6 9 0-0 ♘c6! 10 ♘xe4 de 11 ♗xe4 ♘xd4 12 ♘g5 ♗f5 13 ♗xf5 ♘xf5 14 ♘e6.** This occurred in a game Konstantinopolsky-Keres (Moscow 1940). After 14 ... ♕xd1 15 ♖xd1 ♖fe8! 16 ♘xc7 ♖ad8 17 ♗f4 ♖e2, Black has the better endgame.

In answer to the currently fashionable **3 g3 d5 4 ed ♘xd5 5 ♗g2**, Black can try **5 ... ♘b6!?** The books pass over this possibility in silence, and yet after 6 ♘f3 ♘c6 7 0-0 ♗d6 8 ♖e1 0-0 9 d4 ed 10 ♘xd4 ♘xd4 11 ♕xd4 c6, White has only an insignificant advantage.

Obviously the analysis of the Vienna Game is not exhausted by these variations, but by taking them as a basis you can easily prepare for other possible continuations by White.

Centre Game

These systems are rarely met with in contemporary tournaments, yet it pays to be familiar with them, especially since they all contain a fair amount of poison. Given that the merest slip can have the most dire consequences in positions that depend on forced continuations, an exact knowledge of variations here is quite indispensable.

1	e4	e5
2	d4	ed
3	♕xd4	♘c6
4	♕e3	♘f6
5	e5	♘g4
6	♕e2	d6
7	f3	

White can't manage to win a piece with 7 h3? ♘gxe5! 8 f4, since after 8 ... ♕h4+ 9 ♔d1 ♘d4 10 ♕e4 ♕f2 he has to cope with immensely strong threats. Going after a pawn looks equally suspect: 7 ed+ ♗e6 8 dc ♕xc7, and Black has a big lead in development.

7	...	♘h6
8	♗xh6	♕h4+

Black stands better *(ECO)*. Alternatively: **5 ♘c3 ♗b4 6 ♗d2 0-0 7 0-0-0 ♖e8 8 ♕g3 ♖xe4! 9 ♗d3 ♖g4 10 ♕h3 d6** *(87)*

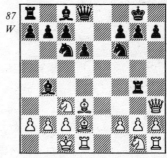

– with advantage to Black (Zinn-Sax, Baja 1971).

Centre Gambit

1	e4	e5
2	d4	ed
3	c3	♕e7
4	cd	

On 4 ♕e2 ♘f6 5 ♘d2 d5 6 e5 d3, Black wins a pawn (Spielmann-Réti, Baden 1914).

4	...	♕xe4+
5	♗e3	

Or 5 ♗e2?! ♕xg2 6 ♗f3 ♕g6 7 ♘c3 ♗b4, and White hasn't enough compensation for the lost pawns.

5	...	♘f6
6	♘c3	♗b4
7	♘f3	♘d5
8	♕d2	♘xe3 *(88)*

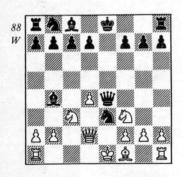

88
W

– with equal chances.

Danish Gambit

1	e4	e5
2	d4	ed
3	c3	dc
4	♗c4	cb
5	♗xb2	d5
6	♗xd5	♗b4+
7	♘c3	

Or 7 ♔f1 ♘f6! 8 ♕a4+ ♘c6 9 ♗xc6+ bc 10 ♕xb4 ♖b8, when Black regains his piece and obtains the advantage.

7	...	♗xc3+
8	♗xc3	♘f6
9	♘f3	♘xd5
10	ed	♕e7+
11	♔f1	0-0 *(89)*

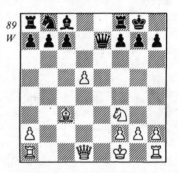

89
W

Black's extra pawn ensures him the advantage (Radevich-Asuturian, 1968).

Scotch Gambit

1	e4	e5
2	♘f3	♘c6
3	d4	ed
4	c3	♘f6
5	e5	♘e4
6	♕e2	f5
7	ef	d5

8	♘xd4	♘xd4
9	cd	♔f7

Another possibility is 9 ... ♗b4+ 10 ♗d2 ♗xd2+ 11 ♘xd2 0-0.

10	fg	♗b4+
11	♔d1	♖e8
12	♗e3	♔g8
13	♕h5	♗e6
14	♗d3	♕d7
15	h3	♗f5
16	♗c2 *(90)*	

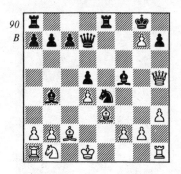

With 16 ... ♘g3! Black could have put White in a difficult situation (Levy-Boey, Siegen Ol 1970).

Scotch Game

1	e4	e5
2	♘f3	♘c6
3	d4	ed
4	♘xd4	♗c5

In recent years this move has become highly popular again, and has nearly caused 4 ... ♘f6 to be discarded from practice.

5	♗e3	

Or 5 ♘b3 ♗b6 6 a4 ♕f6 7 ♕e2 ♘ge7 8 a5 ♘d4 9 ♘xd4 ♗xd4 10 c3 ♗c5 11 g3 (11 e5 ♕c6! 12 b4? ♗xb4, and Black wins) 11 ... 0-0 12 ♗g2 a6, with a level game.

5	...	♕f6
6	c3	

On 6 ♘b5?! the familiar continuation is 6 ... ♗xe3 7 fe ♕h4+ 8 g3 ♕xe4!? 9 ♘xc7+ ♔d8 10 ♘xa8 ♕xh1 11 ♕d6 ♘f6 12 ♘d2 ♘e8 13 ♕f4 ♕d5. Although the resulting position is judged by the books to be in Black's favour, in a game Bašagić-Ivkov (Sarajevo 1976) the still more decisive 7 ... ♕d8! 8 ♘1c3 a6 was played, when White is left with a battered pawn structure and no compensation at all.

6	...	♘ge7
7	♘c2 *(91)*	

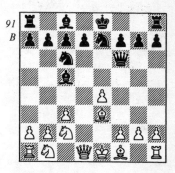

It isn't hard to see that in reply to the development of White's bishop Black carries out the central counterstroke ... d5. For example, 7 ♗c4 (on 7 ♗e2, the immediate 7 ... d5 follows) 7 ... ♘e5 8 ♗e2 ♕g6! 9 0-0 d5 10 ed ♗h3 11 ♗f3 0-0-0, re-establishing the material balance.

7	...	♗xe3
8	♘xe3	♕e5
9	♕f3	0-0
10	♗c4	d6
11	♘d2	♗e6
12	0-0	♕g5
13	♕e2	♘g6

With a level position (Tartakower-Tarrasch, Pecs 1922).

In view of this, White has been trying a different move-order to reach the Scotch Game: **1 e4 e5 2 ♘f3 ♘c6 3 ♘c3 ♘f6 4 d4** But now, without any risk, Black can evade the Scotch formation – and also, incidentally, the Belgrade Gambit (4 ... ed 5 ♘d5!?) – by playing **4 ... ♗b4!? 5 ♘xe5** On 5 d5, there is no need at all to go in for the variation that has been analysed in detail: 5 .... ♘e7 6 ♘xe5 0-0 etc. It's preferable to clear up all problems quickly with 5 ... ♘b8!? 6 ♗d3 (6 ♘xe5? ♕e7 leads to a difficult position for White) 6 ... d6. But with **5 ♘xe5** White can hardly achieve more, because of **5 ... ♘xe4 6 ♕g4 ♘xc3 7 ♕xg7 ♖f8 8 a3 ♗a5 9 ♘xc6 dc 10 ♕e5+ ♕e7 11 ♕xe7+ ♔xe7 12 ♗d2 ♗f5 13 ♗d3 ♗xd3 14 cd ♖g8!** (92)

The game is level.

Four Knights' Game

1	e4	e5
2	♘f3	♘c6
3	♘c3	♘f6
4	♗b5	♗b4
5	0-0	0-0
6	d3	d6
7	♗g5	♗xc3

Continuing to play for symmetry can lead to loss after 7 ... ♗g4? 8 ♘d5 ♘d4 9 ♘xb4 ♘xb5 10 ♘d5 ♘d4 11 ♕d2! c6 (11 ... ♗xf3? 12 ♗xf6 gf 13 ♕h6, and White wins the queen) 12 ♘xf6+ gf 13 ♗h4! ♗xf3 14 ♕h6 ♘e2+ 15 ♔h1 ♗xg2+ 16 ♔xg2 ♘f4+ 17 ♔h1 ♘g6 18 f4, with a lost position for Black.

8	bc	♕e7
9	♖e1	♘d8

The simplest way of freeing himself from the pin.

10	d4	♘e6
11	♗c1	♖d8 (93)

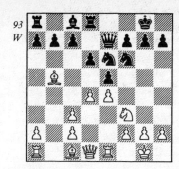

93
W

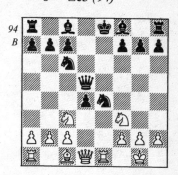

6	♖e1	d5
7	♗xd5	♕xd5
8	♘c3	*(94)*

94
B

– with equality.

Two Knights' Defence

In answer to 1 e4 e5 2 ♘f3 ♘c6 3 ♗c4, the moves 3 ... ♗c5 and 3 ... ♘f6 are of equal worth. However, constructing your repertoire in keeping with your chosen tactics – with your aim of playing openings that give initiative – you have reason to settle for the Two Knights' Defence. We should observe, by the way, that a knowledge of variations in this opening can help you steer towards familiar positions when the opponent employs an unexpected system. For example, 1 e4 e5 2 ♗c4 ♘f6 3 d4 ed 4 ♘f3 ♘c6; or 2 ♘f3 ♘c6 3 d4 ed 4 ♗c4 ♘f6, etc.

One possible continuation is:

1	e4	e5
2	♘f3	♘c6
3	♗c4	♘f6
4	d4	ed
5	0-0	♘xe4

8	...	♕h5!

At this point all the opening books examine 8 ... ♕a5 in detail, while devoting just a few brief lines to 8 ... ♕h5 – which is at least as good!

9	♘xe4	♗e6
10	♗g5	

The routine 10 ♘eg5?! can even lead to loss: 10 ... 0-0-0 11 ♘xe6 fe 12 ♖xe6 ♗d6 13 ♕e2? d3! 14 cd ♘d4.

10	...	♗b4?!
11	♘xd4	

A bad line is 11 c3 bc 12 bc ♗a5 13 ♘c5 0-0 14 ♘xe6 fe 15 ♖xe6 ♖xf3 etc.

11	...	♕xd1
12	♖exd1	♘xd4
13	♖xd4	♗a5
14	♘c5	♗b6
15	♘xe6	fe
16	♖e4	0-0
17	♗e3	♗xe3

18	♖xe3	♖ad8
19	♖ae1	♖d2
20	♖3e2	♖fd8 *(95)*

In this position White can scarcely count on success. But even if he could, Black has at his disposal a further possibility, which was employed in a game Bondarev-Shifman (Schoolboys' Championship, Leningrad 1979). Instead of 10 ... ♗b4, Black chose the other move that is known in the position – **10 ... ♗d6!?** *(96)*

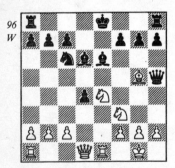

In answer to the move recommended by *ECO*: **11 ♗f6** Black played the unexpected **11 ...**

♗xh2+! 12 ♘xh2 ♕xd1 13 ♖axd1 gf 14 ♘xf6+ ♔f8 – and remained with an extra pawn. An equal game would have resulted from 11 ♘xd6+ cd 12 ♗f4 0-0.

One must add that as an alternative to 5 ... ♘xe4, Black should be prepared to go into the highly complex variations of the Max Lange Attack with 5 ... ♗c5!? – so as to retain the possibility of playing for the win.

Another variations is:

1	e4	e5
2	♘f3	♘c6
3	♗c4	♘f6
4	d4	ed
5	e5	d5
6	♗b5	♘e4
7	♘xd4	

The well-known continuation here is 7 ... ♗d7 8 ♗xc6 bc 9 ♗e3 ♗c5 10 0-0 (10 f3 ♕h4+ 11 g3 ♘xg3 12 ♗f2 ♕h6 13 ♗xg3 ♗xd4 14 ♕xd4 ♕c1+ 15 ♕d1 ♕e3+ 16 ♕e2 ♕c1+ draws) 10 ... 0-0 11 f3 ♘g5 15 ♕d2 f6! with equality. Apart from this, a game Karaklaic-Trajković (Yugoslavia 1968) offers wide scope for analysis:

7	...	♗c5?!
8	♗e3	

He can't play 8 ♘xc6? ♗xf2+ 9 ♔f1 ♕h4 10 ♘d4+ c6 11 ♘f3 ♘g3+ 12 ♔xf2 ♘e4+ with a winning attack for Black.

8	...	0-0
9	♘xc6	bc

10	♗xc5	♘xc5
11	♗xc6	♗a6

The game now continued 12 ♕xd5 ♕g5! with advantage to Black. Instead, referring to the game Henkin-Vasyukov (Moscow 1954), the books recommend 12 ♘c3! and if 12 ... ♕g5, then 13 ♕d4! is unpleasant for Black. To anticipate, we will say that 12 ♘c3 does indeed give White the advantage. But in order to convince yourself of this, you have to analyse in detail the position after 12 ... d4 13 ♗xa8, and now not 13 ... ♕xa8? 14 ♕xd4 ♖d8 15 ♕g4 (*ECO*), but 13 ... dc!? *(97)*

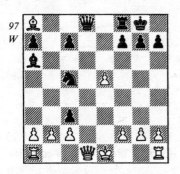

97
W

After 14 ♕xd8 ♖xd8, White has two main possibilities:
a) **15 ♗c6?** ♖d2 16 b4 ♖e2+, and whichever way his king goes, White has nothing.
b) **15 b4!** ♘e6 16 ♗c6 ♗c4 (16 ... ♖d2? 17 b5 ♘d4 18 0-0! is hopeless for Black) 17 ♖d1 ♘d4 18 ♗e4? f5! 19 ef?? (better 19 ♗d3 ♗xd3 20 cd ♖b8) 19 ... ♘xc2+!

and mate in two.

It is unfortunate that these lines are ultimately unconvincing. By continuing the analysis, the reader can, without any particular trouble, discover for himself the right continuation for White. He should therefore go back to the tried and tested 7 ... ♗d7!

What conclusion can be drawn from examining these variations? That the study of an opening goes hand in hand with diligent analysis of the middlegame, or even endgame, that results from it.

There are further lines in the Two Knights' Defence that give great scope for analytic investigations. Not to speak of the Traxler Attack (Wilkes Barr), particular interest is offered by the relatively little studied position after:

1	e4	e5
2	♘f3	♘c6
3	♗c4	♘f6
4	♘g5	d5
5	ed	♘a5
6	♗b5+	c6
7	dc	bc
8	♗e2	h6
9	♘f3	e4
10	♘e5	♕d4!?
11	f4	♗c5
12	♖f1	*(98)*

Black would have had a substantial initiative after 11 ♘g4 ♘xg4! 12 ♗xg4 e3 13 ♗xc8 ef+ 14

98
B

10 ♕e4 b5 11 ♗xb5 ♘a5! *(99)*

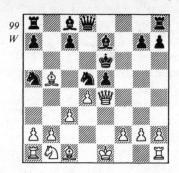

99
W

♔f1 ♖xc8 15 ♕e2+ ♗e7 16 ♕xf2 ♕d7.

In the diagrammed position, instead of the generally accepted move 12 ... ♘d5?! it's worth trying out 12 ... ♗b6!? 13 c3 ♕d8 14 b4 ♘b7 15 ♘xc6 ♕c7. White has won two pawns, but it isn't simple for him to remove his king from the centre.

It's interesting that in spite of the severe verdict that has long been passed on it, even the old line **5 ... ♘xd5?!** conceals unexpected possibilities which can be unearthed only by diligent analysis:

a) After **6 ♘xf7** ♔xf7 7 ♕f3+ ♔e6 8 ♘c3 ♘e7 9 d4, a game Ujtumen-Miagmasuren (Ulan Bator 1963), continued 9 ... b5 10 ♘xb5 c6 11 ♘c3 ♕b6?! 12 de? ♕d4 13 ♗b3 ♕xe5+ 14 ♗e3 ♕f5 15 ♕e2 ♔f7 16 0-0-0 ♗e6, with a winning position for Black.

b) Nor is everything clear in the modernised system: **6 d4** ♗b4+ 7 c3 ♗e7 8 ♘xf7 ♔xf7 9 ♕f3+ ♔e6

White can obtain as many as four pawns for his piece, but Black is much better developed and therefore has quite good counter-chances.

Of course, knowing the variations we have quoted is not enough to repulse all possible tries by White in the Two Knights' Defence. In the line with 5 ... ♘a5 6 ♗b5+, the move 9 ♘h3, which occurred in the Steinitz-Chigorin match of 1892, should not be forgotten; nor should the interesting piece sacrifice which Bronstein played against Rojahn (Moscow 1956): 6 d3 e4 7 de!? (another possibility is 7 ♗b5+ c6 8 de!?). You must acquire a good feel for, and knowledge of, the various attacking methods at Black's disposal in the line 7 ♕e2 ♘xc4 8 dc ♗c5 etc.

From all that has been said, a conclusion may be drawn. Your detailed analysis of opening variations can confirm, or actually sometimes refute, the categorical verdicts of contemporary works of theory; yet the most valuable thing is not this, but the experience you gain from analysing and studying the many tactical and strategic ideas for the resulting middlegame – which appreciably facilitates the working-out of variations in practical play.

Ruy Lopez

For several centuries now, the Ruy Lopez has held the attention of all accomplished chessplayers. The abundant possibilities, both for White and Black, inherent in the various branches of this opening afford any player a rich choice of continuations suited to his individual style. For this reason we will not detain the reader with any concrete variations, but will remind him once again that the study of openings has to contain a core of investigative work.

This last point is tellingly illustrated by the examples which follow.

Bezman-Ehlvest
USSR Junior Ch, Dushanbe 1980
English Opening

1	c4	♘f6
2	♘c3	e6
3	e4	d5
4	e5	♘e4

5	♘xe4	de
6	♕g4	c5!?

A new move. In Taimanov's opinion, the familiar 6 ... ♘c6 7 ♕xe4 ♕d4 8 ♕xd4 ♘xd4 9 ♔d1 ♗d7 10 d3 0-0-0 11 ♗e3 is in White's favour.

7	♕xe4	♘c6
8	♘f3	♕d7
9	♗e2?!	

By returning the pawn with 9 d4! cd 10 ♗d3 White could have obtained a good position, whether Black continued 10 ... ♘b4 11 0-0 ♘xd3 12 ♕xd3 – when the defence of the d-pawn would have caused a good deal of trouble – or 10 ... ♗b4+ 11 ♔f1! after which the placing of the bishop on b4 could be utilised by White for a queenside offensive.

9	...	b6
10	0-0	♗b7
11	♕f4?	

White is playing planlessly, and – what is most important – fails to make out the fairly clear plan of his opponent. As will be seen from what follows, a better move was 11 ♕e3.

11	...	h6
12	b3	g5
13	♕e3	g4
14	♘e1	h5
15	f4	

The consequences of White's unfortunate 11th move are emerging. The further weakening of his position is forced; he can't develop his bishop because of the threatened 15 ... ♝h6.

| 15 | ... | ♞d4 |
| 16 | ♝d3 | |

Guarding himself against unpleasantness after 16 ... ♞f5.

16	...	♛c6
17	♝b2	0-0-0
18	♝xd4	♜xd4
19	♜f2	♝h6
20	♚f1	

The advance of the black rook's pawn is threatened, so the white king tries to leave the danger zone in good time.

| 20 | ... | ♜hd8 |
| 21 | ♜c1 (100) | |

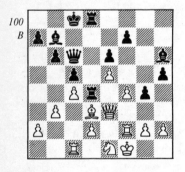

100
B

| 21 | ... | ♜xf4! |

Black has attained a large positional plus, and this beautiful combinative stroke, leading to a forced win, forms the logical culmination of his previous play.

22	♜xf4	♝xf4
23	♛xf4	♜xd3
24	♞xd3	♛xg2+

25	♚e1	♝f3
26	♛e3	♛h1+
27	♚f2	♛xh2+
	0-1	

White resigned in view of 28 ♚e1 ♛h1+ 29 ♚f2 g3+ 30 ♚xg3 ♛g2+ and 31 ... ♛g4 mate.

Cvitan-Short
World Junior Ch Mexico 1981
Queen's Indian Defence

1	d4	♞f6
2	c4	e6
3	♞f3	b6
4	a3	c5
5	d5	♝a6
6	♛c2	ed
7	cd	♝b7
8	e4	

In this fashionable variation, new paths are being sought for both White and Black. In this connexion, a game A.Petrosian-Zaichik (Frunze 1981) is of interest: 8 ♞c3!? ♞xd5 9 ♝g5 ♝e7! 10 ♛e4 ♞xc3! 11 ♛xb7 ♞c6 12 ♝xe7 ♚xe7! 13 bc ♜b8 14 ♛a6 b5!! with a won position.

8	...	♛e7
9	♝d3	♞xd5
10	0-0	♞c7
11	♞c3!	

A new move! Before, 11 ♝g5 had been played with no particular success, so Short cannot be blamed for selecting this sharp variation – where Black has an extra pawn in return for White's freer game – in his encounter with the tournament leader.

However, the decisive range of his repertoire (against 1 e4, as a rule, Short chooses the French or Pirc, and against 1 d4 the Nimzo-Indian or Queen's Indian), the position arising in the game had not been analysed by him deeply enough.

11	...	♛d8
12	♘d5	♘e6
13	♘e5	♘c6
14	f4	♘xe5?

This is the mistake referred to. Now White achieves a large preponderance in the centre, and Black is in no position to cope with the increasing difficulties. 14 ... d6 was undoubtedly stronger.

15	fe	♝e7
16	♛e2	*(101)*

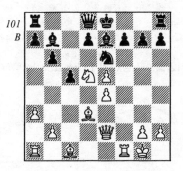

101
B

What is Black to do about the threat of 17 ♛h5? The most natural-looking continuation, 16 ... 0-0, loses to 17 ♛h5 g6 18 ♛h6 ♝xd5 (18 ... ♝g5 19 ♘f6+)

19 ed ♝g5 20 ♝xg5 ♛xg5 21 ♛xg5 ♘xg5 22 h4, winning a piece.

Alternatively: 17 ... f6 18 ef gf 19 e5! f5 20 ♝xf5 ♖f7 (or 20 ... ♖xf5 21 ♘xe7+) 21 ♝xe6 etc. An attractive line could occur after 19 ♝h6?! ♖f7 20 ♖f3 ♝d6 21 ♖af1 ♝e5 22 ♛xe5! fe 23 ♖xf7 ♛h4 24 ♘e7+ ♚h8 25 ♝g7+ ♘xg7 26 ♖f8+ ♖xf8 27 ♖xf8 mate. However, 20 ... ♛e8 allows Black to prolong his resistance.

Having evidently seen these variations, Short plays a move which only emphasises how forlorn Black's position is.

| 16 | ... | h6?! |

It's hard to see what else to suggest.

| 17 | ♛h5 | ♖f8 |
| 18 | ♝xh6?! | |

Characterising Lasker's achievements, Grandmaster Fine wrote: "Don't resign before your position is absolutely, definitely, hopeless. Keep on fighting, never mind whether analysis can show that the situation is dismal. Don't cling to any sort of stereotyped dogma ... Believe firmly that in chess there are no rules without exceptions – this is what we learn from studying Lasker's games."

White's last move lets slip the win which was attainable by the quiet 18 ♝d2! For example, 18 ... ♝g5 19 ♖xf7 ♖xf7 20 ♖f1 ♝f4 21 ♘xf4! ♛g5 22 ♛xf7+ ♚xf7 23

♘xe6+ ♚xe6 24 ♗xg5 hg 25 ♖f5
followed by 26 ♗c4+ and 27 ♗d5
(Cvitan)

18	...	gh
19	♖xf7	♖xf7
20	♖f1	♘g5
21	♗c4	

We can imagine that Lasker
would have succeeded in saving
the game by 21 ... ♕b8! (the only
move) 22 ♖xf7 ♘xf7 23 ♘xe7
♚d8! 24 ♗xf7 ♚xe7 25 ♕h4+
♚xf7 26 ♕f6+ – draw (Cvitan).

Short didn't find this variation . . .

21	...	♚f8??
22	♖xf7+	♘xf7
23	♘f6	

1-0

Mate is unavoidable.

Kouatly-Petursson
World Junior Ch Groningen 1977
Nimzo-Indian Defence

1	d4	♘f6
2	c4	e6
3	♘c3	♗b4
4	♗g5	h6
5	♗h4	c5
6	d5	b5
7	de	

The complications arising from
7 e4?! lead to a draw after 7 ... g5 8
♗g3 ♘xe4 9 ♗e5 0-0 10 ♕h5 d6 11
♗d3 ♘xc3 12 ♕xh6 ♘e4+ 13 ♚f1
de 14 ♗xe4 f5 15 ♕g6+ ♚h8
16 ♕h6+.

| 7 | ... | fe |
| 8 | cb | d5 |

| 9 | e3 | 0-0 |
| 10 | ♗d3! | |

Considerably stronger than
10 ♘f3?! as played by Spassky
against Tal (Tallinn 1973). After
10 ... ♕a5 11 ♗xf6 ♖xf6 12 ♕d2
(better 12 ♕c1!) 12 ... a6! 13 ba
♘c6 14 ♗e2 d4! White had to lose
material.

10	...	d4
11	ed	cd
12	a3	♗a5
13	b4	dc
14	ba	♗b7
15	♘e2!?	

Playing more sharply than in
Spassky-Unzicker (Bath 1973):
15 ♘f3 ♕xa5 16 0-0 ♘bd7 17 ♕e2
♗xf3! 18 ♕xf3 with equality.

| 15 | ... | ♗xg2! |

In Timman-Unzicker (22nd Ol,
1976) Black refrained from this
move, and after 15 ... ♕xa5 16 0-0
♘bd7 17 ♗c4 ♘d5 18 ♗e7! ♖f7
19 ♗b4 ♕b6 20 ♗xc3 ♘e3 21
♗d4! White obtained a good
game.

| 16 | ♖g1 | ♗f3 |
| 17 | ♗c2?! | |

In G.Ligterink's view, a stronger
line is 17 ♖g3 ♕d5 18 ♗xf6 ♖xf6
19 ♕c2 ♘d7 20 0-0-0!

| 17 | ... | ♘bd7 |
| 18 | ♕d6 | *(102)* |

All this had been seen for the
first time in Cooper-Adamski
(21st Ol Nice 1974). That game
continued 18 ... ♗xe2 19 ♚xe2

♕xa5 20 a4. Kouatly evidently had no objection to this position, but it is precisely here that a complete surprise awaits him.

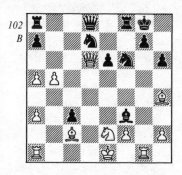

18 ...   ♘e5!

The Leningrad Variation of the Nimzo-Indian is favoured by a large group of players headed by grandmasters Spassky and Timman. They have done much to demonstrate its viability. Yet Petursson's last move invalidates what had hitherto been regarded as an extremely strong continuation.

The position turns out to be bad for White, for example:

a) 19 ♕xe5 ♕d2+ 20 ♔f1 ♕xc2 21 ♘xc3 (21 ♗xf6 ♖xf6 22 ♕xf6? ♕xe2 mate) 21 ... ♕d3+ 22 ♘e2 ♗xe2+ 23 ♕xe2 ♕h3+ and 24 ... ♕xh4. Black comes out a piece up.

b) 19 ♕xd8 ♖axd8 20 ♖d1 ♖xd1+ 21 ♔xd1 (or 21 ♗xd1 ♘d3+ 22 ♔f1 ♘e4, and White can save himself from mate only at further costs in material) 21 ... ♗h5! 22 ♗xf6 ♖xf6 23 b6 ab and now:

b1) 24 ab ♘f3 25 b7 ♖f8 26 ♖g3 ♘d4 27 ♖xc3 (27 ♗d3 ♖b8 deprives White of his last hope – the pawn on b7) 27 ... ♗xe2+ 28 ♔d2 (or 28 ♔e1 ♗f3 and 29 ... ♘xc2+; or 28 ♔c1 ♗a6, threatening ... ♗xb7 or ... ♘e2+) 28 ... ♗f3 29 ♖c7 ♘b5 30 ♖d7 ♗c6 31 ♖e7 ♖d8+ and 32 ... ♘d6, winning the b-pawn.

b2) 24 a6 ♘f3 25 a7 ♖f8 26 ♖g3 ♘d4 27 ♗e4 ♘xe2 28 f3 ♘xg3 29 hg ♖xf3 30 a8♕+ ♖f8+ 31 ♔c2 ♖xa8, and Black's extra pawns ensure the win.

c) 19 ♕xe6+ ♔h8 20 ♖d1 ♕e8, and Black has a winning attack.

It follows that the adherents of this system have no alternative but to try out the line recommended by Ligterink.

19 ♖d1   ♕xd6
20 ♖xd6   ♗d5

A pity! A fitting conclusion to this game would have been 20 ... ♗xe2 21 ♔xe2 ♘f3 22 ♔xf3 ♘e8+ 23 ♔e2 ♘xd6 24 ♗e7 ♘xb5, with a won ending.

21 ♘d4   ♖ac8

21 ... ♘e8? appears dubious: 22 ♖a6 ♖f4 (on 22 ... ♗b7 23 ♖xe6 ♖f4 24 ♖xe5 and 25 ♖e7, White even has the better position) 23 ♗g3 ♖xd4 24 ♗xe5 ♖d2 25 ♗a4 ♗c4 (25 ... ♖d3 can be met by 26 ♖g3 ♖xg3 27 hg ♖c8 28 ♔d1, blocking the black passed pawn while White's pawns on the

queenside move irresistibly forward) 26 ♗xc3 ♖e2+ 27 ♔d1 ♖d8+ 28 ♔c1 ♖d3 29 ♗b4, and White's bishops are safely protecting his king.

Now the game unexpectedly ends in a draw:

22	f4	♘c4
23	♘xe6!	♘xd6
24	♖xg7+	♔h8
25	♗xf6	♖xf6
26	♖h7+	♔g8
27	♖g7+	♔h8
28	♖h7+	

½-½

Miles-Short
British Ch 1979
French Defence

1	d4	e6
2	e4	d5
3	♘c3	♗b4
4	ed	ed
5	♗d3	♘c6
6	a3	♗xc3+

ECO gives preference to 6 ... ♗e7, judging that 6 ... ♗xc3+ 7 bc ♘e7 8 ♕h5 gives a position slightly in White's favour.

7	bc	♘f6!?

The French Defence is Short's favourite opening, and he has an excellent feel for its various refinements. With his last move he forestalls White's queen sortie and compels his distinguished opponent to seek other ways of fighting for the initiative.

8	♗g5?!

This turns out badly. He had to take account of possible queenside castling by Black – in which event the position of White's bishop will help Black to develop a pawn attack.

8	...	♕e7+!
9	♘e2	♗d7
10	0-0	h6
11	♗f4	0-0-0
12	c4	

At first sight, White might seem to have a good position. In actual fact he has not. His weak queenside pawns are deprived of mobility, and it is difficult for him to organise active operations against the black king.

12	...	♗e6
13	c5	

13 cd ♘xd5 14 ♗g3 ♘b6 is no better.

13	...	g5
14	♗d2	♘e4
15	♖b1	f5
16	f3?!	

The fact that Black has come out of the opening with a good position may psychologically have been a surprise for Miles, and he loses his composure. His last move plays into his opponent's hands, for now a further weakness – the e3 point – is formed in the white camp. A preliminary 16 ♗e1! would have saved White from a good deal of unpleasantness.

16	...	♘xd2
17	♕xd2	f4
18	♗b5	

Other attempts to gain the initiative are also ineffective, for example: 18 c3 ♖de8 19 ♕b2 ♘d8 20 c6 b6, and to White's many worries an extra one is added – the defence of his pawn on c6.

18	...	♗d7
19	♖fe1	♕f6
20	♕c3	♖de8!
21	♕b3	♖e3!
22	♗d3	

22 ♕xd5? loses to 22 ... ♗e6, while 22 c3 could be met by 22 ... ♕e6! 23 ♗a4 ♘d8 24 ♗xd7+ ♔xd7! and the pin on the e-file should bring victory to Black.

22	...	♘d8
23	c4	♗f5
24	♗xf5+	♕xf5
25	♕a2	♖he8
26	♖b2	

No other way of shaking off the pin is to be found. On 26 ♔f2, Black would easily win: 26 ... g4 27 ♘g1 g3+ 28 hg fg+ 29 ♔f1 ♕d3+ 30 ♘e2 ♖xf3+! etc.

26	...	g4
27	♖f1	gf
28	gf	

28 ♖xf3? leads to loss after 28 ... ♕d3!

| 28 | ... | ♖g8+?! |

By now there are several ways of winning, but 28 ... ♕d3! was immediately decisive – since 29

♖d2 loses to 29 ... ♖xe2, while 29 ♖f2 loses to 29 ... ♖g8+ and 30 ... ♕d1+.

29	♔h1	♕h3
30	♖f2	♖xf3
31	♘g1	*(103)*

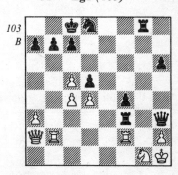

103
B

| 31 | ... | ♖e3! |

Simple but pretty.

32	♖g2	♕e6
33	♖xg8	♕xg8
34	cd	

At last White has managed to activate his pawns. But meanwhile his right flank has been shattered, and irresistible threats have been created against his king.

34	...	f3
35	d6	♕g5
36	d7+	♔xd7
37	♕b1	♘e6
38	♕h7+	♔c6
39	♕f7	♘xd4!
40	♕c4	♕xc5
41	♕a4+	b5
42	♕d1	♕d5
43	♖f2	♖e2!
44	♕c1+	♔b7

45	♘xe2	fe+
46	♖g2	♘c2!

0-1

Lelchuk-Sitnikova
USSR Women's Ch 1979
Ponziani Opening

1	e4	e5
2	♘f3	♘c6
3	c3	

An unexpected opening choice. In her preceding games Lelchuk had used the Ruy Lopez.

Evidently wishing to avoid prepared lines, she has now decided to play this ancient opening in which a whole range of variations are of a forcing nature.

3	...	d5
4	♕a4	♘f6!?

Notwithstanding the youthfulness of the two opponents, a notable psychological duel is being conducted in the opening of this game. The usual continuation is 4 ... de 5 ♘xe5 ♕d5 6 ♘xc6 bc 7 ♗c4 ♕d7 8 0-0 ♘f6 9 d3 ed, with slightly the better position for White. Realising that it was this variation that had received her opponent's chief attention in preparation for the game, Sitnikova steers clear of it and adopts a rarely seen gambit line.

5	♘xe5	♗d6
6	ed?	

It turns out that White's prepared line is not backed up by adequate knowledge and is superficial in character. Nor is this failing unique. Among young players, the desire to startle the opponent with something unexpected rarely coincides with serious study of the variation, so that this kind of 'prepared line' tends to boomerang. In place of this last move, White should have continued 6 ♘xc6 bc 7 d3 0-0 8 ♗e2 ♕e8 9 ♘d2 ♖b8 10 0-0, with some advantage after 10 ... c5.

6	...	♗xe5
7	dc	0-0
8	d4	

A game Rabinovich-Alekhine (Moscow 1920) went 8 ♗e2 ♖e8, with a dangerous initiative.

8	...	♗d6
9	♗e3	♘d5
10	♘a3	

The obvious 10 ♘d2 is weaker – it deprives the king of an important flight square.

10	...	♘xe3
11	fe	♕h4+
12	♔d2	♖e8
13	♖e1	♗g4
14	♘c4?!	

In the present situation, the problem that White faces consists not only in evacuating the king to safety but also in bringing the queen to the defence of the key central squares as quickly as possible. This could have been achieved by the transposition

14 ♗e2! ♛f2 15 ♘c4, and now:

a) **15 ... b5?** 16 ♛xb5. If now 16 ... ♖ab8, White has the reply 17 ♛g5! available, after which none of Black's attacking tries work. On the other hand, if Black continued as in the actual game but with the *omission* of 16 ... ♖ab8, the exchange sacrifice which occurs on move 20 would not be playable (see the note to Black's 22nd move).

b) The rook sacrifice **15 ... ♖xe3?** is attractive but inadequate: 16 ♘xe3 ♗f4 17 ♔c2! (after 17 ♛d1? ♗f5!! an unexpected mate could occur) 17 ... ♗xe2 18 cb ♖d8 19 ♛xa7, and Black is helpless in the face of White's threat to queen the pawn. Therefore:

c) Black would have to resort to the immediate **15 ... ♗f4** 16 ef ♗xe2 17 ♔c1 b5 18 ♛xb5 ♖ab8 19 ♖xe2 ♛xe2 20 ♛a4 ♛xg2. The ensuing position is of course won for Black, but there would be quite a few obstacles to surmount before victory was achieved.

> **14 ... b5!**

An obvious and at the same time very strong move, which quickly decides the game.

> **15 ♛xb5 ♖ab8**
> **16 ♛a6!**

The crucial square e2 needs defending by all available means.

> **16 ... ♛f2+**
> **17 ♗e2 ♗f4**

> **18 ♖hf1 ♗xe3+**
> **19 ♔c2 ♔xg2**
> **20 ♘e5 *(104)***

White had been pinning her last hopes on this move. But Black's position is such that she shouldn't feel any worries about the outcome. The unsafe position of White's king, and the lack of harmony in the actions of the white pieces, supply ample grounds for a combination. Sure enough, the following exchange sacrifice settles the issue at once.

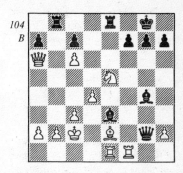

104
B

> **20 ... ♖xe5!**

Reaping the fruits of her well-laid plan.

> **21 de ♗xe2**
> **22 ♖xe2**

White must part with a piece, otherwise Black would win the queen after 22 ♛xe2 ♛e4+ 23 ♛d3 ♖xb2+.

> **22 ... ♛xf1**
> **23 b4 ♖d8**
> **24 ♔b3 g6**

Nothing remains but White's

unwillingness to face the hard facts.

25	e6	♕d1+
26	♖c2	♖d2!
27	ef+	♔xf7
28	♕c4+	♔f8
29	♕e4	♕b1+

0-1

Vladimirov-Mestel
Pont-Sainte-Maxence 1974
Sicilian Defence

1	e4	c5
2	♘f3	d6
3	d4	cd
4	♘xd4	♘f6
5	♘c3	g6
6	f4	

There are few lines in opening theory that have undergone such detailed investigation as the Dragon Variation. Therefore Vladimirov should not be blamed for sidestepping the strongest, but most intensively studied, continuations – 6 f3 or 6 ♘b3. However, when evading a theoretical contest, you have to have in reserve a solid system that you have analysed well. As will appear from what follows, Vladimirov's knowledge of the variation he had chosen was superficial.

6	...	♗g7?!

The usual continuation is 6 ... ♘c6 7 ♘xc6 bc 8 e5 ♘d7 9 ed ed, for example 10 ♗e3 ♕e7?! (stronger 10 ... ♗e7 11 ♕f3 d5 12 0-0-0 ♗f6

13 ♗d4 0-0) 11 ♕d4 ♗g7 12 ♕xg7 ♕xe3+ 13 ♗e2 ♖f8 14 ♖f1 ♗a6 15 ♖f3 ♕g1+ 16 ♗f1 ♗xf1 17 0-0-0 0-0-0 18 ♖dxf1 ♕xg2 19 ♕d4 ♘b6 20 a4! ♔b7 21 a5 ♘c8 22 ♘d5! with a strong attack for White.

7	e5	♘h5

Black has a bad position after 7 ... de 8 fe ♘g4 9 ♗b5+ ♘c6 10 ♘xc6 ♕xd1+ 11 ♘xd1 (11 ♔xd1 is also good: 11 ... ♘f2+ 12 ♔e2 ♘xh1 13 ♘d4+ ♗d7 14 ♗f4, and with two pieces for a rook White has sufficient advantage to win) 11 ... a6 12 ♗a4 ♗d7 13 h3 ♘h6 14 ♘xe7! ♗xa4 15 ♘d5 ♖d8 16 c4. White retains his extra pawn.

8	♗b5+	

8 g4? loses to 8 ... ♘xf4 9 ♗xf4 etc.

8	...	♗d7
9	♕f3?	

Vladimirov may not have known about the line recommended by theory: 9 e6! ♗xb5 (9 ... fe? 10 ♘xe6 ♗xc3+ 11 bc ♕a5 12 ♗d2 ♗xb5 13 c4, winning the piece back with an excellent position) 10 ef+ ♔xf7 11 ♘cxb5 ♘f6 12 0-0, with the better game for White; but such a variation isn't difficult to find over the board for a master of his class. For some reason or other he failed to do so; evidently he wasn't in the right frame of mind for the game.

9	...	de
10	fe	♗xe5
11	♗e3	♗xb5

12	♘cxb5	♕a5+!
13	c3	

13 b4?! would be answered, not by 13 ... ♕xb4+? 14 c3 ♕c4 15 ♕xb7 0-0 16 ♕xa8 a6 17 ♕e4 ♗g7 18 ♘a7 ♕xc3+ 19 ♔e2 ♕b2+ 20 ♘c2 – when White beats off the attack, remaining a rook up – but by 13 ... ♕b6! followed by 14 ... ♘c6 or 14 ... 0-0.

A possible answer to 13 ♘c3 would be 13 ... ♘d7 14 ♕xb7 ♖b8 15 ♕c6 0-0! (15 ... ♖xb2?! is inferior: 16 ♕c8+ ♕d8 17 ♕xd8+ ♔xd8 18 ♘c6+ ♔c7 19 ♘xe5 ♘xe5 20 ♗d4) 16 ♕xd7 ♖fd8 17 ♕g4 (it may be better to give back the piece at once with 17 ♕a4!?) 17 ... ♘f6 18 ♕h4 ♕b4 19 ♖d1 ♘d5 20 ♗f2 (20 a3? ♘xe3!) 20 ... ♘xc3 21 bc ♕xc3+ 22 ♔e2 ♖b4 23 ♖d3 ♖8xd4 24 ♗xd4 ♕xc2+ 25 ♖d2 (25 ♔e3? loses to 25 ... ♗d4+ 26 ♖xd4 ♕c3+) 25 ... ♕xd2+ 26 ♔xd2 ♖xd4+ 27 ♕xd4 ♗xd4. In the ensuing endgame, White will have to struggle to draw.

13	...	a6!

The only move to maintain Black's advantage.

| 14 | ♕d5 *(105)* | |

14 ♕e4 would be answered by the simple 14 ... ♘d7.

14	...	♗xd4!
15	♘d6+	

Or 15 ♕xd4 0-0 16 ♘a3 ♘c6, with a winning position.

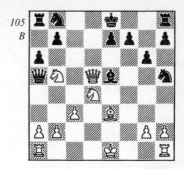

105
B

15	...	ed
16	♕xa5	♗xe3
17	♔d1	

It's hard to give good advice in such a position. But perhaps White should stock up with material, even though after 17 ♕c7 ♘d7 18 ♕xb7 ♖b8 19 ♕xa6 0-0 20 b4 ♖bc8 it isn't clear how he rescues his king from the attack by Black's numerous pieces. White would gain no relief from 17 ♔f1 ♘c6 18 ♕c7 0-0 19 g3 ♖fe8 (threatening 20 ... ♖e7) 20 ♕xb7 ♘e5. And of course he can't play 17 ♕a4+ ♘c6 18 ♕e4+ ♔d7 19 ♕xe3? ♖he8.

17	...	♘c6
18	♕c7	0-0
19	♖f1	♖ab8
20	♔c2	♘d4+!

This unpleasant blow is made possible by the placing of White's queen and king on the c-file.

21	♔b1	♘e6
22	♕xd6	

This hastens defeat; he shouldn't

have opened the file for Black's rooks.

22	...	♖bd8
23	♕e7	♖d2
24	a3	♘hf4
25	♕xb7	

So White does decide to pick up Black's queenside pawns – in worse circumstances than before.

25	...	♘c5
26	♕f3	♘d5!
	0-1	

White resigned in view of the variations 27 ♖c1 ♘d3 28 ♖c2 ♘xc3+! or 27 ♖a2 ♘xc3+ 28 bc ♖b8+ 29 ♔a1 ♘b3+ 30 ♔b1 ♘d4+.

Many a joke has been made at the expense of Grandmaster Bronstein for taking five or ten minutes over his opening move in serious competitions. A fact not known to all the jokers is that the grandmaster was not thinking about what first move he should make. His thoughts were ranging far beyond the confines of the starting position – contemplating a position twelve or fifteen moves ahead, which he had been analysing at home.

It just shows Bronstein's way of preparing himself for the coming struggle . . .

Augousti-Uzman
19th Olympiad Siegen 1970
Ruy Lopez

| 1 | e4 | e5 |

2	♘f3	♘c6
3	♗b5	a6
4	♗a4	♘f6
5	0-0	b5
6	♗b3	♗b7
7	♖e1	

This is considered strongest. A gambit lines that's interesting to try out is 7 d4 ♘xd4 8 ♘xd4 ed 9 e5 ♘e4 10 c3 d3 (a bad alternative is 10 ... dc? 11 ♕f3 d5 12 ed ♘xd6 13 ♗xf7+, or 11 ... ♕e7 12 ♘xc3 ♘c5 13 ♘d5) 11 ♕f3 ♕e7 12 ♘d2 ♘c5 13 ♗d5 c6 14 ♘e4!

| 7 | ... | ♗c5 |
| 8 | c3 | ♘g4? |

In the hope that White will fall into a trap, Black makes a bad move. The correct line was 8 ... 0-0 9 d4 ♗b6 10 ♗g5 h6 11 ♗h4 d6.

| 9 | d4 | ed |
| 10 | cd?? *(106)* | |

The trap succeeds. However, had White played 10 h3! with 11 cd to follow, Black's position would not have been enviable.

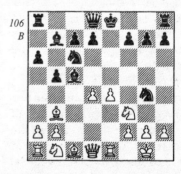

106
B

| 10 | ... | ♘xd4! |

11	♘xd4	♛h4
12	♘f3	♛xf2+
13	♔h1	♛g1+!
14	♖xg1	♘f2 mate

How do we explain a player's choice of a discredited variation in a high-level contest? Sometimes it happens accidentally – when the player experiences intense excitement at the board, and, playing quickly in an opening he knows well, forgets to make some necessary move. Thus, for example, in a game Zubova-Esterkina, (Leningrad Championship 1978), after 1 e4 c6 2 d4 d5 3 ♘c3 de 4 ♘xe4 ♗f5 5 ♘g3 ♗g6 6 h4 h6 7 ♘f3 ♘d7 8 h5 ♗h7 9 ♗d3, Black played 9 ... e6?!

On seeing such a spectacle, we say that an 'accident' occurred. However, if we try to imagine the circumstances that preceded the Augousti-Uzman game, we must suppose that Black's decision to test out his opponent's knowledge had been taken 'at home'. The dubious variation had been selected deliberately, on the assumption that the opponent wouldn't find the correct rejoinder. It was a case of playing for a trap. Such tactics deserve the harshest criticism.

Yet despite the primitiveness of the conception in the case we are discussing ('White's knowledge of the theoretical lines is weak, he makes his move quickly ... maybe

he'll play the obvious 10 cd?? without looking into it' – such, more or less, was Uzman's train of thought), the win was achieved – with no difficulty, either. We have thus come upon a highly important issue, which no strong player in our time can pass over – the problem of preparing for your opponent psychologically.

At the root of it there is a fairly complex task – that of finding out your rival's weak and strong points. Once you succeed in this, you can try to make every opponent conduct the game in a manner that he finds unpleasant – forcing him to defend if he's used to attacking, provoking him into an unclear attack if he likes quiet positional manoeuvring; luring him into the complexities of an opening line he doesn't know much about, even if it's favourable for him; blunting his alertness by appearing to want a quick draw, when all the time your thoughts are on winning ... etc. etc.

These notions were put into a concrete form by Nimzowitsch: "Try to give your opponent the kind of pawn formation he doesn't know how to handle.'

This dangerous weapon was wielded with virtuosity by Lasker, Alekhine and Botvinnik. Lasker was always saying that "the struggle on the chessboard is between human beings, not chessmen". Alekhine and especially Botvinnik developed this thought and erected the foundation for a new branch of sporting knowledge, which in our day is the object of expert attention.

In the next three games, the player with White succeeded in saddling his opponent with an opening scheme he hadn't adequately studied. It was not easy for Black to discover the right arrangement of his pieces, and the errors he committed led to defeat.

Sturua-Estrin
Kutaisi 1978
King's Indian Attack

1	♘f3	♘f6
2	g3	d5
3	♗g2	g6
4	0-0	c5
5	d3!	

This move appears to have been prompted by psychological considerations. Of course, it is no stronger than a number of others. The point is, though, that International Master Estrin virtually always opens with the king's pawn in his games with White, and defends against 1 d4 with the Nimzo-Indian or the Grünfeld. Therefore in practice he has rarely come up against the complicated problems of the King's Indian Defence. This fact had been very

astutely discerned by his young opponent, who, with his fifth move, goes into a King's Indian set-up.

5	...	♘c6
6	♘bd2	♗g7
7	e4	0-0
8	♖e1	♗g4?!

One of the unobtrusive inaccuracies which decisively contribute to the outcome of this game. With 8 ... e6 9 c3 ♕c7 Black could have satisfactorily solved the problems that faced him, for example 10 a3 de 11 de ♖d8, with 12 ... b6 to follow, equalising.

| 9 | ed! |

A typical King's Indian Defence has now been reached with colours reversed.

9	...	♘xd5
10	h3	♗c8

Of course Black is loth to exchange this bishop. But why not 10 ... ♗f5?

11	c3	b6
12	♘c4	♗b7
13	a4	♕c7
14	♕b3	♖fd8?!

The rooks should have been placed on d8 and e8 – that is, 14 ... ♖ad8! was in order.

| 15 | a5 | ♗a6? |

And this already is a serious mistake. In spite of the slight inaccuracies he had committed, Black's position was still quite defensible. He should have con-

tinued 15 ... ♖ab8! so as to answer
16 ♘g5 with 16 ... ♘xa5! 17 ♘xa5
ba, and in view of Black's pressure
on the b- and d-files, his chances
are no worse.

16 ♘g5   e6 (107)

This appears forced, for the
threat was 17 ♗xd5 ♖xd5 18
♘xb6, winning at once.

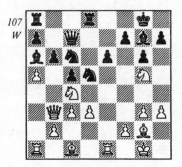

107
W

17 ♖xe6!
Wins by force.

17	...	fe
18	♘xe6	♕d7
19	♘xd8	♖xd8
20	ab	♗xc4
21	♕xc4	ab
22	♗g5	♘e5
23	♕a2	c4
24	♗xd8	♕xd8
25	♕a8!	

1-0

Yurtayev-Rozental
USSR Junior Ch, Riga 1977
King's Gambit

1	e4	e5
2	f4	

The King's Gambit is not often
seen in modern tournaments.
More's the pity! There is no better
opening for developing the tactical
skills of juniors, and yet trainers
and young players alike have been
scared away from it by the
dogmatic controversies of the
'authorities', as to whether the
gambit gives an opening advantage
to White or to Black.

In this game, the choice of
opening was most likely made on
psychological grounds. The point
is that Lithuanian chessplayers
have a detailed analysis of Petroff's
Defence and employ it with
success. Generally wishing to
avoid that opening, players with
White have been obliged to turn to
the Four Knights or the Scotch
Game – for which Black is well
prepared too. All that remains is
to see how Black feels defending
the King's Gambit.

The answer is, uncomfortable –
as the game will show.

2	...	ef
2	♘f3	♗e7
4	♗c4	

White has some quite good
possibilities after 4 ♘c3 ♗h4+
5 ♔e2 d5 6 ♘xd5 ♘f6 7 ♘xf6+
♕xf6 8 d4 ♘c6 9 c3 ♗g4 10 ♕d2!

4	...	♘f6
5	e5	♘g4
6	0-0	d5?!

The first inaccuracy. With 6 ...

♘c6 7 d4 d5 8 ed ♗xd6 9 ♘c3 0-0, Black would obtain good play (Keres-Alatortsev, Moscow 1950).

7 ed ♕xd6?!

The second inaccuracy. 7 ... ♗xd6 8 ♖e1+ ♔f8 9 d4 g5 would lead to a position where White's advantage is not easy to demonstrate.

8	**d4**	**0-0**
9	**♘c3**	**♘c6?**

A third inaccuracy which already loses the game. Black played more strongly in Bronstein-Koblenc (Moscow 1949): 9 ... ♘e3 10 ♗xe3 fe, and now, by continuing 11 ♘b5 ♕d8 12 ♘e5 ♗e6 13 ♗xe6 fe 14 ♖xf8+ ♗xf8 15 ♕g4, White could have obtained good attacking prospects. (Boleslavsky).

10	**♘b5**	**♕b4?**

As a result of the errors he has made, Black's position is lost. Rozental naturally doesn't like 10 ... ♕d8 11 ♗xf4 ♗d6 12 ♘xd6 cd 13 ♗g5! ♕b6 14 h3 h6 15 ♗f4 ♘f6 16 ♗xd6 ♖d8 17 ♗c5 ♕xb2 18 ♕d3! – so, with his last move, as often happens, he tries to stir up complications in the hope that a chance mistake by the opponent will allow him to recover.

But such a method is faulty and doomed to failure.

11	**b3**	**♗d6?** *(108)*

Black is thoroughly demoralised. Over the past five moves he has committed two inaccuracies and

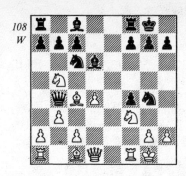

108
W

three errors. Instead of losing his queen, he could have got off with the loss of a pawn: 11 ... ♘e3 12 ♗xe3 fe 13 ♘xc7 ♖b8 14 ♘d5 and 15 ♘xe3.

12	**♗d2**	**♘e3**
13	**♕c1**	
	1-0	

Everybody has some weakness, which mostly results either from insufficient boldness or from the reverse – too much of it.

Emanuel Lasker

Short-Biyiasas
Hastings 1979-80
Ruy Lopez

1	e4	e5
2	♘f3	♘c6
3	♗b5	a6
4	♗a4	d6
5	d4	

International Master Biyiasas became known to chess enthusiasts after the Brazil Interzonal in 1973. His calm, well balanced play enabled him to finish successfully in that distinguished contest. Since then, his style has hardly altered. As before, he avoids sharp forcing variations in the opening, and tries to postpone the weight of the struggle until the middlegame. On the occasions when he succeeds in gaining the initiative, he plays with complete assurance, obtaining good results from his encounters with the strongest grandmasters.

These characteristics of his style were very acutely discerned by his young opponent, who endeavours by a pawn sacrifice to work up sharp play right from the first few moves.

5	...	b5
6	♗b3	♘xd4
7	♘xd4	ed
8	c3	♗b7?!

Short's psychological reasoning proves correct. Biyiasas doesn't want to be tied down to prolonged defence after 8 ... dc 9 ♘xc3 ♘f6 10 0-0 ♗e7 11 ♖e1 0-0 12 ♗g5, so he selects an old and little investigated continuation.

| 9 | cd | ♘f6 |

After refusing the pawn one move earlier, there is hardly any sense in taking it now, especially since the conditions for this have become still less favourable: 9 ... ♗xe4?! 10 0-0 ♗e7 11 ♖e1 ♗b7 12 ♗g5! and difficulties of kingside development arise for Black. But

even after the move played, it isn't easy for him to solve the problem of how to combat the enemy centre.

As we shall see from the following, Black was not to succeed in doing so.

10	f3	♗e7
11	0-0	0-0
12	♗e3	c5
13	♘c3	

There is nothing new in all this. The position that has arisen is assessed by theory as favouring White.

| 13 | ... | ♖e8?! |

Finding himself in an unfamiliar position, Biyiasas makes a move on general considerations, whereas the circumstances demanded concrete, well thought-out actions. He ought not to have weakened the f7 point. 13 ... ♖c8 was correct, preparing 14 ... cd and 15 ... d5.

| 14 | ♕e1 | ♗f8 |

It's now too late for 14 ... cd? 15 ♗xd4 d5 16 ♖d1! de 17 ♘xe4! (on 17 ♗xf6? ♗c5+ 18 ♔h1 ef! Black wins) 17 ... ♕c7 (17 ... ♘xe4 18 fe) 18 ♗xf6 ♗xf6 19 ♘xf6+ gf 20 ♕h4, and White has a won position.

| 15 | ♖d1 | c4? |

The most distinguished of chess-players have happened to make errors of calculation, blunders throwing away pieces or allowing one-move mates. But Black's last move comes into no such category, since it is contrary to the spirit of the position. It is impossible to explain it. After all, one cannot imagine Biyiasas failing to consider that by taking the pressure off the centre and closing the c-file, he was untying his opponent's hands for a direct kingside attack!

16	♗c2	♘d7
17	d5	g6
18	♕g3	♕c7
19	a3	♗g7
20	f4	♘c5 (109)

109
W

21 e5!

Short makes good use of the opportunity presented to him. The attack initiated by this move is not original in conception. But then, completely comparable positions hardly ever occur in chess – the slightest dissimilarity between them can radically alter the state of affairs. Therefore White's achievement in the next phase of the game, when energy and precise calculation bring him victory,

should not be underrated.

21	...	♘d3

White's threats are very dangerous. 21 ... de would be met (as in the actual game) by 22 f5. Then 22 ... ♘d3 would be unavoidable, since on 22 ... ♖ac8 there could follow: 23 d6 ♕d7 (or 23 ... ♕c6 24 ♘d5 ♕xd6 25 fg fg 26 ♘f6+ ♕xf6 27 ♖xf6 ♗xf6 28 ♗xc5 ♖xc5 29 ♕f2 ♗e7 30 ♖d7, winning a piece) 24 ♗xc5 ♖xc5 25 ♗e4 ♗xe4 26 ♘xe4 ♖c6 27 f6 ♗f8 28 ♖d5, and Black is completely paralysed.

22	♗xd3	cd
23	♖xd3	de
24	f5!	♕c4
25	♖d2	♖ad8
26	h4!	

Against the further advance of the rook's pawn, there is no defence. Black's many weaknesses and insecure king give Short the possibility of a pretty finish.

26	...	a5
27	h5	♖d6
28	fg	fg
29	h6	♗f6
30	♗g5	♗xg5
31	♕xg5	b4
32	♘d1	♖xd5
33	♘e3	♕c5
34	♖df2	♖dd8
35	♘g4	♖f8
36	♘f6+	♔h8 (110)
37	♘e4!	♕d4
38	♕xe5+	

1-0

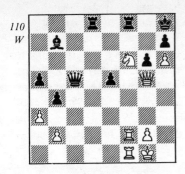

**A. Petrosian-Panchenko
Odessa 1973**
French Defence

1	e4	e6
2	d4	d5
3	♘d2	♘c6
4	♘gf3	♘f6
5	e5	♘d7
6	♗e2	

One of the best lines in this system, although 6 ♘b3 enjoys greater popularity; there can follow 6 ... ♗e7 7 c3 0-0 8 ♗d3 f6 9 ♕e2 ♕e8 10 0-0 fe 11 de ♕h5 12 ♖e1 ♘c5 13 ♘xc5 ♗xc5 14 b4, with the freer game for White (*ECO*).

6	...	f6
7	ef	♕xf6
8	♘f1	e5?! *(111)*

Panchenko is used to working hard – and fruitfully – at raising the level of his mastery. In each of the multifarious variations that make up his vast repertoire, he strives to find fresh possibilities instead of confining himself to playing out familiar continuations. Here is a case in point; while he was looking over some old games, a pawn sacrifice played in Bogatirev-Magergut (Moscow 1947) did not escape his keen eye. After adding a few refinements to it, he resolves to try it out in practice. The customary continuation is 8 ... ♗d6 9 ♘e3 0-0 10 0-0 ♕g6 11 c4 ♘f6 12 g3, with advantage to White (*ECO*).

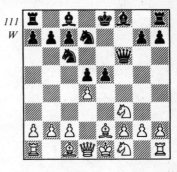

9	de?!

It would be very interesting to know what Panchenko had prepared against the strongest move 9 ♘e3!

In practice Black has been unable to maintain the balance after this move. For example:

a) 9 ... ed 10 ♘xd5 ♕d6 11 ♗c4 ♘de5 12 ♘xe5 ♕xe5+ 13 ♔f1! and it isn't easy for Black to parry the threat of 14 ♗f4 (Korchmar-Hudoshin, Saratov 1948).

b) 9 ... ♘xd4 10 ♘xd4 ed 11 ♘xd5.

c) 9 ... ♘b6 10 de ♘xe5 11 ♘xd5; in both these last variations,

White's position is preferable (*ECO*).

d) 9 ... e4 10 ♘xd5 ♕d6 11 ♗c4 (also 11 c4!? ef 12 ♗f4 fe 13 ♕xe2+ ♘de5 14 de ♕d8 15 0-0-0 ♗f5 16 ♖he1 ♗b4 17 g4! ♗g6 18 ♘f6+ with quick win in Korchmar-Arartovsky, Saratov 1948) 11 ... ef 12 ♗f4 fg 13 ♖g1 ♕e6+ 14 ♔d2 ♗d6 15 ♖e1 ♘de5 16 de ♗b4+ 17 c3 0-0 18 ♘f6+ gf 19 ♕g4+ ♔f7 20 ef ♗xc3+ 21 bc ♖d8+ 22 ♔c1, and Black resigned (Varlamov-Monin, Leningrad 1979).

9	**...**	**♘dxe5**
10	**♕xd5?**	

Accepting the pawn sacrifice is dangerous, not merely because Black obtains a formidable initiative in return – as had been shown in an article by A. Hachaturov and R.Isaakian as long ago as 1948 – but also because Panchenko is sure to have given the resulting position a thorough analysis, so that in the intricate middlegame which lies ahead, it will be easier for him to find his way in the mounting complexities.

The Bogatirev-Magergut game saw 10 ♘e3, with equal chances.

10	**...**	**♗e6**
11	**♕b5**	**a6!**

An important refinement compared with the previously known move 11 ... 0-0-0?!

12	**♕a4**	

He could have lost his queen with 12 ♕xb7?? ♖a7.

12	**...**	**0-0-0**
13	**♘xe5**	**♕xe5**
14	**c3** *(112)*	

White is already consenting to the drawing line 14 ... ♘d4?! 15 cd ♖xd4 16 ♕e8+ (16 ♕c2? loses to 16 ... ♗f5 17 ♕b3 ♗b4+ 18 ♗d2 ♗d3 19 0-0-0 ♗xe2 20 ♖e1 ♖hd8) 16 ... ♖d8 17 ♕a4 ♖d4.

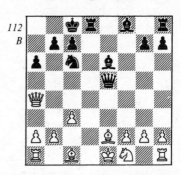

112
B

14	**...**	**♗b4!!**

A beautiful combinative stroke, which results in irreparable weaknesses being formed in the White camp. Once the material balance is re-established, the outcome of the game will be clear.

15	**cb**	**♗c4**
16	**♘g3**	**♗b5!**
17	**♕a3**	**♖d3**
18	**♗f4**	**♕e6**
19	**b3**	**♖xg3**
20	**0-0**	**♖xg2+**
21	**♔xg2**	**♗xe2**
22	**f3**	**♖f8**
23	**♗g3**	**♕e3**
24	**♕c1**	

The unfortunate thing, from White's viewpoint, is that his queen is taking no part in the struggle. With his last move he tries to bring it into play, but already it is too late; he has to forfeit material, since 24 ♖f2? loses to 24 ... ♗xf3+ 25 ♔g1 ♘d4.

24	...	♗xf3+
25	♖xf3	♕xf3+
26	♔g1	♖e8
27	♕f1	♕e3+
28	♔g2	♕e4+

and White resigned a few moves later.

When going over games from current tournaments, you ought to subject the most interesting ones to a meticulous analysis taking into account all the available relevent material. Skimped work here is impermissible. Poor-quality analysis or the specious assessment of positions can have catastrophic results – as in the following encounter.

Makarichev-Vaganian
Tbilisi 1973
French Defence

1	e4	e6
2	d4	d5
3	♘d2	♘c6
4	♘gf3	♘f6
5	e5	♘d7
6	♗e2	f6
7	ef	♕xf6
8	♘f1	e5?!

9	de?!	♘dxe5
10	♕xd5?	♗e6
11	♕b5	a6!
12	♕a4	0-0-0
13	♘xe5	

The following comments were made by Makarichev: "13 ♘e3 was stronger, but I was repeating the game A.Petrosian-Panchenko (Odessa 1973), in which Black had played what I thought to be an incorrect piece sacrifice."

13	...	♕xe5
14	c3	♗b4!!
15	cb	♗c4
16	♘e3	

"It seemed to me that this move refuted the sacrifice."

16	...	♗xe2
17	♔xe2	♘d4+
18	♔e1	*(113)*

"On 18 ♔f1 Black wins with 18 ... ♖hf8, for White cannot satisfactorily protect the f2 point. However, danger now strikes suddenly from a direction I least expected."

113
B

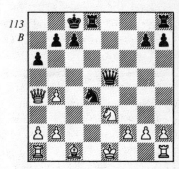

18	...	♖he8!
19	♗d2	♕e4

"Now there is no defence against the threatened ... ♕xg2 and ... ♘c2+. Relatively the best move is 19 f3, which would prolong White's resistance."

20	♔d1	♕d3
21	♖e1	♘b3
22	♖e2	♘xa1
23	♔e1	♖xe3!
24	fe	♘c2+
25	♔d1	♘xe3+
26	♔e1	♕b1+
27	♔f2	♘g4+

0-1

During a tournament, just as much depends on a player's physical as on his mental condition.

Spielman

Taking part in tournaments demands a great expenditure of mental and psychic energy. Chess contests are of prolonged duration – three or four weeks of concentrated mental labour. In the struggle for the highest honours, the lengths of time involved are magnified. Let us recall, for example, the match in Baguio City that lasted more than three months, with all the goings-on which took place there – not only at the chessboard. What with many sleepless nights spent in analysing unfinished games – quite apart from the five-hour playing session itself, in which all one's physical and intellectual powers have to be mobilised to overcome the opponent's resistance – players vary as to how they endure this burden. "Every chessplayer posseses his own work capacity, his own individual powers", writes V.Malkin, a doctor of medicine. These powers vary not only when play (or adjournment analysis) is in progress. To quote Malkin again: "Many chessplayers dream about positions they have played. Some of them work out variations in their sleep . . . It follows that the game of chess is not confined to the period when the clocks are going – it carries on far longer."

Playing a game of chess means mental effort of tremendous intensity, leaving a durable trace on the cortex of the brain. Investigations by Professor G.Kukolevsky have revealed that "the period of recovery after a five-hour tournament game often lasts twelve to sixteen hours, or more."

Therefore every player who takes part in competitions has to work out a routine for himself which will guarantee his health, his physical and nervous stamina, for the full length of the contest. Disturbance of the routine is capable of producing chronic mental stress.

An acute mental tension is something we often encounter in everyday life. It is a perfectly natural physiological phenomenon which is dispelled in a few hours of good sound sleep. Chronic mental stress, however, is a pathological condition, which harmfully influences all the workings of the human organism – including the nervous and endocrine systems which support the normal functioning of the brain cells. When this happens, sleep is disrupted, abnormal irritability arises, tiredness sets in more quickly than is usual, and even a state of full-scale neurosis may develop.

A chessplayer should adhere to a regular mode of living and observe a constant routine for work, relaxation and nourishment; each day he should keep to the same times for going to bed, getting up, taking his meals and exercise.

G.Kukolevsky

In nearly every game it is possible to achieve a winning position. But if you don't have a clear head at the crucial moment, all your previous exertions can be reduced to nothing.

Euwe

Vladimirov-Ftačnik
World Junior Ch Groningen 1977
King's Indian Defence

1	♘f3	♞f6

2	g3	g6
3	♗g2	♝g7
4	0-0	0-0
5	c4	d6
6	d4	♞bd7
7	♘c3	e5
8	e4	ed
9	♘xd4	♜e8
10	♗e3	c6?!

This move, which is played in analogous positions, is quite out of place just here, since it doesn't give Black the possibility to rearrange his pieces in the required manner.

The correct line was **10 ... ♞c5 11 f3 ♞fd7 12 ♕d2 ♞e5 13 b3**, and only then 13 ... c6, as in a game Furman-Geller (Moscow 1949). Another possibility is **10 ... ♞e5 11 b3 ♞fg4 12 ♗c1 ♞c6 13 ♞xc6 bc**, with a slight advantage to White (Sajtar-Lilienthal, match Prague-Moscow, 1946).

11	h3	♞f8

Even now 11 ... ♞c5 was preferable, although after 12 ♕c2 a5 13 ♜ad1 Black can't get in 13 ... a4 followed by 14 ... ♕a5, because of 14 ♞xc6 and 15 ♗xc5. He would have to make do with 13 ... ♕c7, since the more 'active' 13 ... ♕e7?! leads to another bad position after 14 ♜fe1 ♞fxe4? 15 ♞xc6 bc 16 ♗xc5 dc 17 ♜xe4 ♕f8 18 ♜xe8 ♕xe8 19 ♕a4.

12	♕c2	♛e7
13	♜ad1	♞e6

14	♘b3	♘d7
15	f4	♘b6
16	♘a5	f5

Black is suffocating from lack of counterplay, and decides on this continuation in order to free himself. But no good comes of opening up lines when in a cramped position.

17	♖fe1	♘c5
18	♗d4	fe
19	♗xg7	♕xg7 *(114)*

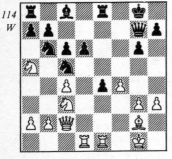

114
W

This game was played in round nine of the tournament. There were four further rounds to go. At this stage Vladimirov was sole leader; having conceded only two draws, he was a point clear of his nearest rival. After his logical conduct of the first phase of the game, he has reached a winning position. As Grandmaster Kavalek indicates, after 20 b4! the situation would be catastrophic for Black:
a) **20 ...** ♘d3 21 ♖xe4 ♖xe4 22 ♘xe4 ♘xb4 23 ♕b3 c5 24 ♖xd6 ♕e7 25 ♕e3 ♗f5 26 ♕xc5 ♗xe4 27

♖xg6+ ♔f8 28 ♖g8+, winning the queen; or 24 ... ♕a1+ 25 ♔h2 ♕xa2 26 ♖d8+ ♔f7 27 ♕c3, with a mating attack.
b) **20 ...** ♘a6 21 ♖xd6 ♘xb4 22 ♕b3 c5 23 ♘xe4 ♔h8 24 ♖ed1 ♘a6 25 ♘f6 ♖f8 26 ♘d5 ♘xd5 27 ♗xd5. White's positional preponderance is beyond doubt.

Instead of this, White commits an error which throws away all the advantage he has acquired with so much effort.

| 20 | ♖xd6? | ♗f5 |
| 21 | g4 | ♘d3! |

This powerful intermediate move places the initiative in Black's hands.

| 22 | ♖d1? |

Vladimirov possesses a fortunate combination of healthy optimism, physical fitness and quite a high level of chess mastery. Nonetheless, in this game a familiar syndrome emerges – the oversight on move 20 sets off a chain reaction producing a new mistake, this time a decisive one.

Nor is this accidental. Réti has written: "Every chess game is accompanied by a war of nerves. Tournament play is not like working at leisure in the quiet of your study, with the chance of a break when you are tired. No – it is acute mental strife ... The feeling of responsibility is intensified to the utmost; with every move, the master's reputation is at stake. Understandably, therefore, any oversight that is subsequently detected, and especially any lost game, can bring most masters to the point of nervous collapse."

Everything that has just been said applies all the more to contests on a high level, where an insufficiently hardened nervous system very often proves unable to cope with those unexpected vicissitudes which inevitably arise in the course of a game. Sometimes a contestant will be seized with a feeling of terror induced not by his opponent but by the thought of failing to achieve the goal he was set. A psychological blockage will be set up, fettering a chessplayer's creative thought and hence impairing his competitive results . . .

Black would have been confronted with complex problems after 22 ♖e3! ♕c7 (not 22 ... ♘c8? 23 ♖dxd3) 23 gf ♕xd6 24 ♘xe4 ♖xe4 25 ♗xe4 *(115)*.

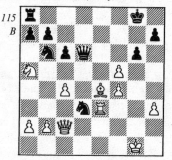

*115
B*

An interesting position – finding

the right continuation is not easy:
a) **25 ... ♘b4** 26 ♕c3, and now:
a1) **26 ... ♘xa2** 27 ♕e5 ♕xe5 (White has an irresistible attack after 27 ... ♕d1+ 28 ♔h2 ♕d2+ 29 ♗g2) 28 fe gf 29 ♗xf5, with a won position.
a2) **26 ... ♕xf4** 27 a3! (considerably stronger than the tempting 27 fg hg 28 ♗xg6 ♘6d5! 29 cd ♘xd5 30 ♗f7+ ♕xf7 31 ♖g3+ ♔h7, when White's attack runs out) 27 ... ♘a2?! 28 ♕d2 ♕g5+ 29 ♔h1 ♖d8 30 ♗d5+ ♔g7 31 ♕d4+ ♔h6 32 h4! with a quick win.
b) **25 ... ♘xf4!** 26 c5 and now:
b1) **26 ... ♕e5?!** 27 cb ♕xa5 28 ♕c4+ ♔g7? 29 ♕d4+ ♔g8 30 ♕d6 ♘d5 (30 ... g5 31 ♕e7) 31 ♕e6+ ♔h8 (or 31 ... ♔g7 32 f6+ ♔h6 33 ♗xd5 ♕xd5 34 ♕xd5 cd 35 f7, and one of the pawns will queen) 32 fg hg 33 ♗xd5, and White wins.

Alternatively: 28 ... ♘d5 29 fg! (White obtains nothing much from 29 ba?! ♖xa7 30 ♗xd5+ ♕xd5, or from 29 ♗xd5+ cd – but not 29 ... ♕xd5? 30 ♕xd5+ cd 31 ♖a4! a6 32 ♖c3, with winning chances in the rook ending) 29 ... hg 30 ba ♖xa7 31 ♗xd5+ ♕xd5 32 ♕xd5+ cd 33 a3. In the resulting endgame, despite the reduced material, it is not easy for Black to defend.
b2) **26 ... ♕d4!** 27 ♕f2 ♕d1+ 28 ♕e1 ♕xe1+ 29 ♖xe1 ♘bd5, or 28 ♔h2 ♘bd5 29 ♖e1 ♕h5 30 ♕g3 ♖f8! Although in these last two

variations White still retains the better chances, Black can very likely hold the draw.

22	...	♘c8
23	♖6xd3	ed
24	♕f2	♗e6
25	♖xd3	♘b6
26	c5	♘c4
27	♘xc4	♗xc4
28	♖d4	♖e1+!

Black energetically exploits White's errors. The routine retreat with the bishop would have led to an unclear position after 29 ♘e4.

29	♔h2	♗a6
30	g5	♖f8! *(116)*

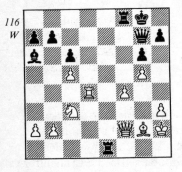

116
W

Black's last move is directed against 31 ♘e4, which would be met by 31 ... ♖e2! 32 ♕g1 ♖xb2! 33 ♘f6+ ♖xf6 34 gf ♕xf6, with a won position.

Incidentally, 32 ... ♖xf4? instead would not work. The reply 33 ♘f6+? would lose to 33 ... ♖xf6 34 gf ♕xf6, threatening 35 ... ♕e5+ and 36 ... ♖e1. On the other hand, the intermediate 33 ♖d8+! would

lead to a level position: 33 ... ♖f8 34 ♘f6+ ♔h8 35 ♕d4 ♖fe8 36 ♘xe8 ♕xd4 37 ♖xd4, or 35 ... ♖ee8 36 ♖d7 ♖e7 37 ♖xe7 and 38 ♘d7+. It's interesting that on the careless 35 ... ♖e7? White wins with the striking 36 ♘h5! (pointed out by L.Yudasin).

31	a4	♕e5!

Again the strongest. On 32 fe ♖xf2 33 ♘e4, the simplest answer is 33 ... ♖xe4! 34 ♖xe4 ♗f1 35 ♖g4 ♔f7 36 ♔g1 ♖xg2+ with a won pawn endgame.

32	b4	♕e3
33	♕xe3	♖xe3
34	♘e4	♖d3
35	♖d6	♗c4
36	♘f6+	

He couldn't save himself with 36 ♗f1 ♖xd6 37 ♗xc4+ ♖d5 38 ♘f6+ (or 38 ♘d6 ♖xf4 39 ♗xd5+ cd 40 b5 d4 41 ♔g3 d3 etc) 38 ... ♔g7 39 ♗xd5 (or 39 ♘xd5 cd 40 ♗xd5 ♖xf4 41 b5 ♖f5 42 c6 bc) 39 ... cd 40 ♘xd5 ♖f5 41 ♘c7 ♔f7 42 ♔g3 a5, breaking up the white queenside.

36	...	♔g7
37	♖xd3	♗xd3
38	♔g3	♖d8
39	h4	

Or 39 b5 cb 40 ♗xb7 ba 41 c6 ♗f5.

39	...	♖d4
40	b5	cb
41	♗xb7	

and White resigned without waiting

for the reply.

On the day after the game, Vladimirov lost again. Then he scored three draws, to finish in 4th-7th place.

The majority of players, including some masters, don't possess the gift of creativity in a sufficient measure. Against such players, the golden rule is: come up with something new in the opening.

Nimzowitsch

Kouatly-Liu
World Junior Ch Groningen 1977
Dutch Defence

1	d4	f5
2	♗g5	

A rare variation, which is mentioned in beginners' textbooks in connexion with a quaint checkmate: 2 ... h6 3 ♗h4 g5 4 ♗g3 f4 5 e3 h5 6 ef h4 7 ♗d3 ♖h6 8 ♕h5+ ♖xh5 9 ♗g6 mate.

2	...	h6?!
3	♗h4	c5?!

Black reacts to White's chosen continuation in a highly individual manner. With the move played, he prepares to bring his queen out to b6, freeing d8 as a flight square for the king. However, as we shall see, this whole plan is faulty. When encountering a new idea in the opening, you must first and foremost be sure that your reply is a solid one, and not permit

yourself any doubtful experiments which often will lead to loss. These requirements were fully met by 2 ... ♘f6 3 ♘c3 d5.

4	e3!?	

Black's dubious play could have been refuted by 4 e4! ♕b6 5 ef ♕xb2 6 ♘d2 ♕xd4 7 ♘gf3 ♕d5 8 ♗d3 ♘f6 9 0-0. White has an overwhelming position for the pawn.

4	...	♕b6
5	♘d2!?	

A sounder idea was to protect the d-pawn with 5 c3 ♕xb2 6 ♘d2 ♕xc3 7 ♖c1 ♕a3 8 ♖xc5 ♘c6 9 ♕h5+ ♔d8 10 ♕xf5, when White has an excellent game.

5	...	cd
6	♘c4??	

The forced variation that follows after this move leads to a loss for White. Mistakes of this kind do not always stem from a player's lack of calibre. Sometimes they occur in games by masters and grandmasters. The straightforward continuation 6 ed would have secured White an excellent position after either 6 ... ♘f6 7 ♗xf6 (7 ♘c4? ♕e6+ and 8 ... g5) 7 ... ♕xf6 8 ♘gf3, or 6 ... ♕xd4? 7 ♕h5+ ♔d8 8 ♕xf5 ♘f6 9 ♗xf6 ♕xf6 10 ♕xf6 gf 11 0-0-0. In this last variation, White could also continue more sharply with 9 ♘gf3 ♕xb2 10 ♖b1 ♕xa2 11 ♗c4 ♕a3 12 ♕g6! For the sacrificed pawns, he has a big lead in development.

6	...	♛b4+
7	c3	dc
8	a3	c2+

We can readily assume that this move, which leaves him a pawn down with no compensation, was just what White had overlooked. We are unable, on the other hand, to explain exactly why this happened. Various reasons are possible. For example, in examining this variation Kouatly may have forgotten that after 8 ... c2+ 9 ab cd♛+ the newly promoted black queen would not yet have been taken, and may have imagined White could win with 10 ♞b6?? This hypothesis may sound far-fetched. But let us recall what happened in the game Petrosian-Bronstein (Candidates' Tournament, Amsterdam 1956):

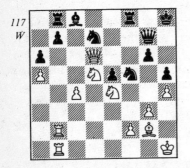

117
W

In this position, the player who was later to be World Champion forgot that his queen was attacked by the black knight, played 36 ♞g5?? and resigned after 36 ...

♞xd6.

Similar occurrences are not uncommon in chess history. In a tournament in Munich (1979), another player who has been World Champion – Boris Spassky – lost the following game with Black against H.Lieb: **1 e4 e5 2 ♞c3 ♞f6 3 ♝c4 ♞c6 4 d3 ♝c5 5 f4 d6 6 ♞a4 ♝xg1 7 ♜xg1 ♞g4 8 g3 ef 9 ♝xf4** *(118)*

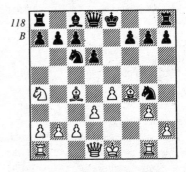

118
B

9 ... ♞xh2?? 10 ♛h5 1-0.

In the USSR Junior Championships, Tbilisi 1976, the following miniature was played: **1 e4 e6 2 d4 d5 3 ♞c3 ♞f6 4 ♝g5 ♞fd7??** **5 ♝xd8** 1-0. On Black's scoresheet the move 4 ... ♝e7 was written down. The player imagined he had already made that move when he retreated his knight.

The list of such curiosities could be added to, but let these suffice. The cause of all of them is that the player's normal process of thought is upset by some extraneous disturbance. How true it is that the chess struggle takes place not between automata but between human beings who are prey to the most varied emotions. During the game they can suddenly be overcome by either joy or distress, or disappointment, or perplexity, or other feelings. It may be, for example, that Kouatly was experiencing dissatisfaction with the opening set-up he had selected, and, instead of bracing himself for a hard struggle, was merely regretting he had not chosen some other particular line. After all, a look at his game against Petursson (page 152) will convince you that he is a perfectly knowledgeable player in the field of the openings.

It is not impossible that before the game even started Kouatly had been struck by some vivid impressions from which he couldn't free himself in the course of playing. Uncontrollably, they surfaced in a most unexpected form in the middle of his thought process, and, distracting him from the precise analysis of variations, induced an error.

9	♕d2	♕xd2+
10	♔xd2	♘c6
11	♘f3	d6
12	♔xc2	g5
13	♗g3	♘f6
14	♖d1	♗g7
15	b4	b5
16	♘xd6+?	

Admitting defeat.

16	...	ed
17	♗xb5	♗d7
18	♗c4	

The pawn on d6 is invulnerable owing to the threat of 18 ... ♘xb4+. The remaining moves were:

18	...	♖c8
19	♔b3	♘e4
20	♖he1	♔e7
21	♖d3	♖c7
22	♗d5	

and without waiting for his opponent's reply, White resigned.

Notwithstanding the successful outcome of this game from the Singapore player's viewpoint, Nimzowitsch's maxim should be treated with caution. We should not forget that by deviating from tested patterns of play in the opening (especially with Black), we incur the risk of slipping into an inferior position which may afterwards turn into a lost one at the slightest inaccuracy.

Plaskett-Hawelko
European Junior Ch Groningen 1979
Modern Defence

1	e4	g6
2	d4	♗g7
3	♘c3	d6
4	f4	a6
5	♘f3	b5
6	a4!?	

Black has played an unpopular opening line which had been shown by earlier games to lead to a difficult position for him. White's last move had not previously been seen in serious competitions. The familiar continuation was 6 &d3 &b7, and now:

a) 7 ♕e2 ♘d7 8 e5 e6 9 a4 b4 10 ♘e4 with a substantial central plus (Jansa-Vogt, Leipzig 1973).

b) 7 0-0 ♘d7 8 e5 e6 (8 ... c5? is a mistake leading to a quick loss: 9 ♘g5 ♘h6 10 f5 cd 11 fg! dc 12 gf+ and Black can cease resistance; I. Zaitsev-Adamski, Polanica Zdroj 1970) 9 a4 b4 10 ♘e4 &xe4 11 &xe4 d5 12 &d3 ♘e7, and the white position is preferable (*ECO*).

6	...	b4
7	♘a2	&b7
8	&d3	a5?!

It was not worth weakening the b5 point, although after 8 ... c5 9 dc dc 10 ♕e2 White's game is to be preferred.

9	0-0	♘d7
10	♕e2	d5?!

A more cautious choice was 10 ... e6 11 f5 e5! 12 ♘g5 ♘h6 13 &c4 0-0, when Black manages to defend.

11	e5	e6
12	g4!	c5

There's no time for 12 ... h5 13 f5 hg 14 fe gf 15 ♕xf3, with a won position for White.

13	dc	h5?

Black's effort to wrest the initiative from White without delay will prove his undoing. At first sight 13 ... ♘xc5 14 &b5+ looks unattractive, yet this is the very line that Black should have chosen. After 14 ... &f8! he could have consolidated his position, establishing his knight on the central square e4 with the intention of later going over to active operations by ... h5. In that case, not the least important factor in an assessment of the position would be the unfortunate placing of White's knight on a2.

14	f5!	hg
15	fe	gf
16	♖xf3!	♘xe5

16 ... ♕h4 17 ed+ &e7 18 &f4 is no better.

17	&b5+	&e7

This leads quickly to loss, but already there was no saving him. On 17 ... &c6 18 ef+ &f8 19 fg♕+ &xg8 20 &xc6 ♘xc6 21 ♕e6+, White forces his opponent's resignation. Alternatively, 18 ... &d7 19 f8♘+ &xf8 20 ♕xe5 ♖h5 (the threat was 21 ♕xd5+) 21 ♖f7+ ♘e7 22 ♕d6+ &e8 23 ♖xe7+ &xe7 24 ♕xg6+ &f8 25 &xc6 and 26 &h6+; or 22 ... &c8 23 ♕xd8+ &xd8 24 &xc6, and the result is not in doubt.

18	&g5+	f6
19	♕xe5	♖h5 *(119)*

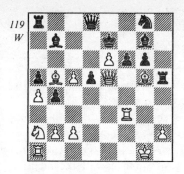

119
W

20   &d7!

A remarkable move. Mate is threatened. Black can't play 20 ... ♖xg5+? 21 ♕xg5 fg 22 ♖f7 mate. On 20 ... ♕b8, White plays 21 ♕xb8 ♖xb8 22 ♗f4, followed by 23 ♗d6+.

20   ...   ♖a6
21   ♖af1   ♕f8

Stopping the threatened 22 ♖xf6! But other misfortunes now await Black.

22   h4!

Aiming at the c7 point.

22   ...   ♖xg5+
23   hg   fe
24   ♖xf8   ♘f6
25   gf+   ♔xf8
26   e7+

                   1-0

As the opening phase of the game passes, the tasks that take shape for the middlegame consist primarily in being able to contend for small advantages and accumulate them, until the time is ripe for a tactical stroke or for favourable simplification and the transition to a superior endgame.

Zaid-Chekhov
USSR Junior Ch Sochi 1975
King's Indian Defence

1	d4	♘f6
2	c4	g6
3	♘c3	♗g7
4	e4	d6
5	f3	0-0
6	♗e3	c5?!

Recommended by Georgian players at the end of the 1960s. At the cost of a pawn, regardless of the exchange of queens, Black attempts to seize the initiative. A more usual continuation is 6 ... b6, and only afterwards 7 ... c5.

7	dc	dc
8	♕xd8	♖xd8
9	♗xc5	♘c6

The root position of the variation. Despite Black's practical success in many games, he is inadequately equipped for this kind of activity. This is confirmed by the game Karpov-Barle (Ljubljana-Portorož, 1975): 10 ♘d5! ♘xd5 11 cd ♗xb2 12 ♖b1 ♗c3+ 13 ♔f2 b6 14 ♗a3 ♘e5 15 ♘e2 ♗d2 16 ♗xe7 ♖e8 17 ♗f6 ♘d3+ 18 ♔g3. White's position is preferable.

Karpov indicates that after 11 ... b6 12 ♗e3 ♗xb2 13 ♖b1 ♗d4 (the verdict isn't altered by 13 ... ♗c3+ 14 ♔f2 ♘a5 15 ♗b5 e6 16 ♘e2, when White's central passed pawn becomes very dangerous) 14 ♗xd4 ♘xd4 15 ♔d2, White's chances are again preferable, thanks to the insecure position of Black's centralised knight.

The game just quoted was as yet unknown to both Chekhov and Zaid. Chekhov did, however, know about another one. In 1974, Zaid had unsuccessfully employed this variation against Ubilava – a circumstance which played, perhaps, none too insignificant a part in deciding the opening for the present game. It is appropriate here to recall how Botvinnik used to prepare for his opponents:

"My chess preparation begins with looking over the published material that has collected since I left off last. This is indispensable for acquainting yourself with new interesting games; scanning this material, I make notes for myself about questions that have interested me. At the same time I pay attention to all games by players I shall be facing in the contest I am preparing for. I study the peculiarities of these masters' play, their favourite variations – this stands me in good stead when preparing for specific games during the tournament itself"

10   ♗a3?!

Played in order to protect the pawn on b2, but from the point of view of fighting for the central squares it looks better to place the bishop on e3.

10   ...   b6
11   ♘ge2   e6

Nor is development easy for White after the natural 11 ... ♗b7 12 ♘d5 e6 13 ♘e7+ ♘xe7 14 ♗xe7 ♖d7 15 ♗a3 ♘h5. With the move played, Black provokes White into the variation which now follows.

12   ♘b5   a6
13   ♘d6   ♘d7
14   0-0-0   ♘c5
15   f4?

It isn't simple for White to defend. It appears he should have tried to connect his rooks as quickly as possible. This could have been done by 15 g3 ♘e5 16 ♗xc5 bc 17 ♗g2 ♖b8 18 b3! (18 ♘xc8? loses to 18 ... ♘d3+ 19 ♖xd3 ♖xd3 20 ♘f4 ♖d7) 18 ... ♘c6, and although Black definitely has compensation for the pawn, the position must be rated as roughly equal.

The move Zaid plays pours oil onto the flames.

15   ...   e5!
16   f5   gf
17   ef   ♗h6+
18   ♔c2   ♘d4+!

Leads by force to a won position.

19   ♘xd4   ♖xd6
20   ♗xc5   bc

21	♘b3	♗xf5+
22	♗d3	e4
23	♗e2	e3+
24	♔c1 *(120)*	

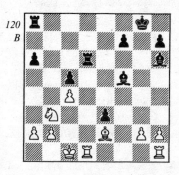

120
B

| 24 | ... | ♖d2! |

An elegant move that forces White into a *zugzwang* position.

25 ♘xd2

There is no improvement in 25 ♖xd2 ed+ 26 ♔d1 ♗b1! (the most decisive) 27 ♖f1 ♗xa2 28 ♘xc5 ♗e3! (the transposition 28 ... ♖c8? 29 ♖f6! ♗e3 30 ♖xa6 jeopardises Black's win) 29 ♖f5 ♖c8, and Black wins.

25	...	ed+
26	♖xd2	♖d8
27	♖d1	♖d4
28	♗f1	♔f8
29	♗e2	

White is completely helpless and can only move his bishop. Any move by a pawn would create additional opportunities for the black king to penetrate into the enemy camp.

29	...	♔e7
30	♗f1	♗e4
31	b3	♔d6
32	g3	

White can't avoid this weakening move, since after 32 ♗e2 ♔e5 33 ♗f1 a5 34 ♗e2 ♖xd2 35 ♖xd2 ♗xg2 36 ♔c2 ♗xd2 37 ♔xd2 ♔d4 Black obtains an easily won endgame.

32	...	♔c6
33	♗e2	♔b6
34	♗f1	a5
35	a4	

Otherwise 36 ... a4 is decisive, for the black king cannot be stopped from reaching c3.

35 ... ♔c6 36 ♗e2 ♔d6 37 ♗f1 ♔e5 38 ♗e2 ♗e3 39 ♗f1 h5 40 ♗e2 h4 41 g4 f6 42 ♗f1 ♔f4 43 ♗h3 ♔g5 44 ♗f1 ♔xg4 45 ♗e2+ ♔g5 46 ♗f1 f5 47 ♗e2 f4 48 b4 cb 49 c5 b3 50 c6 ♗xc6 0-1.

I would like to teach pupils who know how to think independently and take a critical view of what they are taught.

Emanuel Lasker

5 The Experiences of a Chess Trainer

Assessing Games of Young Players

Looking at young players' games, you can quite often form an opinion of their trainer – of his erudition, his relationship with his pupils as individuals or as a team, his efforts to keep informed about their rivals, and, finally, the mistakes he makes when preparing young players for competitions. Here are some notable examples.

A game from the USSR Junior Team Ch, Tashkent 1978

Sicilian Defence

1	e4	c5
2	♘f3	d6
3	d4	cd
4	♕xd4	a6
5	♗e3	♘c6
6	♕d2	♘f6
7	♘c3	e6
8	0-0-0	b5?
9	e5!	de
10	♕xd8+	♘xd8
11	♘xb5!	ab
12	♗xb5+	♗d7
13	♖xd7	♘xd7
14	♖d1	♖a5
15	♗xd7+	♔e7
16	♗b6	♖d5

17	♖xd5	ed
18	♘xe5	♔d6!
19	♗xd8	♔xe5
20	♗b6	*(121)*

Let us note, first of all, that Black's choice of variation in this game was hardly accidental. Obviously the game Dolmatov-Yermolinsky (see page 80) had been subjected to detailed analysis by the Ukranian chess coaches, who concluded that Black can obtain a draw. But even if that is the case, they were scarcely helping their pupil by recommending this line to him, since, without having any chance of victory, Black may end up in a lost position as a result of the slightest inaccuracy.

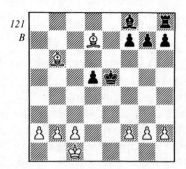

121
B

20 ... ♗e7!

The strongest move!

21 a4

On 21 c3, the continuation could be 21 ... ♔d6 22 ♗f5 ♔c6 23 ♗d4 ♗c5 24 ♔d2 ♗xd4 25 cd, and Black should draw, since White has difficulty controlling both open files and stopping the rook from penetrating.

21 ... ♔d6

22 ♗f5?!

Inconsistent. Having played 21 a4, White should definitely have withdrawn his bishop to b5, where it would keep an eye on the important c6 square. Black would then have found it much harder to carry out his plan, which consists in exchanging off the black-squared bishops. All the same, even in this line Black could have obtained a position with good drawing chances after 22 ... ♗g5+! For example:

a) 23 ♔d1 ♗f6 24 c3 ♖b8 25 ♗e3 d4! 26 ♗f4+ ♗e5 27 ♗xe5+ ♔xe5 28 c4 d3 29 a5 ♖b7! (otherwise, after 30 a6, Black's rook can't get to the e-file) 30 a6 ♖a7! (not immediately 30 ... ♖e7, because of 31 ♗c6 and 32 ♗b7). After 31 c5 ♔d4 32 c6 ♖e7, White can't improve his position.

b) 23 ♔b1 ♖b8 24 ♗d4 ♔e6! (24 ... ♗f4!? followed by 25 ... ♗e5 also looks adequate) 25 f3! (25 ♗xg7? f6) 25 ... ♗f6 26 ♗f2 ♖b7! 27 ♔a2

d4 and 28 ... ♔d5.

22 ... ♗g5+

23 ♔d1 ♖b8

24 a5 ♗d8

25 ♗xd8 ♖xd8

So the first part of Black's plan is accomplished: the bishop exchange has come about.

26 ♗d3 d4

27 a6 ♔c5

28 b3

There was no hurry for this move. In some variations White is now deprived of the possibility of undermining the black d-pawn with c3, and – most important – he can face difficulties in transferring his king to the kingside. The right continuation was 28 ♔e2! against which Black should set up a defensive position with king on b6, rook on d7 and pawns on h6, g7, f6 and d4.

28 ... g6?

One of the unobtrusive errors which lead Black to defeat. As already indicated, the pawns ought to have been arranged on black squares, and to begin with Black should have cut the white king off from the kingside with 28 ... ♖e8!

29 ♔d2? f5?

Black continues to weaken his own pawn chain. It was still not too late for 29 ... ♖e8 30 ♗c4 ♖e7 31 ♔d3 f6.

30 ♔e2

At last White finds the winning plan.

30	...	♖e8+
31	♔f3	♖e1
32	♔f4	♔b6
33	h3?	

Better 33 h4! at once. After 33 ... ♖g1 34 g3 ♖g2 35 f3 ♖g1 36 b4 ♖g2 37 b5 ♖g1 38 h5 g5+ 39 ♔xf5 ♖xg3 40 ♗e4, White creates a passed pawn on the kingside.

33	...	♖g1
34	g3	♖g2
35	♔f3	

35 f3 g5+! leads to unnecessary complications.

35	...	♖g1
36	b4	♖b1
37	b5	♖h1
38	♔f4	

After 38 h4 ♖h2, it's hard for White to strengthen his position.

38	...	♖e1

38 ... ♖xh3? loses to 39 ♔e5 ♖h1 40 ♔xd4 h5 41 c4 ♖c1 42 ♗e2 ♖c2 43 ♗f3 ♖xf2 44 c5+ ♔a7 45 ♗b7.

39	h4	♔a7
40	h5	♔b6
41	hg	hg
42	♔g5	♖e6
43	f4	♔a7
44	g4	fg
45	♔xg4	♔b8
46	♔g5	♖b6
47	♔h6	

47 ♗xg6 would also win.

47	...	♖f6

48	♔g7	♖xf4
49	b6	g5
50	a7+	♔b7
51	♗a6+	♔xa6
52	a8♕+	

1-0

Kasparov-Ehlvest
USSR Junior Ch, Tashkent 1978
Sicilian Defence

1	e4	c5
2	♘f3	d6
3	d4	cd
4	♘xd4	♘f6
5	♘c3	a6
6	♗g5	e6
7	f4	b5
8	e5	h6?!

The books assess this continuation as insufficient for equality. But considering the surprise effect and the ensuing sharp play for which Ehlvest was undoubtedly prepared, it might seem that the Estonian trainers were not to be blamed for their recommendation. And yet there is a flaw in this reasoning – the variation was used against the wrong opponent.

Everyone knows that Kasparov is one of those players who love sharp positions. He calculates variations accurately and quickly; he conducts the attack imaginatively and doesn't shrink from sacrificing material.

In the position we have now reached, he is in his element.

These circumstances had evidently not been taken into account in Ehlvest's preparation, and his chosen variation boomerangs.

| 9 | ♗h4 | g5 |
| 10 | fg!? | |

Kasparov has forgotten the continuation known to theory – or perhaps is consciously deviating from it. Paoli-Primavera, Italy 1959, went: 10 ♗g3! de (Black loses after 10 ... gf? 11 ♗h4! de 12 ♘xe6! ♕xd1+ 13 ♖xd1 fe 14 ♗xf6 ♖g8 15 ♖d8+ ♔f7 16 ♖xc8 ♔xf6 17 ♗d3 b4 18 ♘a4 b3 19 0-0 ba 20 ♗e4 – Boleslavsky) 11 fe ♘d5 12 ♘xd5 ♕xd5 13 ♗e2 with a big advantage for White.

10	...	♘h7
11	♕h5	hg
12	♗g3	♗g7
13	0-0-0	d5
14	♗d3	*(122)*

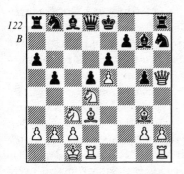

Boleslavsky considers that the position which has arisen is perfectly accpetable for Black. After this game, the assessment

will evidently have to be revised. How, indeed, is Black to continue here? The threat is 15 ♖hf1, followed by a knight sacrifice on b5. It's no good trying to defend with 14 ... ♘f8 15 ♕f3 ♗d7 16 ♖hf1 ♕e7 17 ♘f5! ef 18 ♘xd5 ♕c5 19 ♘f6+ ♗xf6 20 ♕xa8, and White wins. 15 ... ♖a7 is not much better: 16 ♘dxb5 ab 17 ♘xb5 ♕a5 18 ♘d6+ ♔d8 (18 ... ♔d7? 19 ♕xf7+ ♔c6 20 ♗b5+, and the black king no longer has a satisfactory square to go to) 19 ♘xf7+ ♔c7 20 ♘xh8, or 17 ... g4 18 ♕xg4 ♗h6+ 19 ♔b1 ♕a5 20 ♘d6+ ♔d8 21 ♗c4! In the last two variations, the end positions are completely hopeless for Black.

In the event, Black played:

| 14 | ... | b4 |
| 15 | ♖hf1 | ♖a7 |

15 ... ♘f6? is effectively refuted by 16 ef! ♖xh5 17 fg ♔e7 18 ♘f5+ (18 ♗xb8 is also sufficient) 18 ... ef 19 ♘xd5+, and White wins.

16	♘cb5	ab
17	♘xb5	♘f8
18	♕f3	♕e7
19	♘d6+	♔d8
20	♕e3!	

Of course White cannot be content with the variation 20 ♘xf7+ ♕xf7 21 ♕xf7 ♖xf7 22 ♖xf7 ♗h6.

| 20 | ... | ♘c6 |
| 21 | ♕b6+ | |

Winning the queen with 21

♖xf7?! ♕xf7 22 ♘xf7+ ♖xf7 23 ♕xg5+ ♔c7 24 ♔b1 would lead to unclear play.

21	...	♕c7
22	♘xf7+	♔e8
23	♘d6+	♔d8
24	♕e3	b3

In a forlorn position, Ehlvest strives to find some counter-chances, but accurate play by his opponent, who incidentally was short of time, frustrates these attempts.

25	ab	♘e7
26	♘f7+	♔e8
27	♘d6+	♔d8
28	♘b5	♖a1+
29	♔d2	♕a5+
30	c3	♖a2
31	b4!	

One can only marvel at the coolness of the young Baku player – or perhaps, on the contrary, at his enthusiasm. Although in time trouble, he rejects the obvious 31 ♔c2, which Black would probably have answered with 31 ... ♗a6, and chooses a continuation which looks risky but is nevertheless strongest and quickly leads to the desired result.

31	...	♖xb2+
32	♔e1	♕a6
33	♖f7	

After this there is no defence. The disunity of Black's forces, and the chronic weakness of his black squares in the centre and on the queenside, take their toll.

| 33 | ... | ♕c6 |

33 ... ♗h6 could be answered by 34 ♖xe7 ♔xe7 35 ♕c5+, winning the queen.

34	♖xg7	♗a6
35	♕xg5	♗xb5
36	♕xe7+	♔c8
37	♗xb5	♕xc3+
38	♔f1	

1-0

Zubova-Konstantinova
USSR Junior Ch, Kaluga 1968
King's Gambit

1	e4	e5
2	f4	d5
3	ed	e4
4	♘c3	♘f6
5	♕e2	

Although this old move looks dubious, in fact it inaugurates a logical plan.

Since kingside castling is made difficult by the possibility of ... ♗c5, White brings her queen out with tempo, attacking the central pawn.

| 5 | ... | ♗g4 |
| 6 | ♕b5+? | |

This move incurred unanimous censure from the trainers present at the contest. To be sure, at an early stage of the game White is bringing her queen into play and moving the same piece twice in succession. In other words, the basic principles of development are being violated. In actual fact, though, things are not so simple after the correct move 6 ♕e3! In any case, the shafts of the critics were aimed at the wrong target. The game continuation had been recommended to Natasha Zubova during preparation for the contest, by me. Yes, Black is a little better developed. But for the moment she doesn't seem to be creating any direct threats, while White does already have an extra pawn; and then, it looks as if the bishop will have nowhere to retreat after h3 . . . Alas! Both of us had overlooked Black's cunning 9th move, after which White's position collapses like a house of cards. All I can say by way of excuse is that this isn't the first or the last time that diligent home analysis has been refuted in a tournament game.

6	...	♘bd7
7	h3	a6
8	♕a4	b5
9	♕a5	*(123)*

123
B

| 9 | ... | ♘xd5! |

An elegant although not a complicated rejoinder, which does credit to the girl from Volgograd. It's obvious that mate follows if the knight is taken, while the capture of the bishop allows Black to win the queen. The remaining moves were:

10	♗xb5	ab
11	♕xb5	♘xc3
12	dc	♕h4+

0-1

Kochiev-Miles
World Junior Ch, Manila 1974
Sicilian Defence

1	e4	c5
2	♘f3	d6
3	d4	cd
4	♘xd4	♘f6
5	♘c3	g6
6	♗e3	♗g7
7	f3	♘c6
8	♕d2	0-0
9	g4	

I happened to work together with Kochiev for about six years in the Leningrad Palace of Young Pioneers. From childhood he had had an inclination for quiet manoeuvring play after his favourite 1 ♘f3, and distinguished himself among his contemporaries by his positional flair and excellent technique. His accurate calculation of variations preserved him from error in cases where the game developed into the kind of sharp tactical fight which as a rule he tried to avoid.

His game with Miles was played in the penultimate round. The Englishman was a point ahead.

The choice of opening for this encounter is all the more astonishing. It was possible to ascertain, in preparation and also during the tournament itself, that Miles chose the Dragon Variation with surprising consistency. His crushing defeat at J.Littlewood's hands, a few months before the Manila tournament, was not an adequate reason for hoping to beat him in a variation where all the hidden resources had been thoroughly studied by Miles but known to Kochiev only at second hand. Undoubtedly, if Kochiev's regular trainer had been with him, the opening of the present game would have been different.

9   ...   e6!? (124)

Miles's patent. Against Little-

wood he had played the weak 9 ... ♘d7 10 h4 ♘de5 11 ♗e2 ♘xd4 12 ♗xd4 ♗e6 13 f4! and White obtained an overwhelming attack, since the pawn on g4 cannot be taken without loss of a piece: 13 ... ♘xg4? 14 ♗xg7 ♔xg7 15 f5 gf 16 ♕g5+ ♔h8 17 ef ♖g8 18 ♕f4.

10   ♘db5?!

Naive simplicity! It's clear that this move, first and foremost, had been analysed by Miles at home. Now Kochiev will have some difficult problems to solve over the board.

In this sense one may say that the players were playing under unequal conditions. A less committal line was 10 0-0-0 d5 11 g5 ♘h5 12 ♔b1! although even then White can scarcely count on any advantage.

Evidently, after 9 g4?! the continuation 9 ... e6!? neutralises White's attacking chances.

10   ...   d5
11   ♗c5   a6!
12   ♗xf8   ♔xf8
13   ed?!

As the following will show, it was better to retreat the knight at once, without exchanging pawns.

13   ...   ed
14   ♘a3   b5
15   ♘d1

Indispensable. Nothing good would come of 15 g5 ♘h5 16 ♘xd5 ♗xb2 17 ♖b1 ♗xa3 18 ♕c3

♕xd5; or 16 ♘axb5 ab 17 ♗xb5
♘d4; or 16 ♘d1 b4 17 ♘b1 ♕e7+
18 ♗e2 ♘d4, followed by 19 ...
♘f4.

In all these variations Black's
loss of the exchange is of no
consequence at all, whereas the
unfortunate placing of White's
pieces (including his king) and his
battered pawn structure on the
kingside create insurmountable
difficulties for the defence.

15	...	b4
16	♘b1	♗xg4!
17	♗g2

Of course, the sacrifice cannot
be accepted because of 17 ... ♘e4!

| 17 | ... | ♕e7+ |
| 18 | ♕e3 *(125)* |

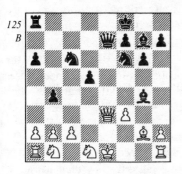

18 ... ♘e4!

Black conducts the attack
imaginatively. Now 19 fg? leads to
immediate loss: 19 ... ♕h4+ 20
♔f1 ♗d4 21 ♕f4 g5! 22 ♕f5 ♖e8,
and without great material losses
no defence is to be found against
the threatened 23 ... ♘d2+ with

mate next move.

19 fe?

After this, Black acquires two
pawns for the exchange while
retaining a powerful position, and
gradually conducts the game to
victory. If Kochiev had felt greater
confidence from the psychological
standpoint, he would surely not
have missed his last chance to
confuse the opponent with 19 c3!?
(pointed out by Marjanović).
After 19 ... ♕h4+ 20 ♔f1 bc! the
following possibilities arise:

a) **21 ♘bxc3?** d4 and now:

a1) **22 ♕xe4 ♖e8 23 ♕xe8+ ♔xe8
24 fg ♕f6+** and 25 ... dc. Despite
material equality White's position
is hopeless, in view of his exposed
king.

a2) The attempt to preserve the
queen leads to an even bigger
advantage for Black: **22 ♕f4 dc 23
bc ♗h6 24 ♕xg4 ♘d2+ 25 ♔e2
♖e8+ 26 ♔d3 ♘e5+** and Black
wins the queen all the same.

a3) Nor is it any better to try a set-
up with **22 ♕e1+ ♕xe1+ 23 ♔xe1
dc 24 fg cb 25 ♖b1 ♖e8**. After the
forced **26 ♗xe4 ♖xe4+ 27 ♔d2
♖xg4**, White can't touch the pawn
on b2. (**28 ♘xb2 ♖g2+ 29 ♔c1
♘b4** etc.)

b) **21 bc ♖e8 22 fg** (or **22 fe ♗xd1
23 ♕c5+ ♔g8 24 ♕xc6 ♕f4+ 25
♔g1 ♕e3+ 26 ♔f1 ♗e2+** etc.)
21 ... d4! and now:

b1) **23 ♕f4 dc!** (even more

energetic than 23 ... ♗h6 24 ♕xe4 ♖xe4 25 ♗xe4) 24 ♗xe4 c2 25 ♗xc2 ♕h3+ or 25 ♕d6+ ♔g8 26 ♘bc3 ♖xe4! 27 ♘xe4 ♗xa1, and White can't stop the pawn from queening.

b2) White would preserve drawing chances in the variation 23 ♕xe4!? ♖xe4 24 ♗xe4 dc 25 ♘bxc3 ♗xc3 26 ♘xc3 ♕h3+.

19	...	♗xd1
20	♘d2	♗xc2
21	♖c1	d4
22	♕h3	d3
23	0-0	♔g8
24	e5	♖d8
25	e6	fe
26	♖ce1	♘d4
27	♔h1	♘f5
28	♖e4	♕g5
29	♘f3	♕h6!
30	♖h4	

After a queen exchange there is no stopping the black d-pawn.

30	...	♕e3

Towards the end of the game Miles even shows a superfluous degree of accuracy. He doesn't permit the complications after 30 ... ♘xh4!? 31 ♕xe6+ ♔h8 32 ♕e7. In fact, a fairly straight-forward analysis shows that in that line too White's position is without hope: 32 ..∴ ♖f8! and now:

a) 33 ♕xh4 ♖xf3.

b) 33 ♘e5 ♘f5 34 ♘f7+ ♖xf7 35 ♕xf7 ♘g3+ 36 ♔g1 ♕e3+ 37 ♖f2 (37 ♕f2 ♘xf1) 37 ... d2.

c) 33 ♘xh4 d2 34 ♖xf8+ ♗xf8 35 ♕f6+ ♕g7.

31 ♖xb4 d2 32 ♘xd2 ♕xh3 33 ♗xh3 ♖xd2 34 ♖e1 ♗f8 35 ♖b8 ♔f7 36 ♖b7+ ♗e7 37 ♗f1 ♗a4 38 ♖b6 ♗d6 39 ♖e2 ♖d1 40 ♔g2 ♗b5 41 ♖f2 ♗c5 42 ♖b7+ ♔f6 43 ♗xb5 ab 44 ♖e2 ♖g1+ 45 ♔h3 g5! 46 ♖g2 ♖d1 0-1.

The anxiety of a trainer

In the course of a game, a participant, gearing himself to the logic of the struggle, will expend his energy in searching for the best continuation, usually without even suspecting what opportunities he has missed. A trainer, in company with his colleagues, will, as a rule, see many things a good deal more quickly than the player. With trepidation he waits to see whether his protégé will find the strongest move and whether the opponent will react to it correctly. Ideas that have not been realised appear before his mind's eye as on an x-ray photograph.

Soviet Master A. Nikitin has most tellingly described his state of mind while watching the game Kasparov-Kupreichik in the USSR (Top League), Minsk 1979. I shall now reproduce his account. *(126)*

"The minute which Gary had taken over his last move, 13 ♘h7xf8, had been spent by me in working out a different and more

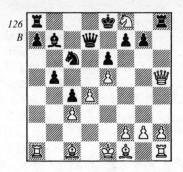

126
B

striking one – the knight jumping to f6. Now, however, the demonstration board operator had no sooner removed the bishop from f8 and replaced it with the white knight, than the reply 13 ... ♕xd4! came into my head. Any chessplayer is familiar with such sudden moments of 'illumination', when just after moving a piece on the board you all at once notice your opponent's terrible reply. The inevitability of a dismal result (from our point of view), after 14 cd ♖xh5, was so obvious that I instantly jumped up and reached into my pocket for a tranquiliser. What a string of disasters! I cast a glance at the stage, at the young man responsible for my tribulations, who had taken a 'full' five minutes over his last eight moves, eight exceedingly sharp moves which (a crucial point) he had never before encountered in practice. I looked ... and knew at once that he too had noticed his opponent's possible

reply. After the event, that is.

"Yet once he had seen it, Gary took a decision which, in the circumstances, was the only psychologically correct one. He didn't leap up from his chair and go pacing up and down the stage, as he would often have done previously; instead, with an imperturbable, and, I would even say, self-confident expression, just as if nothing had happened, he sat up before the table, showing his readiness to . . . make his next move instantaneously. On the other hand, though, it was with an equally imperturbable expression that the wily and sharp-sighted tactician Viktor Kupreichik was sitting and deliberating. What about? Five minutes, ten minutes passed . . . It was hard to believe that he – of all people – would overlook the queen 'sacrifice'. All that remained was for me to think up something to say to the boy in another hour and a half or so, on his departure from the arena . . .

"Another ten excruciating minutes passed. A strong local junior player who was sitting next to me suddenly asked me: "What if Black plays ... ♕xd4 . . . ?" Good Lord! I rushed off into the foyer. "No", I thought to myself, "a raw sixteen-year-old and a southern temperament – that just *doesn't* go together with trying to get into big-time chess and playing in the Top League. What'll come of it is that Gary's nerves will take a terrible hammering. His character won't be steeled here – just the reverse, it'll be shattered. It's my fault! I ought to have made the lad aim for a 'peaceful' score such as +2 –1 =14, instead of driving him hell for leather all the time – in this slush-and-'flu-ridden city, too. But then" – so I argued to myself – "he doesn't like to, he *can't* play a nice, quiet, simple sort of game. In that sort of game, the top brass here would devour him whole. Or *would* they? . . . Suppose he came through unscathed. Then another three years, and with his nerves hardened he could start to play more boldly, in some not too important game he could sacrifice the odd pawn or two . . ."

"Imperceptibly, half an hour of this torment had somehow gone by, and still Kupreichik hadn't moved! He sat placidly at the board like a sphinx, scarcely moving a muscle. And then he began to look as if he wasn't too happy; somehow he showed signs of losing his assurance. Surely he couldn't have . . . missed it? *Hadn't* he seen it? He hadn't! Finally, Viktor took the queen with his rook, and in a flash the black queen too disappeared from the board.

"About four hours later, young Gary rejoined us. He hadn't yet recovered from what he had just been through, but he was in good spirits, satisfied with his precisely played endgame and his much-needed victory. We were quick to assure him (and ourselves too) that all's well that ends well, that everyone gets 'nerves' towards the finish, that it was splendid how he hadn't batted an eyelid ("You're learning, old chap!"), and that generally this tournament wasn't such a 'fierce' one as all that . . .

"The main thing now was – the next game."

The satisfaction of success

I shall conclude with two games by gifted chessplayers whom I happened to coach for a number of years at the Leningrad Palace of Young Pioneers. The reader should note that these games are highly characteristic of the players' respective achievements.

Alexey Yuneyev was born in 1957. He has sytematically occupied himself with chess since the age of eight. From the very beginning it was clear that the boy had uncommon abilities – an excellent memory, good understanding of the positional elements, lightning-quick reactions and fine combinative vision. Nevertheless, over a long period, in the vast majority of cases his most interesting conceptions failed to receive their logical consummation, as a result of crude one-move blunders. Even today, after he has become a master, his games very often remind you of adventure films in which the scales are tipped now this way, now that way, without warning.

Karasev-Yuneyev
Kronstadt 1981
King's Indian Defence

1	♘f3	♘f6
2	c4	g6
3	♘c3	♗g7
4	e4	d6
5	d4	0-0
6	♗e2	e5
7	d5	a5
8	a3?!	

The usual move in this variation is 8 ♗g5! restraining Black's kingside initiative, but Soviet Master Karasev – like his opponent, as it happens – tries to avoid well-worn paths in the opening.

| 8 | ... | ♘a6?! |

8 ... ♘h5 or 8 ... ♘bd7 was undoubtedly more logical.

| 9 | b4 | ♘h5 |
| 10 | g3?! | |

After 10 0-0 ♘f4 11 ♗e3, Black would face difficulties in view of the threatened 12 c5.

| 10 | ... | f5 |
| 11 | ♘g5? | *(127)* |

A stock manoeuvre, but out of place here. With 11 ♘d2 ♘f6 12 f3, the defects of Black's careless play could have been exposed. But now, Yuneyev's plan justifies itself. Tactical complexities arise, connected with the undefended position of the rook on a1 and the knight on c3. And it is on tactics that the ideas of this gifted player have been based, in the majority of his games ever since childhood.

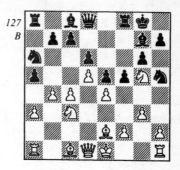

127
B

| 11 | ... | ♘f4! |
| 12 | h4 | |

There is nothing else. 12 gf ef would lose, while after 12 ♘e6 ♘xe6 13 de ♗xe6 White is a pawn down with a bad position into the bargain.

| 12 | ... | h6! |
| 13 | ♘h3 | |

As before, the black knight cannot be taken: 13 gf ef 14 ♗d2 hg 15 h5 fe, and White can resign.

| 13 | ... | fe! |

Forcing White to take the knight at last. It's clear that the tempting 13 ... ♘xh3? would be much weaker: 14 ♖xh3 fe 15 ♖h2 ♗f5 16 g4, with equality.

| 14 | gf | ef |
| 15 | ♕b3 | |

In an attempt to remove his king from the danger zone after 15 ... ♕xh4? 16 ♗b2 ♗xh3 17 0-0-0, White misses one more tactical stroke, whereupon resistance becomes hopeless for him.

15	...	ab
16	ab	♘c5!
17	♕b2	♖xa1
18	♕xa1	♘b3
19	♕b2	♘xc1
20	♕xc1	♕xh4

Black has three pawns for the piece. In addition he threatens 21 ... e3, so White's next move is forced.

21	♘xe4	f3
22	♗d3	♗f5!
23	♕e3	♗xe4

Of course not 23 ... ♖e8 24 ♘f6+.

| 24 | ♗xe4 | ♖e8 |
| 25 | ♘f4 | ♗c3+! |

The quickest way to settle matters.

26	♔d1	♕xh1+
27	♔c2	♕e1
28	♕xe1	♗xe1
29	♗xg6	♖e5
30	♘d3	♖e2+
31	♔d1	♗xf2

In this completely hopeless position, White lost on time. (Notes to the game were prepared in collaboration with the winner.)

Alexey Yermolinsky was born in 1958. Like Yuneyev, he began receiving tuition from me at the age of eight. His temperament is more balanced, and his progress towards distinguished results and high creative achievements has been swift and largely untrammelled. At the present time Yermolinsky is one of the strongest masters in the USSR.

This game which he annotated at my request makes a powerful impression and shows that his play is in the grandmaster class.

Yermolinsky-Shashin
Leningrad 1980
King's Indian Defence

1	♘f3	♘f6
2	c4	g6
3	♘c3	♗g7
4	e4	d6
5	d4	0-0
6	♗e2	e5
7	0-0	♘c6
8	d5	♘e7
9	♘e1	♘e8
10	♘d3	f5
11	♗d2	♘f6
12	f3	

This is one of the contemporary standard positions in the King's Indian. The most widespread move here is 12 ... f4, but my opponent adopts one of Fischer's recommendations.

12	...	c5
13	♖b1	f4
14	b4	b6
15	bc	bc
16	♖b2	g5
17	♘f2	h5
18	h3	♖f7
19	♕a4	♗f8
20	♖fb1	♖g7

Fischer's idea is that it isn't simple for White to develop an initiative here. 21 ♖b8 is met by 21 ... ♖xb8 22 ♖xb8 ♕c7 23 ♖b2, and already Black threatens ... ♘h4 followed by ... g4. Nor does 23 ♕b3 work, in view of 23 ... ♘d7, winning the exchange (24 ♖b5 a6). Another plan – 21 ♘b5, threatening 22 ♗a5 – comes up against the powerful reply 21 ... a5! when White's play, once again, is halted.

At all events, in spite of its blocked nature, the position is a dynamic one, and the slightest inaccuracy by either side could be fatal.

21   ♘cd1!

This seemingly paradoxical but very strong move had already been seen in Loginov-B.Vladimirov, Leningrad 1979. It combines two ideas – while threatening 21 ♗a5, White keeps the b-file open, which is of decisive importance in the variation 21 ... a5 22 ♖b8 ♖a7 23 ♖1b5 ♘d7 24 ♖xa5! winning a pawn.

21	...	♗d7
22	♕a6	♕e8!

In the game mentioned, Black went wrong straight away: 22 ... g4 23 hg hg 24 fg, and it emerged that Black must part with his pawn, since 24 ... ♘xg4? would fail against 25 ♗a5 ♕e8 26 ♘xg4 ♗xg4 27 ♗xg4 ♖xg4 28 ♕xd6.

But what is White to do now? 23 ♕xd6? is of course unplayable because of 23 ... ♘exd5! There remains one last resource.

23   ♗a5!   ♘g6

After 23 ... ♗c8 24 ♕xd6 ♘exd5 25 ♕d8, White has a big endgame advantage.

24	♗c7!	♗c8
25	♕a5	

A key position for the assessment of the variation. White's very powerful queenside initiative nullifies Black's attempts to work up an attack against the white king.

25   ...   g4?

In a later game between the same players, Black played 25 ... ♕d7 26 ♗d8 ♗e7 27 ♗xe7 ♖xe7 28 ♘c3 ♕c7 29 ♕xc7 ♖xc7 30 ♘b5 ♖d7 31 ♘d3, and in view of the unanswerable threat of 32 ♘xd6! White has an obvious advantage.

26	fg	hg
27	hg	♘h4
28	♖b8	♕g6!?

There is nothing else. After

28 ... ♖xb8 29 ♖xb8, Black has no useful moves.

29   ♖xa8   ♘xg4

30   ♘xg4!

Of course not 30 ♖xc8? ♘xf2 with an irresistible attack.

30   ...   ♗xg4

31   ♖xf8+!   ♔h7!

The reply that Black had been preparing, but nonetheless insufficient. He would lose at once with 31 ... ♔xf8 32 ♗xd6+! ♕xd6 33 ♗xg4 ♖xg4 34 ♕xa7.

Now White could have beaten off the attack with 32 ♖bb8 ♗c8 33 g4 ♕xe4 34 ♔f2, but he succeeds in finding a way to decide the game by force.

32   ♗xd6   ♗h5 *(128)*

There is no hope at all in 32 ... ♘xg2 33 ♕d8, or in 32 ... ♗xe2 33

♖h8+ ♔xh8 34 ♕d8+ and 35 ♕xh4+. The move played is prettily refuted.

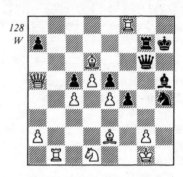

128
W

33	**g4!**	**♗xg4**
34	**♖h8+**	**♔xh8**
35	**♕d8+**	**♔h7**
36	**♕xh4+**	**♗h5+**
37	**♗g4!**	
	1-0	

Index of Complete Games

Index of Openings